Balanced Scorecard
Diagnostics

Balanced Scorecard Diagnostics

Maintaining Maximum Performance

PAUL R. NIVEN

WILEY

John Wiley & Sons, Inc.

Published by John Wiley & Sons, Inc., Hoboken, New Jersey.
Published simultaneously in Canada.

No part of this publication may be reproduced, stored in a retrieval system, or
transmitted in any form or by any means, electronic, mechanical, photocopying,
recording, scanning, or otherwise, except as permitted under Section 107 or 108 of
the 1976 United States Copyright Act, without either the prior written permission
of the Publisher, or authorization through payment of the appropriate per-copy
fee to the Copyright Clearance Center, Inc., 222 Rosewood Drive, Danvers, MA
01923, 978-750-8400, fax 978-646-8600, or on the web at www.copyright.com.
Requests to the Publisher for permission should be addressed to the Permissions
Department, John Wiley & Sons, Inc., 111 River Street, Hoboken, NJ 07030,
201-748-6011, fax 201-748-6008, or online at http://www.wiley.com/go/permission.

Limit of Liability/Disclaimer of Warranty: While the publisher and author have
used their best efforts in preparing this book, they make no representations
or warranties with respect to the accuracy or completeness of the contents of this
book and specifically disclaim any implied warranties of merchantability or
fitness for a particular purpose. No warranty may be created or extended by
sales representatives or written sales materials. The advice and strategies contained
herein may not be suitable for your situation. You should consult with a professional where appropriate. Neither the publisher nor author shall be liable for
any loss of profit or any other commercial damages, including but not limited to
special, incidental, consequential, or other damages.

For general information on our other products and services, or technical support,
please contact our Customer Care Department within the United States at
800-762-2974, outside the United States at 317-572-3993 or fax 317-572-4002.

Wiley also publishes its books in a variety of electronic formats. Some content
that appears in print may not be available in electronic books.

For more information about Wiley products, visit our web site at *www.wiley.com*.

Library of Congress Cataloging-in-Publication Data:

Niven, Paul R.
   Balanced scorecard diagnostics : maintaining maximum performance /
Paul R. Niven.
      p. cm.
   Includes index.
   ISBN-13 978-0-471-68123-7
   ISBN-10 0-471-68123-7 (cloth)
   1. Organizational effectiveness—Measurement.   2. Performance—Measurement.
3. Industrial productivity—Measurement.   I. Title.
HD58.9.N578 2005
658.4'01—dc22   2004025807

Printed in the United States of America.

10 9 8 7 6 5 4 3 2 1

To the many organizations, especially those I am privileged to have worked with, dedicated to the use and ongoing evolution of the Balanced Scorecard.

Contents

Preface

The Balanced Scorecard drumbeat has grown increasingly loud and clear over the past 14 years, supplying a soundtrack of performance management wisdom to accompany us on our journey into the new and uncharted territory of the knowledge economy. The tool's beginnings were humble enough, based on the notion that our traditional performance measurement systems—featuring an overwhelming reliance on financial metrics—were ill-suited to meet the demands of a modern business world characterized by value creation stemming from intangible assets such as employee know-how, deep customer relationships, and cultures capable of innovation and change. The notion was simple, but the ramifications profound. Organizations around the globe quickly began to embrace the Balanced Scorecard system. The idea of four distinct yet balanced perspectives of performance resonated with an enthusiastic audience weaned on shaky financial yardsticks used to quantify results for the past hundred years.

Co-created by Robert Kaplan and David Norton, the Balanced Scorecard has grown tremendously both in stature and adoption since its inception; it has been hailed as one of the 75 most influential business ideas of the 20th century and relied on in thousands of organizations spanning every conceivable type and size across the globe. It began as a measurement system, translating an organization's strategy into an interconnected set of financial and nonfinancial measures used to communicate strategy, build alignment, inform decision making, power performance management, and prioritize resource allocation. The early adopters of the model derived benefits from this measures-based application but then took it to another level by forging linkages between the Balanced Scorecard and critical management processes such as budgeting, compensation, and, more recently, corporate governance. With that, the label of strategic management system was thrust on the Balanced Scorecard, and its legions of practitioners continued to grow. With the advent of strategy maps in the late 1990s, Kaplan and Norton wrote yet another innovative chapter in the deceptively simple creation's life, and it gained a place in the pantheon of management concepts.

But wait, stop the music. Recent findings suggest that as many as half of all Balanced Scorecard users aren't achieving the results they hoped for, and a significant number still rate their performance measurement systems as "adequate."[1,2] So where have we gone astray? Is the Balanced Scorecard system fundamentally flawed, or are the application and implementation practices of certain organizations resulting in these unflattering statistics? This book purports that the Scorecard system remains a robust framework, very capable of helping organizations navigate the challenging seas they face in an ocean of competition and changing dynamics. If anything, the theoretical constructs on which the model is based have grown stronger, as evidenced by the many enhancements made to the model over the past years: from measurement to strategic management to communication and strategy execution.

The trouble, I would posit, lies in the methods used to implement the Balanced Scorecard. Many organizations have been lured by the seductive simplicity of the Scorecard model, believing it could be easily implemented and produce breakthrough results with a minimum of care and feeding. Unfortunately, that is not the case, as the Balanced Scorecard above all other descriptors represents a change initiative: a change in the way you measure, and if utilized to full advantage, a change in the way you manage. As we all know, change is difficult, and hence it is not uncommon for organizations to struggle during their Scorecard implementation period and ultimately question the success of their decision. Troubled implementations stem from any number of deficiencies: a lack of executive sponsorship to reinforce the Scorecard's value within the organization, tired metrics reflecting the past with no regard to the drivers of future success, and management systems that continue to reward unbalanced, largely financial, performance, to list but a few. This is a high-stakes game with significant implications for your success; organizations spend thousands of hours per year on their performance management systems, and therefore they must derive payback from this enormous investment of human and financial resources.

I wrote my first book, *Balanced Scorecard Step by Step: Maximizing Performance and Maintaining Results* (Wiley, 2001), to fill a perceived void between Balanced Scorecard theory and practice. Once again I sense an emerging void—between those questioning the efficacy of the Balanced Scorecard, based on unsuccessful implementation attempts, and what I perceive as the reality: that the Balanced Scorecard framework remains sound, but must be instituted with rigor and discipline if you expect to garner results. This book has been written to provide the tools and techniques necessary to ensure that you're maximizing the benefits of your Balanced Scorecard system.

Over the past 10 years, first as a practitioner and later as a consultant, researcher, and author, I've had a front row seat from which to view the growth of the Balanced Scorecard from New Age measurement device to powerful communication tool to transformative strategic management system. Working with organizations on several continents, I've witnessed highly successful Balanced Scorecard programs built to withstand the considerable vicissitudes of our challenging markets, and those whose foundation is so weak that a subtle wind of trouble could send it toppling down. Those experiences as a participant observer revealed several implementation practices I deem as essential if you hope to effectively install the Balanced Scorecard and have it produce the breakthrough results it has generated for many well-chronicled success stories. Those essentials form the basis for this book, and I believe they are capable of both transforming troubled Scorecard implementations and further strengthening successful initiatives.

WHAT YOU WILL FIND IN THIS BOOK

Breaking new theoretical ground in the Balanced Scorecard field was not my purpose in writing this book; that task is proficiently attended to by many scholars and researchers pushing the academic envelope of the framework. My aim is to provide you with time- and field-tested principles you can use to assess your Balanced Scorecard implementation, along with ideas and recommendations for building a system that will provide results today and sustain that success for many years to come.

The nine-chapter text begins with an examination of the current state of the Balanced Scorecard framework. You'll learn why it has risen to such heights of prominence, receive a refresher course on Scorecard fundamentals, and have the chance to ponder whether the Balanced Scorecard is here to stay. Any guesses as to my answer? You'll have to read on to find out. Chapter Two is titled "First Things First," and examines the foundational elements that must be in place if you hope to effectively employ the Balanced Scorecard. Included in the discussion are determining why the Scorecard is right for your organization and the critical importance of executive sponsorship to this and any change initiative. At the end of Chapter Two, and each succeeding chapter, you'll find self-assessment questions that can be used to critically examine your implementation efforts. I encourage you to take the time to carefully reflect on these queries and use them as the basis for group discussions focused on propelling your Scorecard initiative forward. The theme of "Before You Measure" continues in Chapter Three, as we delve into a critical examination of your Balanced Scorecard team, training and education regimen, and communication planning.

Chapter Four signals a dramatic transition from laying the groundwork for Scorecard success to reaping rewards through the development of a strategy map. You'll be provided with provocative questions you can apply to the objectives appearing in each of your four perspectives and will also discover how personalizing your map can often spell the difference between user apathy and acceptance. The chapter also supplies diagnostics to review the number of objectives on your map and examines the cause-and-effect linkages that tell your strategic story. Measures, targets, and initiatives are the subject of Chapter Five. Testing your current performance measures, questioning the number of measures appearing on your Scorecard, and the vital concept of using measure results to learn—not punish—will all be extensively covered. Many organizations find it difficult to set appropriate targets, thus you will find direction on target setting and sources of target information. The chapter concludes by reviewing how initiatives may be mapped to Scorecard objectives, ensuring that your resources—both human and financial—are directed toward the execution of strategy.

For many organizations, the high-level Corporate Scorecard is simply the first in a series of aligned Scorecards providing all employees with the opportunity to demonstrate how they contribute to overall results. This concept of cascading is the topic of Chapter Six. Cascading principles will be supplied, along with tools to gauge the degree of alignment among Scorecards spanning your organization. In Chapter Seven, we examine the linkage between the Balanced Scorecard and budgeting, compensation, and corporate governance. I'll share proven techniques to effectively forge these linkages and outline how many companies are using the Balanced Scorecard to gauge the performance of their Boards.

Sharing Balanced Scorecard results is our focus in Chapter Eight. Here we'll look at reporting mechanisms—software and lower-tech methods—and also investigate how the Balanced Scorecard can become the centerpiece of your management review process. The book concludes in Chapter Nine with a case study of Aliant, a Canadian telecommunications company that exemplifies many of the principles shared throughout the book.

Eleanor Roosevelt once remarked, "Learn from the mistakes of others. You can't live long enough to make them all yourself."[3] Growth and development in all facets of life result from a willingness to acknowledge our shortcomings and work diligently to overcome them. So it is with the Balanced Scorecard. My hope is that you will employ the principles and lessons found in this book to learn from those who have walked this path before you, and in so doing fortify your Balanced Scorecard for many years to come.

Paul R. Niven
San Diego, California

October, 2004

NOTES

1. Edward A. Barrows, Jr., "Assessing Your Balanced Scorecard's Performance," *Balanced Scorecard Report*, May–June 2004, p. 15.

2. Andy Neely, Chris Adams, and Mike Kennerley, *The Performance Prism* (London: Prentice-Hall, 2002).

3. Quoted in: Jef Nance, *Conquering Deception* (Kansas City, MO: Irvin-Benham, 2000).

Acknowledgments

I feel so fortunate to have had the opportunity to write this, my third book on the subject of the Balanced Scorecard, a topic that first ignited my passion a decade ago and continues to fuel a spirit of inquiry and discovery within me. Of course, an endeavor of this nature is never a singular task, but reflects the work, experience, wisdom, and advice of countless individuals all sharing a fundamental belief in the principles espoused in this text.

Let me begin by thanking some of the many people I've had the great pleasure to serve in a consulting capacity over the past years, and who graciously provided me with a real-world laboratory in which to test my Scorecard hypotheses and theories. From Anheuser-Busch in St. Louis, my thanks go out to Thomasine Joyce. From the U.S. Navy, Captain Bill Wilcox, Commander Mike Sumrall, and Captain Ray Berube. Stan Romanoff at Brother Industries, David Taran and Stephen Pilch of Divco West Properties, Bill Mao and Annette Hess at the Orange County Transportation Agency, Peter Murphy and Sue Patel from EpicData, John Wilcox of World Vision, and Tom Lynch and Vicki Lynn from the Worcester Polytechnic Institute. Special thanks go out to the many people I've had the privilege to work with at Aliant in Halifax, Nova Scotia, Canada. In particular, Jay Forbes, David Rathbun, Allan MacDonald, Dennis Barnhart, Jennifer Dicks, and David Blades.

Many thanks as well to Robert Kaplan and David Norton, whose work and spirit of discovery are a great inspiration to me. Vik Torpunuri of e2e Solutions has been a wonderful friend and strong supporter of my work, and I thank him for both. Thank you as well to Ray Smilor and Rob Fuller of the Beyster Institute in La Jolla, California, who gave me the opportunity to join them in promoting entrepreneurship, highlighted by a trip to Russia during which I delivered a series of Balanced Scorecard workshops. Finally, to my wife Lois: We recently celebrated our tenth anniversary, and I thank her for the love, support, and encouragement she's provided every day of our life together.

CHAPTER 1

The Current State of the Balanced Scorecard

THE ROAD AHEAD

Note to self: Always turn off my e-mail program before working on the book. I've provided myself that reminder because my train of thought was just interrupted by a popup box in the corner of my screen. It gently notified me that a new e-mail was awaiting my immediate attention. Much like the ring of a telephone, the temptation overwhelmed me and I took a quick peek to see who had contacted me. It was a gentleman in Zimbabwe requesting additional information about the Balanced Scorecard. I'm happy to help him and will do so later in the day. Once I reply to his request, I'll file it along with those I've received from China, Fiji, South Africa, Singapore, Finland, the U.K., from small manufacturing firms in the Midwest, and large conglomerates in New York City, from civic governments in California, and nonprofits in Washington, D.C. As the roll call of nations and organization types outlined suggests, the Balanced Scorecard has become a full-fledged worldwide phenomenon. And this phenomenon knows no boundaries; it stretches around the globe and has affected virtually every type of organization known to exist.

There is little doubt that the Balanced Scorecard has joined the pantheon of successful business frameworks; that elite group possessing the dual, and highly elusive, qualities of broad-based appeal and proven effectiveness. The sheer breadth and volume of Scorecard implementations are testament to this fact. Popularity, however, does not guarantee successful outcomes for those treading this road, and in fact it has been suggested that a majority of all Balanced Scorecard initiatives fail.[1] The most commonly cited issues derailing Scorecard implementations are poor design and difficulty of implementation.[2] The purpose of this book is to assist you in clearing those hurdles with proven tools and techniques forged at the crucible of cutting-edge theory and practical experience. Pitfalls await those who are unprepared at any juncture in this journey, from poor planning to ineffective team design to inappropriate objective and measure selection, and many more. During our time together, we'll carefully study the essential elements of Balanced Scorecard implementation, offering tools you can use to ensure that your Balanced Scorecard will help you achieve success today and sustain that success for the long term.

Before we begin to critically examine your Scorecard implementation, however, it's important to step back and cast a trenchant eye on the tool itself. In this chapter, we'll review exactly why the Balanced Scorecard has reached an exalted position as the strategy execution choice of literally tens of thousands of organizations; what it is about this seemingly simple tool, above all others, that quickly captures the attention of senior executives and shop-floor employees alike; and finally, why it remains vitally relevant when hundreds of other potential business panaceas have come and gone.

WHY THE BALANCED SCORECARD HAS RISEN TO PROMINENCE

The reasons for the Scorecard's ascendance are many and varied, but principally I believe the tool's longevity can be traced to an ability to solve several fundamental business issues facing all organizations today. In the pages ahead, we'll look at four pervasive issues that are undoubtedly affecting your business even as we speak: (1) a traditional reliance on financial measures, (2) the rise of intangible assets, (3) the emerging pattern of reputation risk, and finally, (4) the difficulty most organizations face in executing strategy. Some of these issues are age old and have been the nemesis of organizations for decades—relying on financial measures and attempting to implement strategy. The others—a rise in intangible assets and the emergence of reputation risk—are new, and their effects are just now being perceived, evaluated, and monitored. What unites these potentially vexing agents of organizational distress, and serves as inspiration for all of us, is the proven ability of the Balanced Scorecard to overcome every one of them.

Financial Measures: Is Their Time Running Out?

When the uninitiated ask me to describe the Balanced Scorecard "in a nutshell," I get the ball rolling by asking them how most organizations measure their success. A short and reflective pause is typically followed by the confident suggestion of "revenue" or "profits." And they're right, most organizations—be they private, public, or nonprofit—gauge their success primarily by the measurement of financial yardsticks. It's been that way for literally thousands of years, and at the turn of the 20th century, financial innovations, such as the development of the return on equity formula, proved critical to the success of our earliest industrial pioneers, including DuPont and General Motors.

The decades have come and gone, with financial measurement continuing to reach dizzying new heights as the number-crunching savvy among us introduced increasingly sophisticated metrics for the analysis of results. The corporate world readily embraced these developments and, as the prodigious growth of our generally accepted accounting principles (GAAP, in accounting parlance) will attest, financial metrics became the de facto standard of measuring business success. But, as is often the case, too much of a good thing can lead to some unintended consequences. The unrelenting drive to achieve financial success as measured by such metrics as revenue and shareholder value contributed to a round of recent corporate malfeasance unlike anything ever witnessed in the long and storied history of commerce.

Leading the ignominious pack of corporate bad boys is, of course, Enron. Once the seventh largest company in the United States, where did their insatiable thirst for growth and financial success lead them? Right into bankruptcy court, dragging thousands of suddenly poorer and justifiably angry shareholders down the path with them. If we use history as a guide, we'll find that Enron is not the first to apparently run afoul of the law in its tireless pursuit of fortune. A cautionary tale comes in the form of Samuel Insull. Upon migrating to the United States from England in 1881, Insull, through an association with Thomas Edison, co-founded the company that would eventually become General Electric. From his base in Chicago, he assembled a portfolio of holdings that would make any would-be financial impresario envious: Commonwealth Edison, People's Gas, Indiana Public Service Company, and several more. At one point, he held 65 chairmanships, 85 directorships, and 11 presidencies.[3] Sadly, the good times were not destined to roll on forever, and the 1929 crash brought his empire down in a tumultuous thud. Humiliated, and seen as the personification of corporate greed, Insull fled the United States but was later dragged back to stand trial for securities fraud. He was ultimately, and surprisingly, acquitted, but gone were his fortune and reputation. He died, penniless, in a Paris subway station on July 16, 1938.

Since the dawn of the corporation with Sweden's Stora Enso in 1288, companies have walked the delicate line of providing prodigious societal benefits and causing immeasurable harm through questionable, and sometimes unconscionable, acts. Recognizing the need to keep corporations in check, Theodore Roosevelt, the 26th president of the United States, once remarked: *"I believe in corporations. They are indispensable instruments of our modern civilization; but I believe that they should be so supervised and so regulated that they shall act for the interests of the community as a whole."*[4] As the President who took a first step toward bringing big business under federal control by ordering antitrust proceedings against the Northern Securities Company, Roosevelt would likely have welcomed the introduction of the Sarbanes-Oxley Act in 2002. The Act has set some of the toughest corporate governance standards in the world, requiring companies to report on the reliability of their financial controls, and asking CEOs and CFOs to put themselves on the line and acknowledge responsibility for internal controls, verifying their effectiveness.

All companies required to file periodic reports with the Securities and Exchange Commission (SEC) are effected by the Sarbanes-Oxley Act. The sheer magnitude of the work associated with compliance is daunting. To give you some indication, Fortune 1000 companies have earmarked more than $2.5 billion this year in investigation and initial compliance-related work.[5] Proponents suggest that the Act represents the most far-reaching U.S. legislation dealing with securities in many years. While the Act contains many provisions, two are particularly relevant to our discussion. Section 906 of the Act requires certification by the company's chief executive officer (CEO) and chief financial officer (CFO) that reports fully comply with the requirements of securities laws and that the information in the report fairly presents, in all material respects, the financial condition and results of operations of the company. Basically, company executives must pledge that what is in their financial reports is accurate and true. The Act also requires plain English disclosure on a "rapid and current basis" of information regarding material changes in the financial condition or operations of a public company as the SEC determines is necessary or useful to investors and in the public interest.

Undoubtedly, many American investors will sleep more easily knowing the Sarbanes-Oxley Act is ever-present, threatening those even remotely considering anything outside the legal lines with the long arm (and increasingly sharp teeth) of federal prosecutors. But does the increased financial disclosure ensured by the Act really describe the value-creating mechanisms of the corporation? Does it provide us with insight as to how intangible assets are being transformed into real value for consumers and shareholders? To make an informed decision about any organization's true state of affairs, we require information that covers a broader perspective. This is the case whether we're talking about a multinational corporation, a local nonprofit health services organization, or any branch of the federal government. Ultimately, the Act makes reported financial numbers safer for our consumption and analysis, but it doesn't diminish the increasingly apparent limitations of financial metrics. Working in the early 21st century, many organizations are beginning to question the once unquestionable reliance on financial measures. Specifically, they note the following:

- *Financial measures are inconsistent with today's business realities.* When I ask my clients what drives value in their business, it is exceedingly rare for me to hear "machinery," "facilities," or even "computers." What I do hear in near unanimity from everyone in attendance are phrases such as, "employee knowledge and skills," "relationships with customers," and "culture." Intangible assets have become the driving currency of organizations wishing to effectively compete in the modern economy. However, beyond "goodwill," you would be hard pressed to find the valuation of such intangibles on a typical corporate balance sheet. Financial metrics are ill-suited to meet the demands levied by the true value-creating mechanisms of the modern business economy—intangible assets. In the next section of this chapter, we'll take a closer look at their steep rise in prominence.

- *You can't see where you're going when you look in the rearview mirror.* Don't try this at home: driving down the freeway with your gaze cast intently on the rearview mirror. Great view of where you've been, but what does it tell you about where you're going? Very little. Financial measures offer the same limited view of the future. A great quarter of financial success, a great six months, or even a great year are not indicative of what lies in store for you. The business pages are littered with stories of falls from grace by once-lofty companies. The legendary Fortune 500 bears witness to the inability of success to predict success. Two-thirds of the companies listed on the inaugural list in 1954 had either vanished or were no longer large enough to maintain their presence on the list's 40th anniversary.[6]

- *Financial measures tend to reinforce functional silos.* If you were to type "teams" into the search box of Amazon.com, how many hits do you think you'd get? Curious, I did just that and was astonished when the total popped up at over 125,000! Granted, not all of these books embrace the topic of cross-functional teams in the modern organization, but the staggering population of texts about teams lends credence to the well-known notion that in order to get anything done in today's environment, we must work together. Thus, in many respects, and in a growing number of organizations, work flows horizontally across the enterprise. Financial measures, however, are decidedly vertical in nature. A department's numbers are rolled into a business unit, and business units are consolidated into a massive corporate heap of digits. This reporting system does little to encourage cross-functional work patterns.

- *What's the first thing to get cut in a downturn?* Easy question, right? If yours is like most businesses, the first things flung overboard when the economic seas become choppy are those that won't be missed tomorrow or the next day—items like training, employee development, and research. Their effects typically aren't seen for months or even years, and thus they become simple targets for the instant gratification, "must meet the numbers this quarter" paradigm of most publicly traded companies. Focusing on short-term financial numbers can frequently cloud our judgment as to what is going to truly distinguish our business from competitors in the long term. While training may be easy to cut today, what effect will that have on your workforce next year as you attempt to compete in ever-evolving markets?

- *Financial measures aren't always relevant.* We're constantly bombarded with messages about the speed of change these days. I'm guilty of reminding you myself, and did so in the last sentence! Why are these disturbing missives being fired in record numbers? Because it's true. Look at the disruptive technologies we've witnessed in just the past few years that have revolutionized the way business is conducted. Today, more than ever, we need performance information we can act on. Decisions can't be debated endlessly, and the luxury of waiting for complete information is just not an option. Financial measures frequently lack the action imperative necessary to make future decisions. Let's say you pick up your company's monthly income statement and see that sales are 5% off plan. Beyond the obvious, what does that mean, and more important, what do you do? Obviously, declining sales is an important indicator, but what led to that unenviable state of affairs, what was the *leading* indicator? That's the information we need, and fortunately that's what the Balanced Scorecard can supply.

I've charged financial measures with a litany of offenses in the previous paragraphs, so you may be wondering if they even belong in a Balanced Scorecard. The answer is yes, because despite their limitations, no Balanced Scorecard is complete without financial measures. This is the case whether you're reading this as the CEO of a large company, the executive director of a nonprofit, or the senior manager of a state government. An old song reminds us that "money makes the world go round," and so it is with the organizational world. In many cases, the ultimate arbiter of corporate success is financial. Nonprofits and public-sector organizations must also be cognizant of the financial ramifications of their actions and steward their funds in the most efficient manner. This section simply reminds us that financial measures must be balanced with the drivers of future financial success and security. Considered alone, they offer limited value. However, when reviewed in the context of data supplied by nonfinancial measures, they are suddenly imbued with the power of information that can transform decision making and ultimately lead to even greater success.

The Rise of Intangible Assets

The story of intangible assets can sometimes best be told through the prism of your family history, so let me tell you a bit about the Niven clan. My grandfather cut his teeth on the Canadian prairie building railroads for Canadian Pacific. You talk about old economy—the tools of his trade were literally hammer and shovel. It was honorable work, back-breaking of course, but honorable. My father took a different route, opting to be an entrepreneur. He ran a soft-drink business for most of my formative years. Imagine the delight of a youngster whose dad's product is soda pop! Yes, as the "sugar king" I was quite the popular kid in the neighborhood. Dad didn't confine his management to a desk; he was out there on the front lines slinging soda cases from dusk until dawn six days a week. The means of production was a rickety assembly line that produced as many delays and mysterious wheezing sounds as it did soda.

Fast-forward many years, and you have me. I've spent my entire career in some sort of analysis or consulting role, working with others, sharing information and knowledge in an attempt to drive results. I've never swung a pick or hoisted a soda case; in fact, I recently turned 40, and my mother still says I haven't worked a day in my life! Such is the fate of the knowledge worker, and if you're anything like me, that's probably an apt descriptor. In today's economy, things like employee knowledge, relationships with customers, and cultures of innovation and change generate success—in other words, intangible assets.

The power of intangibles manifests in the valuations we see in modern organizations. Margaret Blair of Washington's Brookings Institute explains:

> If you just look at the physical assets of the companies, the things that you can measure with ordinary accounting techniques. These things now account for less than one-fourth of the value of the corporate sector. Another way of putting this is that something like 75% of the sources of value inside corporations is not being measured or reported on their books.[7]

Just 20 years ago, the value of intangible assets in a typical organization rested at around 38%. The value has virtually doubled in the past 20 years. In the United States, spending on intangibles has also grown astronomically, and at around a trillion (yes, trillion!) dollars a year is on par with what companies spend annually on physical assets.[8]

What's become glaringly apparent is that intangible assets are quite different from the "property, plant, and equipment" that have populated fraying general ledger sheets for the better part of the past hundred years. For starters, they may not have a direct impact on financial results. Take training, for example: Many studies have demonstrated that training is positively correlated with financial success, but can we safely say there is a true one-to-one, cause-and-effect relationship evident? Chances are the financial results are a second- or even third-order effect of the training. Perhaps quality improves as a result of better-trained employees. Customers respond favorably to enhanced quality and buy more of the product, which in turn generates financial returns.

There are other differences as well: Tangible assets (as noted previously) are rigorously quantified on our financial statements. Intangible assets, however, can be maddeningly difficult to put a price on. Just what is the value of an innovative culture that consistently delivers new products faster than its competitors?

Tangible assets can be easily duplicated; your company may buy a new machine that increases productivity, but it won't be long before competitors are beating a path to the same supplier. However, intangibles in your possession cannot be bought or duplicated. Relationships with customers that have been cultivated through years of trust and mutual benefit are something your competitors will undoubtedly covet but find it exceedingly tough to beat.

Finally, and this is my favorite, tangible assets depreciate with use. That new computer you bought last week may have the luster of a sparkling diamond now, but just give it a year or two (if that) and then see how much it's worth. Conversely, intangible assets actually appreciate with purposeful use. Consider knowledge sharing: Every time you communicate with a colleague and she expands that knowledge, the circle has been enlarged. Multiply that by dozens, hundreds, or thousands of colleagues on innumerable topics, and the dizzying ramifications will make your head spin. I can scarcely think of a more encouraging fact.[9]

History and tradition yield about as easily as iron bars, so it's not surprising that the rise of intangibles has put tremendous pressure on our performance measurement systems. The antiquated devices employed by most companies simply don't have the capacity to identify, describe, monitor, and provide feedback on these most critical value-creating elements. Going forward, however, there simply is no choice. If 75% of value is generated from intangibles, then we absolutely must develop the ability to measure effectively. As you'll see throughout the book, the Balanced Scorecard has gallantly risen to this vital measurement challenge. In fact, a hallmark of the framework is its ability to track intangible assets and provide intelligence on their transformation into results.

A story from the Balanced Scorecard implementation of the U.S. Army's Medical Department (AMEDD) illustrates the power of the Scorecard in transforming intangible assets. When Lt. General James Peake began his command of AMEDD, he quickly noted: "we recruit soldiers but retain families." Keeping those families happy meant AMEDD had to provide outstanding medical care, and as a result, "quality, compassionate healthcare" became a key objective on the strategy map. The objective sounded noble, but what effect would it have on decision making and action in the field? The test came soon after in the form of a pregnant woman whose unborn child was threatened with a serious neurological defect. Careful diagnosis led to the recommendation of a costly surgery that held the promise of saving both mother and child, but initially the reimbursement was declined because the procedure was deemed experimental. A team of Army medical experts was soon convened, and the promise of compassionate care was put to the ultimate test. After careful reflection the decision was reversed, payment approved, surgery performed, and amid the great joy of all, a beautiful baby girl was born completely free of any complications. As Major General Patrick D. Sculley describes it:

A commander and many consultants went the extra mile, realizing that the initial "no" would have been far more than just a hassle for the family. They wanted to deliver the compassionate care we aspire to on our Scorecard. I'm proud of the way AMEDD could cut through all the red tape and make an informed and appropriate decision.[10]

Reputation Risk

Can you recall where you were on June 13, 2002? I was at home that day, and began my morning as I frequently do, by reading the Wall Street Journal. One headline that day jumped out at me above all others: "ImClone's Ex-CEO Arrested, Charged with Insider Trading."[11] The article described the sorry tale of Samuel Waksal, who had been arrested for allegedly relaying information to family members that the Food and Drug Administration was about to reject his firm's cancer drug, Erbitux. Buried deep within the text was this seemingly innocuous reference to a friend of Waksal's: *"Also implicated is Martha Stewart, who sold 3,928 shares on December 27th the day before ImClone announced the FDA's rejection."*[12] That single sentence was reported to headlines and cable news shows around the world in what seemed like a nanosecond. The government soon shifted its investigative rigor into high gear, and Ms. Stewart was destined for a prodigious fall from grace. Since the implications, and later her arrest, Omnimedia's market value has plummeted, with hundreds of millions of dollars evaporating. It seems like only yesterday that Martha Stewart was ringing the bell of the New York Stock Exchange, a symbolic gesture that signaled her glittering status as a newly minted billionaire. As of this writing, everyone's favorite domestic diva is completing her sentence of five months in prison, to be followed by another period of house arrest, which should offer her plenty of time to consider the perils of reputation risk.

Reputation is truly the ultimate intangible asset, one that must be constantly polished to a sparkling finish in this era of ever-increasing corporate oversight. Earlier in this section, I noted the difficulty in quantifying the worth of an intangible asset. So it is with reputation. However, the stakes here are sky-high, as recent estimates suggest that 5% to 7% of a large corporation's market capitalization is represented by brand value.[13] When we're talking billions of dollars and the ever-watchful eyes of an increasingly suspicious public and hypervigilant regulators, organizations must act and safeguard their reputations. The importance of reputation has not been lost on Wal-Mart, the world's largest retailer. In a teleconference with market analysts, CEO Lee Scott suggested that Wal-Mart management had failed in efforts to repair a reputation tarnished by discrimination cases and charges of worker mistreatment. Many analysts believe bad publicity and the related hit to reputation may be the retailing behemoth's greatest obstacle to store expansion and further growth.[14]

In order to protect reputation, it must be managed, and to manage reputation, it must be measured. Enter the Balanced Scorecard. As previously discussed, a principal benefit of the Scorecard is its ability to shed new light on intangible assets, removing the shroud of mystery and displaying them in the cold light of rational analysis. Leading indicators such as the number of negative news stories or number of audit findings can go a long way toward steering boardroom discussions in a new and provocative direction as leaders openly address this vital asset and put in place mechanisms to protect it for generations to come.

Strategy: It's All About Execution

What do the following words and phrases have in common: *positioning, design, power, emergent, cognitive, learning, cultural, environmental, configuration, disruptive, five forces, and value innovation?* Despite the wide swath of language they cut, each represents a school of strategic thought.[15] The field of inquiry that is strategy has produced enormous volumes of information and insight over the past five decades. Every single piece of work produced, despite the often esoteric jargon, contains at least a few nuggets of extremely practical and valuable information, but the sheer volume of material often leaves us scratching our heads and wondering aloud, "Just what is strategy, anyway?" Every person reading this book could undoubtedly provide a unique response to that question, and while that may lead to initial confusion, the spirit of discovery and debate it spawns holds promise for all of us. While we may never reach a consensus on exactly what strategy is (or is not), one thing most pundits and practitioners alike tend to agree on is the fact that strategy execution is more important than strategy formulation.

It's one thing to sequester yourself and your team away in an off-site location for a few days of chocolate chip cookies and excruciating debate that leads to a fresh new strategy, and another thing entirely to bring that plan to life. But breathing life into the plan on a day-to-day basis is what spells the difference between winning and losing on the front lines of business. As an old Talmudic dictum teaches us, "study is not the essence, but action."[16] And to the victors, go the spoils. One study suggested that a 35% improvement in the quality of strategy implementation for the average firm was associated with a 30% improvement in shareholder value.[17] Sadly, the execution of strategy often falls woefully short, which not only leads to severe bottom-line maladies but can also crumble the often wafer-thin credibility held by senior management when a new plan is introduced. An oft-quoted *Fortune* magazine study from 1999 found that 70% of CEO failures came not as a result of poor strategy, but the inability to execute.[18] So why does strategy execution prove so elusive for the typical enterprise? Scorecard architects Robert S. Kaplan and David P. Norton believe the answer lies in the form of four barriers that must be surmounted before strategy can be effectively executed (Exhibit 1.1):

EXHIBIT 1.1 The Barriers to Implementing Strategy

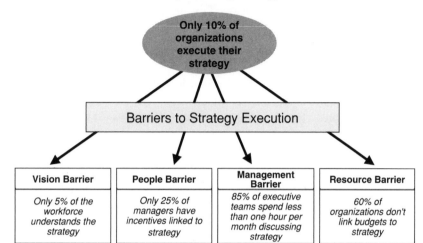

Adapted from material developed by Robert S. Kaplan and David P. Norton.

- *Vision barrier.* Suggests a scant 5% of the typical workforce understands the strategy. As discussed earlier, success in executing a strategy is the product of execution. Execution results from action, action from understanding, understanding from awareness. Right in the middle of that simple equation lies understanding. St. Augustine once remarked, *"one prays for miracles, but works for results."* Leaders who develop strategies and fail to take the requisite time and allocate the appropriate resources to ensure awareness and understanding are doing just that—praying for miracles. Each day your employees are faced with choices: how to handle a customer situation, what to budget for the forthcoming year, how to staff, and a hundred others of practical importance. Informed action is virtually impossible without a sound knowledge of the organization's strategy.

- *People barrier.* Incentive compensation systems have become wildly popular in the corporate world, and with good reason. Linking pay to performance drives focus and alignment around common themes. Problems emerge as a result of the actual construction of the rewards systems, however. Typically, the incentive is linked to a short-term financial target, and that can lead to some less-than-rational decision making as managers seek to maximize short-term gain, often at the expense of long-term sustainable success.

- *Management barrier.* On the topic of brevity in communication, Mark Twain once opined, "I tried to write a short letter, but it was too hard so I wrote a long one." It's a great line, and one that rings absolutely true. In the organizational world, it's difficult to boil things down to their essence, and as a result we tend to spend time on the periphery of issues rather than tackling the core. Management meetings manifest this point well. Rather than examining the blueprint we've developed for success (i.e., the strategy), teams will spend hours debating line items on the income statement such as gross revenue or cost of sales. These are undoubtedly important contributors to success, but are they necessarily strategic?

- *Resource barrier.* Raise your hand if you love budgeting. I'm guessing not a single person will derive any aerobic benefit from that question! Budgets are much-maligned these days, with critics calling their very existence into question. We'll examine the topic of budgets in greater detail in Chapter Seven, but for now suffice it to say that if your budget is not linked to your strategy, then where exactly is it aligned? Strategy should always be the guiding hand in creating the budget, and simple questions employed in crafting them: Based on our strategy, what initiatives will distinguish us from our rivals, and what are the associated resource requirements?

One of the many joys of writing books is having the opportunity to begin a dialogue with people from around the world on a topic of common interest. Since the publication of my first book (*Balanced Scorecard Step by Step: Maximizing Performance and Maintaining Results*), I've received calls and letters from readers around the globe, who have shared their stories and provided feedback on the text. Among the comments I cherish most are those suggesting that my books are "practical and simple." In this age of complexity and constant change, it's comforting to find something that is nonthreatening and approachable. When I reflect on those sentiments, I believe it's not simply my literary style, but the topics I discuss.

Everything I've shared with you thus far in this book is something you face every day—using often outdated financial metrics, harnessing intangible assets, protecting your reputation, and attempting to execute your strategy. These concepts are not particularly challenging from an intellectual standpoint, rather they are "practical and simple." But they are also profoundly important to the success of your business and have led organizations of every conceivable shape and size to embrace the Balanced Scorecard. In the next section, we'll briefly examine the Scorecard model and begin to determine exactly why it has become the tool of choice for those attempting to beat the overwhelming odds and effectively execute their strategies.

THE BALANCED SCORECARD

Origins and Background

The Balanced Scorecard was developed in 1990 by two men: Robert Kaplan and David Norton. Interestingly, Kaplan is an accounting professor at Harvard

University. Given his profession, you might suspect that he had a vested interest in safeguarding the vaunted position of financial numbers, but Kaplan was a visionary; he realized that financial numbers alone would not be enough for organizations attempting to thrive, or even compete, in the 21st century. To that end, he and Norton organized a research study of a dozen companies, attempting to discern best practices in performance measurement. Out of that study, the Balanced Scorecard was born. Just as a person is born and matures, so too has the Balanced Scorecard—from measurement system to strategic management system to a powerful communication tool describing and articulating strategy. We owe a tremendous debt of gratitude to the work of Kaplan, Norton, and their many colleagues who have researched, codified, and published many leading Balanced Scorecard works.

The basic premise behind the Balanced Scorecard is a simple, yet profound, one. Financial measures are, and always will be important, but they must be supplemented with other indicators that predict future financial success. With that as their goal, Kaplan and Norton developed the Balanced Scorecard framework, shown in Exhibit 1.2.

At the center of the diagram we see the words *vision* and *strategy*. Unlike traditional performance measurement systems, which have financial controls at their core, the Balanced Scorecard begins with an organization's vision and strategy. We seek to *translate* the vision and strategy into performance measures, which can be tracked and used to gauge our success in the successful implementation of vision and strategy. This is accomplished by determining objectives and measures in each of the Scorecard's four interrelated perspectives: Financial, Customer, Internal Processes, and Employee Learning and Growth.

Financial Perspective

Financial measures are an important component of the Balanced Scorecard in the for-profit, public, and nonprofit worlds. In the for-profit domain, the measures in this perspective tell us whether our strategy execution—which is detailed through measures chosen in the other perspectives—is leading to improved bottom-line results. In the nonprofit and public sectors, financial measures ensure that we're achieving our results, but doing so in an efficient manner that minimizes cost. We normally encounter classic *lagging* indicators in the Financial perspective. Typical examples include revenue, profitability, and asset utilization.

Customer Perspective

When choosing measures for the Customer perspective of the Scorecard, organizations must answer two critical questions: "Who are our target customers?" and "What is our value proposition in serving them?" Sounds simple enough, but both of these questions offer many challenges to organizations. Most organizations will state that they do in fact have a target customer audience, yet their actions

EXHIBIT 1.2   The Balanced Scorecard

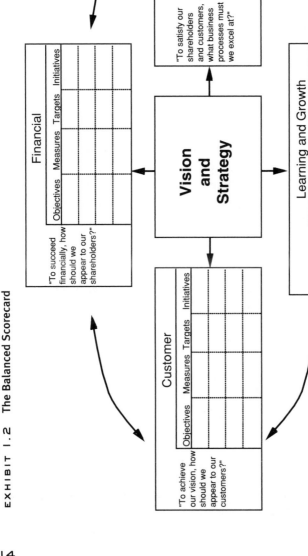

reveal an "all things to all customers" strategy. Strategy guru Michael Porter suggests this lack of focus will prevent an organization from differentiating itself from competitors.[19] Choosing an appropriate value proposition poses no less of a challenge to most organizations. Many will choose one of three "disciplines" articulated by Treacy and Wiersema in *The Discipline of Market Leaders*.[20] They are:

- *Operational excellence.* Organizations pursuing an operational excellence discipline focus on low price, convenience, and often "no frills." Wal-Mart provides a great representation of an operationally excellent company.

- *Product leadership.* Product leaders push the envelope of their firm's products. Constantly innovating, they strive to offer simply the best product in the market. Nike is an example of a product leader in the field of athletic footwear.

- *Customer intimacy.* Doing whatever it takes to provide solutions for unique customers' needs helps define customer-intimate companies. They don't look for one-time transactions but instead focus on long-term relationship building through their deep knowledge of customer needs. In the retail industry, Nordstrom epitomizes the customer-intimate organization.

As organizations have developed, and experimented with, value propositions, many have suggested it is difficult, if not impossible, to focus exclusively on just one. A more practical approach is to choose one discipline in which you possess particularly strong attributes, and maintain at least threshold standards of performance in the other disciplines. McDonald's, for example, is a truly operationally excellent organization, but that doesn't stop the company from continually introducing new menu items. In Chapters Four and Five, we will take a closer look at the Customer perspective and identify what specific steps your organization should take to develop Customer measures. Included in our discussion will be ideas you can use to apply the "value proposition" concept to your organization.

Internal Processes Perspective

In the Internal Processes perspective of the Scorecard, we identify the key processes at which the organization must excel in order to continue adding value for customers. Each of the customer disciplines outlined previously will entail the efficient operation of specific internal processes in order to serve our customers and fulfill our value proposition. Our task in this perspective is to identify those processes and develop the best possible measures with which to track our progress. To satisfy customers, you may have to identify entirely new internal processes rather than focusing your efforts on the incremental improvement of existing activities. Service development and delivery, partnering with the community, and reporting are examples of items that may be represented in this perspective. We will examine the development of performance measures for Internal Processes in greater depth during Chapters Four and Five.

Learning and Growth Perspective

If you expect to achieve ambitious results for internal processes, customers, and financial stakeholders, where are these gains found? The measures in the Learning and Growth perspective (also referred to as the Employee Learning and Growth perspective) of the Balanced Scorecard serve as the enablers of the other three perspectives. In essence they are the foundation on which this entire house of a Balanced Scorecard is built.

Once you identify measures and related initiatives in your Customer and Internal Process perspectives, you can be certain of discovering some gaps between your current organizational infrastructure of employee skills (human capital), information systems (information capital), and climate (organizational capital) and the level necessary to achieve the results you desire. The measures you design in this perspective will help you close that gap and ensure sustainable performance for the future.

Like the other perspectives of the Scorecard, we would expect a mix of core outcome (lag) measures and performance drivers (lead measures) to represent the Learning and Growth perspective. Employee skills, employee satisfaction, availability of information, and alignment could all have a place in this perspective. Many organizations I've worked with struggle in the development of Learning and Growth measures. It is normally the last perspective to be developed, and perhaps the teams are intellectually drained from their earlier efforts of developing new strategic measures, or they simply consider this perspective "soft stuff" best left to the Human Resources group. No matter how valid the rationale seems, this perspective cannot be overlooked in the development process. As I mentioned earlier, the measures you develop in the Learning and Growth perspective are really the enablers of all other measures on your Scorecard. We'll discuss objectives and measures for this perspective in Chapters Four and Five.

The Evolution of the Balanced Scorecard

When Kaplan and Norton developed the Balanced Scorecard some 15 years ago, they were basically attempting to solve a measurement problem: How can we balance the historical accuracy and integrity of financial metrics with the drivers of future financial success? The Balanced Scorecard proved to be an eloquent solution and was ultimately hailed as one of the 75 most influential business ideas of the 20th century by the *Harvard Business Review*. As is the case with any idea whose utility has been forged at the hands of actual practitioners with a real need, the Balanced Scorecard benefited greatly from the constant tinkering and experimentation of organizations bent on deriving ever-greater benefits from the tool.

The second generation of the Balanced Scorecard manifested as what has been termed a "strategic management system," which simply implies linking short-term actions to long-term strategy by way of the Balanced Scorecard. Budgeting and compensation were the logical processes to benefit from a union with the Balanced Scorecard, and so it was as organizations began to find innovative methods of developing budgets linked to strategy, and incentive systems based on balanced metrics of performance.

Perhaps the greatest virtue of the Balanced Scorecard framework is its undeniable power as a communication tool. With the advent of strategy maps in the mid-1990s, organizations discovered a potent new method of clearly and simply describing their strategies in a coherent way to data-rich but information-starved employees. Attempting to discern how strategy could be enacted had for years been an exercise of groping hopelessly in the dark, but with the introduction of the strategy map and Balanced Scorecard, a light literally appeared. No longer is strategy some poorly understood treatise bandied about by executives, but instead it is transformed into simple objectives and measures that drive real people to real behaviors leading to real results.

IS THE BALANCED SCORECARD HERE TO STAY?

Let's put all of our cards on the table and begin with an examination of the "f word." No, not that "f word," the other, far more disturbing one—*fad*. I've been getting the question from conference participants, clients, and readers for the better part of the last 10 years: Is the Balanced Scorecard a fad? Far from resenting this query, I welcome it and the spirit of discourse and discovery it engenders. And why shouldn't we question the longevity of the Balanced Scorecard? In this era of global communication and networks, new ideas flourish and spread faster than chicken pox through a kindergarten class. The metaphor is intentional because many ideas seem to spark more organizational suffering than breakthrough results as originally conceived. Additionally, the longevity of business ideas is gradually diminishing. Back in the 1950s and '60s, the average life of a management theory was around 15 years, whereas today the average idea has a shelf life of approximately three years.[21] Even if you choose to believe in the value of new ideas, where do you begin? Why, just in the last several years, you could:

> Flatten your pyramid, become a horizontal organization, and eliminate hierarchy from your company. You can empower your people, open your environment, and transform your culture. You can listen to your customers, create a customer-focused organization, and commit to total customer satisfaction. You can do the "vision thing," write a mission statement, and put together a strategic plan. You can improve continu-

ously, shift your paradigms, and become a learning organization. You can devote yourself and your company to total quality management. Or you can reengineer your corporation.[22]

Have you sampled any of the tempting delights of this menu? If so, you're certainly not alone. However, as a result of many highly publicized flops, we've become increasingly skeptical of new ideas promising to be the panacea we've been searching for in our quest for business success. But before we write off the entire management idea factory as out of touch or "pie in the sky," let's cast a more critical eye on what goes on when an idea is adopted by an organization.

There is little doubt that some among us are simply idea chasers, rushing wildly from one unproven business nostrum to the next, with little thought of the practical utility of the idea for this business at this time. I believe that virtually all ideas out there contain at least a kernel of value if judiciously implemented in the face of a real business need. Therefore, the first question you should ask yourself when considering the adoption of a new idea or technique (including the Balanced Scorecard) is: "What business need will this tool help us solve right now, and in the future?" If you can't provide a compelling response to that question, one you can sell to your employees who will be looking to you for guidance and leadership, then you must seriously reconsider your intentions. Even if you have a driving business need, a "burning platform," you may still fall victim to lackluster implementation. Frequently, this problem is the real culprit in the ongoing drama being played out in companies around the world. All too often a new idea is sold convincingly, ushered in enthusiastically, but given inadequate resources and lacking the ongoing commitment from senior management to give it any legitimate opportunity to bear fruit.

The Life Cycle of Ideas

As you may have guessed, I'm a fan of new ideas. In fact, I agree with composer John Cage, who once remarked: *"I can't understand why people are frightened of new ideas. I'm frightened of the old ones."*[23] So you can imagine my delight when I recently discovered an entire book dedicated to the topic. *What's the Big Idea?* goes deep into a discussion of business ideas and the gurus who spearhead their acceptance. In an interesting section early in the book, the authors outline the cycle of a successful business idea within an organization.[24] The five phases are outlined in Exhibit 1.3.

Every idea has a *progenitor*, which is represented either by the person introducing the idea to the organization or preceding ideas that sparked interest in the current movement. Once introduced, ideas generally start small in the form of a *pilot*, a limited-scale implementation in one area of the organization. Pilots are conducted to test the rigors of the idea in the real world and to determine if they

EXHIBIT I.3   The Life Cycle of a Business Idea Within the Organization

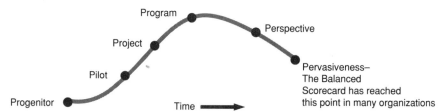

Adapted from material presented in "What's the Big Idea," Thomas H. Davenport and
Laurence Prusak, *What's the Big Idea* (Boston, MA: Harvard Business School Press, 2003).

are appropriate for a wider release throughout the company. Typically, those working on the pilot are the only group aware of the idea, and resources both in the form of budget and management attention tend to be scant.

Once the pilot has been deemed a success, the idea is generally transformed into a *program*, gaining the attention of most senior managers and beginning to attract resources as it spreads throughout the company. The idea is said to have gained *perspective* once it has become part of the everyday routine of the company. While the idea has gained "mind share" in a large percentage of the population, people are still conscious of the idea as they practice it. The final stage in the internal life cycle of a business idea is that of *pervasiveness*. Gone are the consulting projects, conferences, and gurus, which may have originally trumpeted the idea. At this point in its evolution, the idea has become ingrained in the fabric of the organization and is practiced without being overtly discussed.

Organizations that have successfully implemented the Balanced Scorecard have reached the stage of pervasiveness, one in which the Scorecard provides a transparent background for virtually every facet of the operation. The tool has become part and parcel of the everyday running of the company, and while people may be cognizant of the theoretical dimensions of the framework, those underpinnings are simply accepted and no longer expounded in a variety of forums. At this point the Balanced Scorecard has become the cornerstone of management practices, guiding reporting, budgeting, performance appraisal, and frequently, incentive compensation. Organizations implementing the Scorecard could do worse than contemplating this end state of pervasiveness as an initial goal of the implementation. One of my clients did just that. At the outset of their journey, they declared success as *"every employee having the ability to articulate our strategy and how their role contributes to the success we will be achieving in executing our plan."*[25] They realized early on that success lay in commitment, rather than compliance to the notion of the Balanced Scorecard. Once employees were committed through a guiding rationale, extensive communication, and ongoing management support, they would embrace the Scorecard and use it to its full capacity, ultimately resulting in knowledge, focus, and alignment throughout the organization.

The Balanced Scorecard Is on Sound Footing for Longevity

Many business observers suggest that the overwhelming majority of business ideas aren't entirely new.[26] This suggestion most likely results from that uniquely human phenomenon to build on the work of others using the latest data and information to improve or adapt ideas to fit current and anticipated circumstances. In simpler terms, we like to tinker. And let's be thankful for that trait because it has made possible everything from the Constitution under which we live to the modern conveniences of daily life we take for granted. The Balanced Scorecard was put forth by Kaplan and Norton early in the 1990s as a revolutionary idea for measuring organizational performance. I would suggest, however, that the basic tenets of the model map very well to work done by management scholars years, and sometimes decades, earlier. While constantly evolving through the work of academics and practitioners alike, the Balanced Scorecard is on solid theoretical footing, which supports its potential as a business tool for the ages.

Peter Drucker is one of the most widely read and heralded management thinkers of our time. His ideas and musings on the art and science of business have helped shape management direction throughout the world for the past 60 years. Drucker's "The Theory of the Business"[27] argues that all organizations—whether they know it or not—operate under a set of assumptions about market, customers, competitors, technology, competencies, and other fundamental dynamics. The assumptions in all areas must fit one another to produce a valid theory, they must be known and understood throughout the organization, and they must be tested constantly. A Balanced Scorecard approach is remarkably analogous. The "fit" to which Drucker refers is reflected through the cause-and-effect relationships in the Balanced Scorecard. In using the Scorecard as a communication tool, organizations are ensuring that their strategy is known and understood throughout the organization, as Drucker asserts must be the case with any valid theory. Finally, just as assumptions must be tested constantly in Drucker's model, Balanced Scorecard results must be analyzed on an ongoing basis and used to learn about the effectiveness of strategy execution.

In a similar vein, there are striking similarities between the notion of cause and effect as demonstrated in the Balanced Scorecard and the idea of "syndrome dynamics" as put forth by Abraham Maslow. Most of us are familiar with the name Maslow from college courses during which we were introduced to the iconographic "hierarchy of needs." So it may come as a surprise to learn that Maslow also spent time studying organizations, resulting in several provocative ideas, including syndrome dynamics.[28] The basic principle of syndrome dynamics is this: Organizations are "embedded" in their immediate communities; this immediate community is embedded in the larger community, which in turn is embedded in the country, which is embedded in the Western world, and so on. I would suggest that each of the four perspectives of the Scorecard represents syndromes in Maslow's vernacular. The Scorecard perspectives—Financial, Customer, Internal Processes, and Employee Learning and Growth—are contained and structured within the organization. Consistent with Maslow's theory, they share functional relationships in the sense that demonstrable causes and effects can be listed. In fact, the organization would be unable to function without any one of these elements and the myriad of assumed relationships that underlie them.

Finally, no discussion of the Balanced Scorecard's roots would be complete without a reference to the Tableau de Bord, a performance measurement system that emerged in France at the turn of the 20th century. Originally developed by process engineers attempting to improve their production processes by better understanding cause-and-effect relationships (sound familiar?), the Tableau de Bord was soon used by top management as a set of critical indicators used to assess performance in achieving strategic outcomes.[29] Like the Balanced Scorecard, indicators comprising a Tableau de Bord are best generated from a translation of the organization's mission.

Answering the Question

And now the answer you've all been waiting for: Is it or is it not a fad? Based on the undeniable results derived from thousands of organizations of every conceivable type and size in every corner of the globe, and on the constant evolution of the tool to meet the demands and rigor of new practitioners, no, I do not believe the Balanced Scorecard is a fad.

Perhaps the Balanced Scorecard is better wrapped in another colloquialism, "good common management sense." Despite the constant cries of unrelenting change swirling about us, there remain core elements of business that must be managed: strategy, planning, measurement, reporting, and so on. Regardless of what awaits us in the days and years ahead, these pillars will remain, and the Balanced Scorecard (or whatever moniker it's given in the future) will be there, standing resolutely awaiting the challenge of translating inspiring visions and strategies into the day-to-day actions carried out by employees everywhere in making those dreams a reality.

NOTES

1. Mike Bourne and Andrew Neely, "Why Measurement Initiatives Fail," *Quality Focus*, 2000 v4, p. 3.
2. Ibid.
3. John Micklethwait and Adrian Woolridge, *The Company* (New York: Modern Library Chronicles, 2003), p. 187.
4. Ibid., p. 182.

5. Mark A. Stephens and Aaron R. Runk, "Sarbanes-Oxley Compliance Drives Need for Collaborative Management," *Visum Solutions e-paper,* 2004, p. 2.

6. Thomas A. Stewart, *Intellectual Capital* (New York: Currency, 1999), p. xxi.

7. Interview on National Public Radio's Morning Edition, October 27, 2000.

8. Baruch Lev, "Sharpening the Intangibles Edge," *Harvard Business Review,* June 2004, pp. 109–116.

9. Brian E. Becker, Mark A. Huselid, and Dave Ulrich, *The HR Scorecard* (Boston, MA: Harvard Business School Press, 2001), p. 7.

10. Avery Hunt, "Mobilizing for Well-Being: The Army Medical Department's Balanced Scorecard Transformation," *Balanced Scorecard Report,* May–June 2003, pp. 9–10.

11. "ImClone's Ex-CEO Arrested, Charged with Insider Trading," *Wall Street Journal,* June 13, 2002.

12. Ibid.

13. Roy Harris, "Picking up the Pieces," *CFO.com,* August 2004.

14. Emily Kaiser, "Wal-Mart Looks to Reputation," *USA Today,* September 9, 2004.

15. Henry Mintzbert, Bruce Ahlstrand, and Joseph Lampel, *Strategy Safari* (New York: The Free Press, 1998).

16. Michael Hammer, "Why Leaders Should Reconsider Their Measurement Systems," *Leader to Leader,* No. 24, Spring 2002.

17. See note 9.

18. R. Charan and G. Colvin, "Why CEOs Fail," *Fortune,* June 21, 1999.

19. Michael E. Porter, "Strategy and the Internet," *Harvard Business Review,* March 2001, pp. 62–78.

20. Michael Treacy and Fred Wiersema, *The Discipline of Market Leaders* (Reading, MA: Perseus Books, 1995).

21. Tom Lester, "Pick Your Favorite Fad," *The Times of London,* September 13, 2001.

22. From Eileen Shapiro, as quoted in: Thomas H. Davenport and Laurence Prusak, with H. James Wilson, *What's the Big Idea?* (Boston, MA: Harvard Business School Press, 2003), p. 56.

23. Quotation found on www.quotationspage.com.

24. Thomas H. Davenport and Laurence Prusak, with H. James Wilson, *What's the Big Idea?* (Boston, MA: Harvard Business School Press, 2003), p. 53.

25. Allan A. MacDonald, "Implementing the Balanced Scorecard to Create a Strategy Focused Organization," unpublished dissertation, 2004.

26. See note 24, p. 59.

27. Peter Drucker, *Managing in a Time of Great Change* (New York: Truman Tilley / Dutton, 1995).

28. Abraham H. Maslow, *Maslow on Management* (New York: John Wiley & Sons, 1998).

29. Marc J. Epstein and Jean François Manzoni, "The Balanced Scorecard and Tableau de Bord," *Management Accounting,* August 1997, p. 29.

CHAPTER 2

First Things First

Have you heard the one about Sherlock Holmes and Dr. Watson out on a camping adventure? They'd gone to sleep beneath the night sky when Holmes awoke and shook his companion. "Watson, look at the sky and tell me what you see." "I see millions of bright stars," Watson answered. "And what does that tell you?" Watson reflected and stated confidently: "Astronomically, it tells me that there are countless galaxies and potentially billions of planets. Astrologically speaking, Saturn is in Leo. Theologically, I see that God is all powerful and that we are small and insignificant. And you, Holmes?"

Holmes paused. "What I see, Watson, is that someone has stolen our tent!" Moral of the story: Never overlook the obvious, regardless of the circumstances. So it is with our examination of the Balanced Scorecard. The most logical point of departure on this journey is a discussion of two fundamental aspects of implementation success: why are you developing a Balanced Scorecard, and do you have effective executive sponsorship? You may devise the most ingenious set of measures ever encountered in the organizational universe, but without these two foundational elements in place, your Balanced Scorecard will be in great peril from the beginning. In this chapter, we'll explore these topics and provide you with the opportunity to gauge your success in securing this foundation for your work.

WHY BALANCED SCORECARD AND WHY NOW?

Management guru Peter Drucker once observed that the most common source of mistakes in management decisions is the emphasis on finding the right answer rather than the right question. This is a provocative point, and one that is central to the first theme of this chapter. The single most important question to ask yourself before embarking on a Balanced Scorecard implementation is simply: Why? Why are we developing a Balanced Scorecard for this organization, and why now?

We're all familiar with the impressive statistics surrounding Balanced Scorecard usage in the organizational world: adopted by approximately 50% of the Fortune 1000, hailed as one of the 75 most influential business ideas of the 20th century, embraced by public, private, and nonprofit enterprises alike. Mere adoption of the tool, however, does not guarantee that business results will necessarily begin flowing as rapidly as Niagara Falls. Like any other business tool you employ, the Balanced Scorecard must solve an organizational issue, plug a hole, cure a headache, or the like. You choose the metaphor, but the bottom line is that you must possess a legitimate business reason for implementing the Balanced Scorecard. As we all know, swimming with the tide on all things business-related is not a roadmap for success. True breakthrough results await those with the courage and discipline to pursue a path of differentiation—answering opportunities and challenges with a unique response specifically designed to harness the best the organization has to offer. Organizations of this ilk quickly recognize that the Balanced Scorecard is not to be considered a panacea for all that ails them. Rather, it is a carefully considered tool rendered with surgical precision to solve real business issues.

Let me share with you some of the risks you face if you choose to simply develop a Balanced Scorecard for the sake of developing a Balanced Scorecard—and many companies are guilty of this error in judgment. Last year I began working with a government organization under the sponsorship of a senior executive. To my absolute delight, he was downright inspirational in our initial meetings and training sessions with employees. He frequently repeated such refrains as: "The Balanced Scorecard is the single greatest priority of this unit this year." "My number one priority is the successful implementation of the Balanced Scorecard." "I'm committing all the resources necessary to develop the Balanced Scorecard." These are wonderful statements: inspirational, direct, and indicative of true sponsorship. But have you noticed what is missing? Not once did he address why the organization had determined that the Balanced Scorecard was an appropriate tool at this moment. I suggested he insert the "why" message in all future correspondence, but for some reason he hesitated.

Despite our best efforts, over time the implementation began to struggle, and we were rapidly losing momentum. Eventually, I turned to that most reliable of corporate news sources—the grapevine—to find out what people were saying about the Balanced Scorecard. It turns out that most employees were convinced that in the absence of a stated reason for the Balanced Scorecard, their boss was planning to use it as a tool for generating layoffs within the unit, and as a result they were refusing to provide any support for the implementation. "Why lead ourselves to the chopping block?" was the defining sentiment among the rank and file. The sponsor was shocked by this news because he sincerely saw the Balanced Scorecard as a tool that could eventually lead to the attraction of new resources for the group. He attempted to regroup, but the damage was done, and we spent literally weeks thereafter communicating the true message of why the Balanced Scorecard was being implemented. It's a sad but true fact of the business world—in the absence of a motive for change, employees will generate one, and chances are it won't be the message you had in mind!

Virtually any type of change has the potential to feel threatening to those who are affected by it. We've all experienced the warm and fuzzy comfort of the status quo both in our personal and professional lives. Why, it took my wife 10 years to convince me to change the brand of toothpaste I use! Change is difficult; therefore, it's essential for you to answer the question of why the Balanced Scorecard is a necessary step for your organization and why now. As Larry Weinbach, CEO of Unisys, points out:

> Make sure that you recognize not everybody is going to come on board on day one and that it's going to take a lot of face time to ensure that people understand where you want to go and why....The why becomes a big issue because, it may seem surprising, but a lot of people may not understand why you want to make the strategic change, even if the company is not doing well.[1]

Like the absent tent revealing the sparkling night sky above Sherlock Holmes, the rationale for change may be glaringly apparent to you, but chances are you have far greater access to strategic information than most of your employees, the very group who will ultimately be charged with the responsibility of living the Balanced Scorecard on a day-to-day basis. To them, the case for change may be unwarranted or simply unknown, and without that knowledge it will prove exceedingly difficult for you to gain their true commitment to the implementation.

Determining Why to Use the Balanced Scorecard

Your choice for adopting the Balanced Scorecard must be a personal one, based on the environment you face and your belief in the tool's ability to lead you to improved results for all of your stakeholders. However, there are several commonly cited motivations, and we'll discuss each in the following paragraphs. Upon further reflection, some organizations may appropriately determine that the time is not right for a Balanced Scorecard. To help you make that decision, please refer to the assessment guide in Exhibit 2.1.

Probably the most oft-mentioned impetus for implementing a Balanced Scorecard is the *effective execution of a new strategy*. As discussed in Chapter One, the odds are heavily stacked against those wishing to execute their strategies, and therefore, the Balanced Scorecard has emerged as a very popular, and extremely

EXHIBIT 2.1 **Assessing the Need for a Balanced Scorecard**

To complete the exercise, read each statement and determine how much you agree with what is stated. The more you agree, the higher the score you assign. For example, if you fully agree, assign a score of 5 points.

1 2 3 4 5   1. Our organization has invested in Total Quality Management (TQM) and other improvement initiatives but we have not seen a corresponding increase in financial or customer results.

1 2 3 4 5   2. If we did not produce our current Performance Reports for a month, nobody would notice.

1 2 3 4 5   3. We create significant value from intangible assets such as employee knowledge and innovation, customer relationships, and a strong culture.

1 2 3 4 5   4. We have a strategy (or have had strategies in the past) but have a hard time successfully implementing it.

1 2 3 4 5   5. We rarely review our performance measures and make suggestions for new and innovative indicators.

1 2 3 4 5   6. Our senior management team spends the majority of their time together discussing variances from plan and other operational issues.

1 2 3 4 5   7. Budgeting at our organization is political and based largely on historical trends.

1 2 3 4 5   8. Our employees *do not* have a solid understanding of our mission, vision, and strategy.

1 2 3 4 5   9. Our employees *do not* know how their day-to-day actions contribute to the organization's success.

1 2 3 4 5   10. Nobody owns the performance measurement process at our organization.

1 2 3 4 5   11. We have numerous initiatives taking place at our organization, and it's possible that not all are truly strategic in nature.

1 2 3 4 5   12. There is little accountability in our organization for the things we agree as a group to do.

1 2 3 4 5   13. People tend to stay within their "silos," and as a result we have little collaboration among departments.

1 2 3 4 5   14. Our employees have difficulty accessing the critical information they need to serve customers.

1 2 3 4 5   15. Priorities at our organization are often dictated by current necessity or "fire-fighting."

1 2 3 4 5   16. The environment in which we operate is changing, and in order to succeed, we too must change.

1 2 3 4 5   17. We face increased pressure from stakeholders to demonstrate results.

1 2 3 4 5   18. We *do not* have clearly defined performance targets for both financial and nonfinancial indicators.

1 2 3 4 5   19. We cannot clearly articulate our strategy in a one-page document or "map."

1 2 3 4 5   20. We sometimes make decisions that are beneficial in the short term but may harm long-term value creation.

EXHIBIT 2.1   *(Continued)*

Scoring Key:

20 – 30: If your score fell in this range you most likely have a strong performance measurement discipline in place. The program has been cascaded throughout your organization to ensure that all employees are contributing to your success, and it is linked to key management processes.

31 – 60: You may have a performance measurement system in place but are not experiencing the benefits you anticipated or need to succeed. Using the Balanced Scorecard as a Strategic Management System would be of benefit to you.

61 – 100: Scores in this range suggest difficulty in successfully executing your strategy and meeting the needs of your customers and other stakeholders. A Balanced Scorecard system is strongly recommended to help you focus on the implementation of strategy and align your organization with overall goals.

Adapted from *Balanced Scorecard Step by Step for Government and Nonprofit Agencies* by Paul R. Niven.

effective tool in this regard. A note of caution is in order here, however. Some organizations will embark on a Balanced Scorecard effort in the belief that the implementation will lead to the development of a new and winning strategy. Let's be very clear: The Balanced Scorecard is a tool that was designed to assist you in executing your strategy, not crafting a new strategy. The inherent assumption accompanying the Balanced Scorecard is that your organization possesses a strategy and requires a tool to bring it to life on a day-to-day basis. To be fair, however, I have witnessed implementations in which the building of a Balanced Scorecard has led organizations to reconsider their strategic directions and discover new paths, enlightened from the discussion and debate that characterizes Balanced Scorecard development sessions.

Many organizations may have a clear and concise strategy, forged from the fires of the best available knowledge, but find it difficult to galvanize that vision across a diverse workforce. This dilemma is not surprising when you consider phenomena such as mergers and acquisitions, which are increasingly bringing together cultures that may provide synergies down the road but are vastly different. As the ink is drying on the contracts, employees are faced with the question: "What do we do now?" Many organizations will turn to the Balanced Scorecard in an attempt to *drive focus and alignment* from top to bottom throughout the enterprise. Again, the Scorecard admirably answers this call through the deceptively simple objectives and measures that can be quickly communicated and grasped across the company. Cascading the Scorecard, a topic we'll consider in more detail in Chapter Six, provides every employee with the opportunity to openly declare how his or her actions are contributing to the overall success of the company, and in so doing drives those frequently elusive elements of organizational focus and alignment.

The average tenure of CEOs in the United States is declining rapidly, with the typical stay in the chief executive's chair a scant three years. Given the unrelenting focus on driving value for shareholders, CEOs have precious little time to establish themselves as credible leaders, capable of producing the results craved by markets. A Balanced Scorecard is frequently used to *deliver their change agenda* in a clear and coherent fashion, one capable of being absorbed and acted on quickly. What better way for an ambitious executive to put her stamp on the organization than by creating a compelling set of objectives and measures, emanating from strategy, and aimed at taking the organization to the next level.

Just a cursory scan of the business pages, or even the front page headlines, will reveal the existence of many crises in the corporate world. Barely a day goes by that we don't hear of the impending death of a company, or in some cases, entire industries. *Emerging successfully from a crisis* requires many things, but chief among them is the focus on a few, key business priorities that will right the ship in the short term and lead to ongoing profitability in the long term. When Greg Brenneman and Gordon Bethune were charged with the unenviable task of turning around the fast-sinking Continental Airlines in 1994, they quickly grasped the necessity of getting the struggling company focused on fundamentals. A key component of their "Go Forward Plan" was the relentless tracking of 15 or so key performance measures designed to get everyone from baggage handlers to executives rallying around exactly what it would take to turn the company around.[2] As Brenneman, Bethune, and countless other corporate chieftains have learned, the right performance measures—crafted from strategy and woven together to tell your story—have the unique ability to drive laser-like focus on business results. Within a year of their turnaround efforts, Brenneman and Bethune were able to shepherd the ailing Continental from worst to first in dispatch reliability and shave a hefty $275 million from their maintenance budget.

Companies with their feet to the fire tend to garner the lion's share of business press and generate tantalizing headlines, but what of the vast number of organizations that are moving along very well, making their way in a slow and steady progression of ever-greater results? Is the Balanced Scorecard right for them? The answer is a resounding yes. Proactive organizations currently enjoying success realize that *sustaining prosperity* is a challenge to be confronted every day. In fact, generating enthusiasm for a change vision may pose an even greater challenge to those whose employees are operating in a blissful state of confidence, buoyed by past results. That hasn't stopped organizations like Datex-Ohmeda, the largest division of Instrumentarium and a world leader in the production of machinery used in acute care. When they turned to the Balanced Scorecard, the picture could hardly have been brighter; since their inception as a new division of Instrumentarium in 1998, Datex-Ohmeda had posted double-digit growth figures and achieved the targeted 15% operating profit level ahead of schedule. They realized, however, that past success was in no way indicative of future profits, especially in light of toughening competition and increasing customer demands. The Balanced Scorecard has ensured that their strategy is well-understood across the many languages and cultures of the organization, and it helped build a unified team committed to moving ahead together as one.[3]

Most of what we've discussed thus far in this section can be capably represented by numbers and words. It's easy for a CEO to gather employees in a conference room and enthusiastically announce the company's new strategy, accompanied by mouse pads and coffee cups with slogans emblazoned prominently. It's equally simple to provide the stark reality of a grim situation to a frequently incredulous crowd in the form of distressing financial results, but all too often neither of these approaches produces the intended effect of bringing people to action. Some find the messages remote and abstract, whereas others feel the problem rests solely with senior management, and it's their responsibility to get the company out of any mess, regardless of how it was created.

Encountering this situation, some organizations will take the road frequently less traveled and bring their teams face to face with operational problems. That's exactly what New York City Police Commissioner William Bratton did to bring the harsh reality of the city's crime problems into the laps of his managers.[4] As head of the city's transit police in 1990, Bratton discovered that none of his senior staff officers rode the subway to work. Most commuted, and when they arrived at work, they were shuttled throughout the gridlocked streets of New York in the comfort of city-provided vehicles. Complacency reigned, because it was difficult for staffers to feel the literal pain and fear of subway riders when they were traveling safely and comfortably. Bratton quickly extinguished their self-imposed comfort by insisting that every transit police official—including himself—ride the subway to work, to meetings, and at night. What they experienced came as a cold slap in the face to many: aggressive beggars panhandling relentlessly, winos and homeless people sprawled over benches, and gangs of youths running wild and frequently intimidating those citizens courageous enough to brave the system. No longer was subway crime a nonthreatening statistic on some innocuous report; instead, it was transformed into a living, breathing reality.

The need for change was deeply planted in the psyches of managers, and Bratton used it to push for changes in the transit police, and later throughout the entire department. You may not require such dramatic actions as those enacted by Bratton, but certainly you can take concrete steps to introduce the reality of your situation to your employees. Simply speaking to customers, visiting stores where your products are sold, or requiring all employees to use your products or services for a week and report on their experiences may be enough to jolt some team members out of the comforts of complacency and enhance their willingness to embrace a case for change.

The Benefits of Having a Guiding Rationale

Shallow and vague rhetoric simply won't cut it in today's information economy. Employees want and need to understand the strategy of the company and how they contribute to it in a meaningful way. We're overloaded with data at every turn on the corporate highway, and weary managers need the ability to discern the truly important from the marginally noteworthy. Once you've made the decision to use the Balanced Scorecard, your first obligation is to clearly explain why that choice has been made and what benefits you expect as a result. The more specific you are, the better—outline in vivid detail the challenges you face from competitors, changing customer tendencies, supplier pressures, stakeholder demands, and so on. Demonstrate to your team why change is not simply an option, but an imperative if you are to stay in the game and sustain your success.

Developing a rationale for your Balanced Scorecard is not a one-time, check-that-off-the-list activity. Rather, it is an ongoing anthem for the implementation, one that informs all future decisions regarding your Scorecard development. At each junction on the path of Balanced Scorecard development, you're faced with choices. The guiding rationale you've put forth will help illuminate that path and create sound solutions that further embed the tool in the fabric of the organization. Finally—and you all know this—every implementation will lose momentum at one time or another; the practical realities of modern business and its multitude of attendant priorities make that a virtual certainty. The true test is whether you can emerge from these periods of corporate lethargy with renewed vigor and enthusiasm for the task at hand. A guiding rationale for your Balanced Scorecard can serve as your rallying cry, bringing together the entire organization under the banner of why you made this decision in the first place.

WHO OWNS THE BALANCED SCORECARD?: EXPLORING EXECUTIVE SPONSORSHIP

One of the books I'm currently reading is Stephen Ambrose's utterly engrossing tale of the Lewis and Clark expedition, *Undaunted Courage*. It reads more like a novel than an historical account of two 19th-century explorers, and the twists and turns would make any Hollywood screenwriter envious. One of the many things that fascinates me about the journey of the Corps of Discovery is the innumerable choices faced by Meriwether Lewis and William Clark throughout their epic journey. Supplied with the most rudimentary of maps and lacking any concrete knowledge of geography west of the Continental Divide, they had to make potentially life-altering decisions on a daily basis: which route to take, how to traverse seemingly unconquerable terrain, which Indian tribes to trust and trade with, how to ensure the ongoing fitness and safety of their men, and so on.

It's a long way from Lewis and Clark to the executive floors of our major corporations, but consider for a moment the parallels with the modern executive. Charting the direction of today's business enterprise must sometimes feel strikingly similar to being in an isolated wilderness without a reliable map. The journey to strategic execution is fraught with challenges, each with the potential to severely damage corporate and executive fortunes alike. Like Lewis and Clark, modern executives must continually make effective decisions with limited information. However, unlike those intrepid explorers, there is certainly no shortage of potential assistance available to executives blazing their way, with innumerable tools, techniques, and methodologies available to make their job easier. Being human beings, executives, like the rest of us, have limited capacity to absorb the endless swarm of information swirling about them. What they filter through and ultimately decide to pay attention to is what gets done in the organization and forms the essence of executive sponsorship.

No initiative, regardless of its potential, will survive in the organization without executive sponsorship. It's very simple, really: everyone watches what the boss watches. If executives provide casual support to the Balanced Scorecard, that treatment will instantly be translated by those on the front lines to mean this tool is revving up on the runway, heading for that scrap heap of abandoned ideas in the sky. Why commit yourself to something that your leaders appear reluctant to back themselves? As rational beings, most of us want to grow in our lives and careers, and while we all have time for certain pet projects, the majority of our efforts are directed toward steps that are more likely to yield positive results. Can your Balanced Scorecard achieve success without executive sponsorship? A modicum of success, perhaps. You may develop a set of objectives and measures that captures people's attention and drives an increased amount of alignment and focus. However, for real, sustainable, and breakthrough results to occur, an active, ceaseless, and dedicated executive sponsor is an absolute must. Let's look at how leading enterprises are able to secure executive sponsorship and what you should expect your leaders to demonstrate in this capacity.

Securing Executive Sponsorship

You may have already developed a Balanced Scorecard, and after reading the preceding paragraphs can literally feel the wind coming out of it like an untied balloon tossed from the arms of a carefree child and sputtering rapidly to the ground. It's true that without sponsorship it is most likely just a matter of time before that shapeless balloon falls to the ground, with your hopes and dreams of a successful implementation attached to it. The good news is that sponsorship can be secured even after you've begun the development effort, and your implementation will hold much greater promise as a result. Outlined as follows are several techniques you can use to attract an executive sponsor to your Balanced Scorecard implementation.

Sponsoring any initiative entails an element of risk for the executive involved. After all, there is the possibility the initiative may fail, which will result in a personal loss of face, not to mention the organizational consequences. A first step in the process, therefore, is to ensure that the Scorecard framework will in fact work within your unique organization. This may be accomplished by shopping the idea around and testing it through conversations at your workplace. Mohi Ahmed, an idea practitioner at Fujitsu, follows this approach when attempting to introduce any new idea. After he has developed a "feel and sense for how the idea might work at Fujitsu," he discusses it with trusted sources. If it passes that checkpoint, he discusses it with a potential user. Only then will he begin dialogue with a potential executive sponsor. As the idea passes through each checkpoint, the likelihood increases that the idea could be smoothly introduced into the organization's broader discourse and successfully piloted.[5] Once you're confident of the Balanced Scorecard's efficacy in your context, it's time to secure your sponsor.

In their extremely pragmatic book *Execution*, authors Charan and Bossidy describe the dilemma faced by executives when potentially helpful initiatives fail. Typically, they note, the failure is a result of resistance from managers in the organization who feel this too shall pass, pay little attention, and wait for the idea to wither and die on the vine. The result is wasted time, money, energy, and a loss of credibility to leadership, who frequently don't recognize the failure as a personal indictment. They go on to suggest that:

> The leader's personal involvement, understanding, and commitment are necessary to overcome this passive (or in many cases active) resistance. She has not only to announce the initiative, but to define it clearly and define its importance to the organization. She can't do this unless she understands how it will work and what it really means in terms of benefit.[6]

What a powerful statement, and replete with many provocative elements, but the one I'd like to isolate is that of *understanding*. No executive, facing severe time and attention demands, will provide his support to an initiative he doesn't understand. Therefore, it is of paramount importance that you ensure your potential sponsor understands the Balanced Scorecard, its fundamental principles, and practical applications within your business. A first step is basic Balanced Scorecard training. I can hear you saying to yourselves, "I'll never get Charles, Kim, (fill in the name) to commit the time for a training session." It's a fact that most executives are extremely time-starved and won't consent to an in-depth Scorecard training session. But you don't need Balanced Scorecard boot camp, just an informative session to ensure they understand the tool and how it will provide a real benefit to your organization right now.

This investment will yield significant rewards down the road when Scorecard work products are unveiled and you're counting on your executives to possess the knowledge of Scorecard fundamentals in order to process your work. The importance of executive understanding was demonstrated to me in a recent client engagement with a large nonprofit organization. A Balanced Scorecard core team was assembled to produce the majority of work products: strategy map, measures, targets, and so on. Naturally, they underwent training to ensure understanding of both the fundamentals and the intricacies of the framework. The executive sponsors, however, decided to forego the training. A few weeks went by, and it was time for the first presentation of a deliverable, in this case the draft strategy map, to a small group of senior executives. When we presented the findings, a couple of the executives were resistant of everything the team had developed. I immediately felt that the questions and concerns reflected more of a lack of understanding of the Balanced Scorecard system than anything else. One executive in particular was very concerned about the strategy map being "busy work" and didn't seem to understand the terminology. How could the team expect this individual to sponsor and advocate on behalf of the Scorecard when he didn't even understand the terminology employed in the framework?

Understanding is a huge leap forward, but it will not guarantee sponsorship of the Balanced Scorecard by itself. To continue on that path, a key next step is executive involvement in the process. Just as we would not expect executives to advocate on behalf of an initiative they don't clearly understand, it's folly to believe they will support it without some involvement in its development. Initial involvement may be satisfied in the form of an interview, during which the executive is asked to provide input on several critical Balanced Scorecard building blocks, such as strategy, vision, key objectives, potential measures, targets, and supporting initiatives. Not only will interviews yield insights to be used in the construction of your Balanced Scorecard, but they also provide a unique opportunity to assess the executive's true understanding and support of the process.

In fact, it is the latter benefit I would cite as the key takeaway point from most executive interviews I've conducted over the years as a consultant. I can vividly recall an instant in which this was the case during an interview with the CFO of a large client. The gentleman walked into the room, shook my hand confidently, sat down across from me, scattered his assorted papers across the conference room table, and announced: "I want you to know I don't believe in any of this." So much for a smooth opening! But far from being distressed, I welcomed this admonition because it revealed a sincere belief that was clearly out in the open and not being harbored secretly, which can frequently lead to more insidious results. I tossed away my normal interview script and attempted to determine the source of his discontent with the Scorecard: Was it something inherent in the model, or perhaps an unsuccessful attempt at implementation in the past?

It turns out that was the culprit. Some years back, he worked with another organization that had attempted to literally cobble together a Balanced Scorecard consisting of a few metrics, mostly financial. Needless to say, it was a disaster that left him quite tainted. Once this issue was on the table, I had the opportunity to describe how this implementation would be more effective by following a proven framework, involving executives such as himself, and ensuring employee feedback as well. When the interview concluded, he declared: "I'm still not 100% there, but am now willing to listen." An open mind on his part translated to a huge victory in my book. Interviews can be tricky, and to help you through the process, several tips are presented in Exhibit 2.2.

EXHIBIT 2.2 Tips on Conducting an Effective Interview

Hold the interview in the executive's office: In order to receive candid feedback, it's critical that the executive feels comfortable. People tend to be most comfortable on their own "turf." Therefore, whenever possible, conduct your interviews in the executive's office. In addition to putting the person at ease, by holding the interview in his or her office, you have the opportunity to learn more about him or her based on furniture, pictures, desk decorations, etc. Undoubtedly something in the environment will provide the spark for an "ice-breaking" conversation.

Don't interrupt: I've learned this one the hard way. Some people are measured in their comments, taking time to formulate an appropriate response. Be sure that the executive has completed his or her thought before jumping in or moving on to the next question. When you derail someone, even if just for a second, it may throw the rhythm of the interview off significantly.

Consider having a designated note-taker: I have yet to have someone say yes to the following question: "Do you mind if I take some notes while we speak?" However, I have noticed that some people feel distracted by the note taking. Therefore, if possible, have one person asking the questions and a second person in the room solely to take notes. That way the interviewer can establish a comfortable rapport with the executive.

Be prepared to deviate from the "script:" It's crucial to have questions prepared in advance, but be ready to move from topic to topic as the conversation flows. You may pose a question about financial objectives to which the executive replies, "We have to focus on growing revenue, and we'll do that by educating our employees on the latest customer service skills." You have received not only a financial objective, but an employee learning and growth objective as well. Be sure you capture that information and either follow up immediately or return to it when the time is right.

Be aware of body language (both yours and the executive's): Establishing a comfortable rapport is critical in receiving open, honest feedback. Your body language can either facilitate or inhibit this process. Be sure to show interest through appropriate eye contact and facial expressions. You must also look for potential clues emanating from body language. Does the person physically back up or cross his or her arms when you ask certain questions? If so, you've stumbled into an area the person is either uncomfortable discussing with you or has strong feelings about. Either way, tread carefully to maintain the level of safety and comfort you've worked hard to establish.

You've found the executive, provided her with training, and interviewed her, but she's still not convinced, so what now? Let's conclude this section by dipping into the toolkit for a few additional suggestions you can use to win over even the most recalcitrant executive. First, link the Balanced Scorecard to an idea the executive is already passionate about.[7] Perhaps she is acutely aware of the power of intangible assets such as culture and customer relationships in transforming your business. Discuss the proven ability of the Balanced Scorecard to translate intangibles into real business value. If quality is the executive's first love, demonstrate the idea of cause and effect, outlining the fact that quality is a result of unique organizational elements such as training and culture, and that quality drives customer satisfaction and ultimately financial rewards—all key dimensions of the Scorecard framework. If payback in terms of time or money is an issue, show a quick payoff for the implementation of a Balanced Scorecard. Many organizations, for example, use the Scorecard as a means of prioritizing among competing initiatives, reducing or eliminating those that don't show a direct link to the objectives articulated in the Scorecard. Resources thus freed can now be dedicated to more strategic ends. Finally, have a solid implementation plan at the ready; in other words, manifest your readiness to do this right! Be prepared with responses to virtually every conceivable question, from "How long will this take?" to "What do you need?" to "What can we expect as a result of our investment?"

Sponsorship in Action

It's one thing to find a sponsor who vows to advocate on behalf of the Balanced Scorecard and be the inspirational leader of the implementation, and another thing entirely to find a person who is willing to raise the stakes from words to deeds. Understanding the basics and nuances of the Scorecard model and harboring a belief in its worth is tantamount to intellectual commitment to the idea. For meaningful change to take place, however, that intellectual commitment must be elevated to the demonstration of operational commitment.[8] As the old saying goes, actions speak louder than words, and employees will be watching executives' behaviors closely to determine whether they truly are walking their talk. Virtually every sponsor I've encountered in my consulting career has exhibited intellectual commitment to the idea of the Balanced Scorecard, but to their peril many have failed to take the leap from words to action. For those who do, however, rewards will follow in the form of increased employee buy-in, a smoother implementation, and, most important, improved business performance.

The most obvious manifestation of operational commitment comes in the form of involvement in the Balanced Scorecard development process. I strongly believe that people will only truly support something they help create, something that has been wrought from their own labors and creativity. Therefore, it's vital to have your executive sponsor play some role in the actual building of the Balanced Scorecard. Practical reality reigns over this request, however, and most executives won't have the time to play a full-time role on a Balanced Scorecard team. Fortunately, a full-time role is not required. Simply having the sponsor fully informed of the team's activities and giving him the chance to critically review and provide meaningful guidance will suffice in most cases. A dual purpose is served by this involvement: first, and pragmatically, the Balanced Scorecard produced will be of a higher caliber with the wisdom of a senior executive baked in; and second, the executive's involvement, regardless of the time and effort, helps forge greater commitment to the ideals embodied by the Balanced Scorecard.

Beyond direct involvement in the process, you should expect a true executive sponsor to use every available opportunity to spread the Balanced Scorecard message. A key component of this messaging is demonstrating just how important the Balanced Scorecard is in the organization's pursuit of strategic execution. This may seem basic, and you may not think it's necessary to constantly reiterate the point, but in the heat of everyday battle, many busy managers may lose sight of the overall goals, becoming embroiled in the urgent and missing the truly important. Clever executive sponsors nip this possibility in the bud with on-point messaging at key intervals.

Let me give you an example of what I mean: It's not uncommon for me to hear comments like these at the outset of Balanced Scorecard workshops: "I can't stay past four o'clock today, I have important work to do," or "How long will this take, because I have work to do?" I find such laments extremely discouraging. After all, what could be more important than crafting the tool you'll use to guide your company on a journey to strategic focus and alignment? One client executive shared my sentiments and used the opportunity to deliver the message that what they were engaging in was the most important work they could be doing—translating their strategy into action. He simply wouldn't tolerate comments suggesting that other work was more important. This went a long way toward imprinting just how passionately he felt about the Balanced Scorecard and the high expectations he had for everyone in the room in its implementation. We must never forget that the essence of leadership is effective communication of a vision. Robert A. Eckert of Mattel sums up the power of communication very well in this description of his first days with the company:

> I spent hours and hours describing to all our employees and other stakeholders where we were going and how we were going to get there. I traveled and met with people, of course, but also set up a program of regular e-mail updates, invited two-way communication, and responded personally to employee messages. Today, the company is back on track, but I'm still constantly communicating—in the elevator, in the cafeteria, on the street, on the phone, on planes, and through e-mails. And it's always the same basic message, which is our vision for the company.[9]

What we desire most of our executive sponsors is simply the commitment to actually use the Balanced Scorecard on an ongoing basis within the enterprise. Scorecard considerations should inform every facet of operations, including performance management, strategic resource allocation, employee development, and compensation. Bob Gold, a vice president with the Balanced Scorecard Collaborative, has observed true sponsorship in action:

> My clients' most effective leaders carry a laminated copy of their strategy map with them to all their meetings, not just to those with a Balanced Scorecard agenda. They use the map to briefly set the strategic context for the discussion and invite others to talk about how the organization or group is performing around the relevant objective.[10]

Once again, action illuminates true intent, not words. An executive who espouses the vital nature of intangible assets in one breath but focuses virtually all her attention on this quarter's financial results cannot masquerade her true devotions to employees who are carefully monitoring her every move. For the Balanced Scorecard to stand the test of time within the organization and provide the benefits it is certainly capable of, it must enjoy the sponsorship of an executive who understands, embraces, and utilizes the tool.

A Final Thought on Sponsorship and Leadership

Whether it's Balanced Scorecard, total quality, customer relationship management, or any other of the literally hundreds of initiatives your organization may be engaging in, the common theme uniting them all is the necessity of sincere sponsorship and effective leadership. But you don't have to be at the top of the corporate hierarchy to exercise leadership; every day you have the opportunity to be a positive role model for others in your organization and community. I'll end this section with a simple yet powerful exercise that I'm certain will leave you thinking differently about your impact. I learned of the exercise from the work of Joe Ehrmann. Football devotees among you may remember Ehrmann as a member of the "sack pack" defense with the Baltimore Colts in the mid-1970s. Back in those days, Ehrmann was as gifted at finding parties and trouble off the field as he was in running down opponent running backs on the gridiron. The death of his brother at the age of just 18 opened Joe's eyes and began what became a tidal wave of change in his life.

These days, at age 52, he dedicates his life to serving others through his work as a pastor at Grace Fellowship Church just outside Baltimore and his foundation called "Building Men for Others," one of several groups that he's founded to help those who are less fortunate. Joe frequently speaks to high school and college football coaches and challenges them with the following exercise. He distributes to each person a piece of paper with an empty circle and square, and instructs them to "write in the circle the names or initials of two men in your life through whom you felt affirmation as a boy." Once they've done that, he asks the group to move down the page to the empty square. "In the square, write the initials of one man in your life who shamed you." After providing ample time for his audience to complete the exercise, Joe says, "Twenty years from now I'm going to come back, and sitting here will be the boys that you've coached, and I'm going to take them through the same exercise. Do we want the kids we coach to remember us in that circle—as someone who affirmed them, gave them a vision of what they could be— or would we ever want to be put in that box by any single boy we've coached, any boy that we've come across?" Typically, nobody needs to answer out loud.[11]

The exercise as presented here is aimed at coaches of young men, but my hope is that readers will look beyond the male reference to the deeper question here: How do you wish to be remembered as a team member, manager, or executive? Twenty years from now, do you want your staff reflecting on you as having provided a guiding vision and affirming them or as shaming them and providing a model of how not to be an effective leader? The choice is ours, and we have the opportunity to make that choice every day.

SELF-ASSESSMENT QUESTIONS

This chapter marks the debut of self-assessment questions for your review. The purpose of these queries is to allow you to critically examine your Balanced Scorecard implementation in the context of each of the essential elements discussed in the text. The questions may be administered individually or in a group setting. I would recommend that you use the questions to guide a Balanced Scorecard review workshop, which I often conduct for my clients.

Form small groups of four to six people and begin the workshop by having individuals answer each question, and if desired, assigning a grade—many organizations find the traffic light metaphor of green equals good, yellow equals caution, and red signals improvement required as a useful device. Once team members have had the opportunity to answer the questions, the group will share their results and come to a consensus on the overall score (green, yellow, or red) for each element. To elevate this from a static to dynamic exercise, consider assigning the responsibility for each group to list at least three initiatives or actions to either improve red or yellow performance or sustain green performance.

A Guiding Rationale for Your Balanced Scorecard

1. Have we made the realization that the Balanced Scorecard is more than a measurement project and is in fact a change initiative that must be carefully managed using change management techniques?

2. Why have we specifically decided to develop a Balanced Scorecard? What organizational issue (or issues) does it help us solve?

3. Was our guiding rationale for the Balanced Scorecard (as noted in question 2) communicated broadly to our entire workforce?

Executive Sponsorship

1. Has our senior leadership developed, and are they committed to, a guiding vision and strategy for the organization?

2. Have we provided our potential sponsor(s) with Balanced Scorecard training to ensure they understand both the fundamentals and intricacies of the framework?

3. Have we ensured that our sponsor's voice is heard in the Balanced Scorecard by interviewing him or her and ensuring involvement in the development process?

4. Does our executive sponsor deliver consistent messages at frequent intervals regarding the Balanced Scorecard?

5. Is there accountability for results shared among our senior leadership team (i.e., do they have responsibility for meeting Balanced Scorecard targets)?

6. Is there evidence that our executive sponsor is actively using the Balanced Scorecard in the ongoing management of the organization?

NOTES

1. Elspeth J. Murray and Peter R. Richardson, *Fast Forward: Organizational Change in 100 Days* (New York: Oxford University Press, 2002), p. 28.
2. Greg Brenneman, "Right Away and All at Once: How We Saved Continental," *Harvard Business Review,* September–October 1998, p. 168.
3. Judith Ross, "Integrating a Global Enterprise with the Balanced Scorecard," *Balanced Scorecard Report,* March–April 2003, pp. 6–8.
4. W. Chan Kim and Renee Mauborgne, "Tipping Point Leadership," *Harvard Business Review,* April 2003, pp. 60–69.
5. Thomas H. Davenport and Laurence Prusak, with H. James Wilson, *What's the Big Idea?* (Boston, MA: Harvard Business School Press, 2003), p. 141.
6. Larry Bossidy and Ram Charan, *Execution* (New York: Crown Business, 2002), p. 65.
7. Ibid., p. 34.
8. See note 1, p. 48.
9. Robert A. Eckel et al., "Moving Mountains," *Harvard Business Review,* January 2003, p. 44.
10. Robert S. Gold, "Presenting the Balanced Scorecard Strategy Map," *Balanced Scorecard Report,* July–August 2004, p. 16.
11. Jeffrey Marx, *Season of Life* (Washington, DC: Jam Publishing, 2003), p. 122.

CHAPTER 3

Before You Measure

"That's just the tip of the iceberg" is a phrase we've all heard many times in both our personal and professional lives, suggesting there is much more to a topic than what first meets the eye. We can extend the metaphor to our work with the Balanced Scorecard; while the strategy map and measures used to actually translate your strategy get the bulk of attention within the organization, they truly do represent the tip of the iceberg. The submerged core of the Balanced Scorecard is represented by the many things that precede the actual measurement or reporting of results, elements such as a guiding rationale for your efforts and executive sponsorship, both of which were discussed in the preceding chapter. In this chapter we'll continue focusing on the foundation of Balanced Scorecard success by discussing your Balanced Scorecard team, training, communication planning, terminology, and the implementation planning process.

Did you know that the average age of ice comprising an iceberg is thought to be about 5,000 years?[1] I often talk about the Balanced Scorecard standing the test of time, but I have to admit that's pushing it a bit. But if you want the Scorecard to last and help you sustain your immediate success, the elements we discuss in this chapter must be as rock hard as icebergs floating in the North Atlantic.

YOUR BALANCED SCORECARD TEAM

My wife Lois is an active volunteer with an organization that finds adoptive homes for retired racing greyhounds.[2] As with most volunteers, her roles are many, varied, and often demanding, but she loves the work and finds the rewards—in the form of a happily retired, newly dubbed "forty-mile-an-hour couch potato"—well worth the toil. Taking one of these exquisite animals from the racetrack to a new home sounds easy, but it is actually a complex endeavor involving a web of relationships and processes. Just last night, Lois hosted a meeting of her fellow board members at our house. As I sat in our family room, one ear on the television and the other on their meeting in the next room, I could practically feel the energy emanating from their discussion: how they would work with the tracks and trainers to get the dogs, advertising and promotion ideas, attracting new volunteers, new innovations on their website, and support systems for new adopters. While some members were teeming with ambitious plans and ideas, other more fiscal-minded individuals were tempering their ambitions with a fair dose of reality. What they represented more than anything else was a team, *"a small number of people with complementary skills who are committed to a common purpose, performance goals, and approach for which they hold themselves mutually accountable."*[3]

Regardless of the field of endeavor, whether rescuing greyhounds, installing an enterprise resource planning system, or implementing a Balanced Scorecard, teams have emerged as a powerfully effective way of getting things done in the new economy. Bringing together a group of people with disparate skills, experiences, and personalities, each sharing the common goal of solving a problem or improving performance, provides a far greater probability of success than the outdated myth of the "corporate lone ranger" working in lonely isolation. The Balanced Scorecard is well-suited to a team approach because no single individual, not even the CEO, will possess all of the requisite knowledge of strategy, markets, demographic changes, customer preferences, and so on required to create this strategic management system. In the next section we'll examine the key elements of team composition and designating a Balanced Scorecard champion, and ponder the future of the team once the implementation is well underway.

Balanced Scorecard Team Composition

During client workshops, when the discussion turns to the Employee Learning and Growth perspective, it's becoming more and more common for me to hear at least one person utter: "we need to get the right people on the bus." This phrase has burst onto the business lexicon thanks primarily to Jim Collins and his blockbuster book, *Good to Great*.[4] Before we can scale any heights in business, we need the right people to help us make the ascent; it's as simple as that, and the Balanced Scorecard is no different.

The first consideration in loading people on the Balanced Scorecard bus is what level of the organization they should represent. Must the team consist entirely of executives, or will director level do, or perhaps we need front-line staff to ensure buy-in from all employees? The literature is replete with admonitions regarding the importance of executive involvement in the Balanced Scorecard process, and we discussed that requirement in the form of executive sponsorship in Chapter Two. The reality out there in the world, however, is that many senior executive teams either cannot (because of myriad other issues) or will not consent to providing the necessary time to form part of a Balanced Scorecard team. In my experience as a consultant, it is far more common to see an executive sponsor oversee the work of a lower-level Balanced Scorecard team. Would I like to have senior executives comprise the team? Of course, but will the Balanced Scorecard succeed without it? Also affirmative—with a caveat. Regardless of the level of the team chosen, there must be an executive sponsor in place, one with considerable clout within the inner circle of the CEO who can influence change and ensure that the Scorecard is seen as a key tool in the implementation of strategy. In practice, the higher the level of people you can assemble, the better. The advantages are obvious: with rank typically comes experience and knowledge, frequently credibility, and the ability to interact with the most senior of executives at regular intervals.

Some organizations will take a different tack, delegating the Scorecard's construction to a group of lower-level managers or supervisors in the hope that their participation will influence buy-in from front-line staff. This is a sound idea, but I've seen it cause significant problems in application. For one, lower-level managers typically lack the decision-making authority necessary to develop a monitoring system that will ultimately be owned by the organization's senior executives. As a result, they display a good measure of indecision when it comes time to make the trade-offs and tough decisions that form the basis of a sound Balanced Scorecard. Depth of strategic insight is also an issue. Most people at this level have seen bits and pieces but may not be able to fit together the many and diverse pieces of the entire strategic puzzle.

Ensuring representation from across your organization is also standard practice in assembling a quality Balanced Scorecard team. If your company includes, for example, five distinct business units, each should be included in the development of the corporate Balanced Scorecard to guarantee that the challenges, opportunities, and priorities of all five are reflected in the final product. Support groups such as Human Resources, Finance, and Information Technology (IT) will also be welcome at the Scorecard table. As with all things, however, there are limits to the lofty ideal of balanced representation. I recently worked with a client who has significant operations on both coasts of the United States. Our work was done at the head office on the East Coast, but they insisted on having individuals from the West Coast form part of our team. The idea was borne out of the best intentions, and in fact West Coast representation would make for a more universally accepted Scorecard. The problems were primarily logistic, but nonetheless significant. Getting the folks from the west to spend a week back east was challenging to say the least. And while they were there, because they made the trek infrequently, they took it upon themselves to load up with other meetings, seeing people they rarely had the chance to speak with in person. As a result, although they were ostensibly in town exclusively for the Balanced Scorecard, many of our meetings were delayed and some cancelled because the team members were in other sessions. Understandably, this led to thinly veiled frustration from the east coasters and bogged down the entire process. Cross-functional representation is a positive attribute for any team, but just make sure you keep the practical realities of your team members in mind when creating your roster.

My father is fond of saying "It takes all kinds," referring to the fact that our world is made vastly more interesting—and productive—thanks to the many personalities we encounter every day. In this regard the Balanced Scorecard is a microcosm of everyday living. For your team to function successfully, you should endeavor to include individuals with different skills, problem-solving abilities, and personalities. One type of person who will yield tremendous benefits in the form of sharing Balanced Scorecard knowledge and increasing the likelihood of acceptance are "connectors,"[5] people with a special gift for bringing the world together. We all know people who have the knack of making friends and acquaintances from broad and diverse subcultures of the population. They don't do it for the sake of making friends; it simply comes naturally to them. Delving into the history books reveals one of the best connectors of all time: Paul Revere. *"He was a fisherman and a hunter, a card player and a theater lover, a frequenter of pubs and a successful businessman. He was active in the local Masonic lodge and was a member of several select social clubs. He was also a doer, a man blessed . . . with an uncanny genius of being at the center of events."*[6] With his gregarious nature and connections to die for, who better to make the famed ride from Boston to Lexington with the frightening and provocative news that the British were coming? Within your organization today, there are people with this gift, one minute delivering an important presentation to bosses, the next speaking with a friend in the shipping department, and later in the day having coffee with associates in HR. They move easily throughout the company occupying several social strata, attracting new acquaintances comfortably. I've known plenty of connectors in my day and have always been somewhat drawn to them and interested in their opinions. After all, they're out there moving among the world, gathering information from disparate vantage points and communicating it effortlessly to eager ears. Employing at least one connector on your Balanced Scorecard team increases your communication capacity exponentially and gives you a leg up on the possibility of having your staff accept this new management system.

One trait of all team members will prove extremely valuable during your Balanced Scorecard development period: the ability to work comfortably in an atmosphere of conflict. I recall a former colleague of mine telling me that "creative tension" produced breakthrough results in the work of teams and groups—the abrasive sandpaper that eventually smoothed the rough edges of debate. Conflict introduces a powerful new dynamic into any discussion and shakes things up by frequently stepping on organizational sacred cows and challenging new points of view to emerge. Those who remain silent in the face of conflict will often keep ideas to themselves and fail to explore alternate courses of action that may benefit the overall effort.[7] In many ways, conflict is at the essence of Balanced Scorecard development. Most organizations will cling to the outmoded assumptions inherent in financial measurement, and it takes a good measure of conflict to expose those assumptions to the light of rational analysis. Effective Scorecard systems are molded from the heat of conflict as team members passionately debate the pros and cons of potential objectives and measures in the spirit of creating a tool that will serve as the organization's roadmap to success.

As a consultant I have a unique window on the threshold of conflict acceptance among my clients. Some, despite the drawbacks, seem set on ensuring a congenial environment that does nothing but produce consensus and mediocre results. It's my job as a facilitator to ask the tough questions and stimulate debate, but with some corporate cultures, my challenging queries repeatedly fall on deaf ears. Others thrive on creative conflict, taking the opportunity to unearth hidden assumptions, challenge taboos, and create a product that truly represents the best thinking the team has to offer. Not surprisingly, these teams typically derive the greatest benefits from the Balanced Scorecard.

The Balanced Scorecard Champion

To draw on an oft-repeated sports analogy, your Balanced Scorecard team will perform the "blocking and tackling" of the implementation, getting things done on a day-to-day basis. But every team requires a leader, and in the case of the Scorecard, that person is the Balanced Scorecard champion. Hardly a ceremonial title, the moniker confers on the owner several important duties necessary to ensure that the implementation follows a smooth and steady path.

Pragmatically, the Balanced Scorecard champion is the logistical task master of the process; scheduling meetings, tracking results, ensuring the distribution of materials, and interacting with executive sponsors. Philosophically, the champion represents the subject matter expert, devouring the latest Scorecard literature, attending conferences, networking with other organizations, and ensuring that the implementation is taking advantage of proven best practices. These roles appear on the surface to be significantly different and requiring polar skill sets. On the one hand, the logistical challenges require the champion to possess an analytical and rational point of view. The philosophical requirements, on the other hand, demand a seeker of knowledge and sharing mentality. Your choice of a Balanced Scorecard champion—given the nature of the task and its attendant demands—make it among the most critical selections you will make.

Some organizations have determined that the role requires "fresh blood," someone from outside the organization with the proven capacity to fill these challenging shoes. New entrants into the organizational arena can frequently *demonstrate desired behaviors and 'seed' the organization with new ways of thinking. Such individuals not only signal that there are new and different ways of thinking, but they can also quickly transfer critical knowledge and skills early on in the change process.*"[8] Credibility is a huge ally in the early stages of a Balanced Scorecard implementation, and if you can recruit a champion who has demonstrated the ability to successfully lead an implementation, then you're stacking the deck of change in your favor. Of course, the stamp of credibility may reside in the personage of someone currently roaming your hallways. At its core the issue is not whether you should recruit a champion from the outside or look within; it is simply that you must assign a champion if you expect your implementation to enjoy success.

We've all seen television shows or movies during which some poor wretch experiences a medical emergency in the middle of a bustling street in a big city only to be ignored by seemingly preoccupied bystanders as they hurry past. Social psychologists term this phenomenon "diffusion of responsibility"; in other words, when several people are confronted by a situation that requires action, there may be no response from anyone.[9] I'm certain we've all experienced this phenomenon at work in cross-functional teams and groups at our own companies. Lots of potentially great ideas are tossed around, sticky notes representing breakthrough processes are pasted to the wall, and recommendations are triumphantly declared. Once the meeting is over, however, the balloon of ambition is pierced, nobody acts on the suggestions, and the process repeats itself. A Balanced Scorecard implementation is no different. In order for the process to move swiftly and progressively, there must be a capable leader at the helm, guiding the team every step of the way. Team members will look to the champion to provide guidance on tough issues, work with executives to secure valuable resources, provide best practices, and soothe interpersonal issues that can sometimes cramp the work of even the best teams.

Role of the Balanced Scorecard Team beyond the Implementation Phase

Picture this: Your Balanced Scorecard team has just put the finishing touches on your new strategic management system and handed it off to an enthusiastic executive team, promising to live by the ideals embodied in the framework. So now what? Do you follow in the rich tradition of organizations around the globe and hold the celebratory lunch? You know the kind: Everyone gathers at a slightly, just slightly, better restaurant than you'd normally treat yourself to, you joke about how big a bill you're going to stick the boss with, listen to the "thank you for your great efforts" speech from the executive who will inevitably leave before dessert arrives, then, when it's all over, head back to your desks, wonder where you're going to store your six three-inch binders, and ponder the next project. I sincerely hope this is not the approach you're planning to take with your Balanced Scorecard.

Depending on the size and scope of engagement, your team has most likely invested hundreds of hours in the Balanced Scorecard development process. They began by learning about the model, then developed objectives on a strategy map, created measures, targets, and initiatives, and assisted with communication planning to ease the transition for the rest of your staff. Why let this incredible pool of resources be drained from your company? The Balanced Scorecard team can, and should, have a life beyond the initial implementation of the tool. I frequently admonish my clients that the Scorecard is not a one-time, check-off-the-list type of endeavor, but instead represents a new way of managing for the long term. As such, the role of the Scorecard within the organization will evolve over time— entering life as a measurement system, emerging into a strategic management system, and forever standing resolute as a powerful communication tool. Your Balanced Scorecard team can provide the grease that moves this squeaky wheel from one phase to the next.

Given their practical experience, the team should be in the position to provide recommendations regarding everything from how the Scorecard is linked to compensation and budgeting to what method of reporting you'll utilize. Additionally, with experience and use comes knowledge, and your cross-functional Balanced Scorecard team should be relied on to confer at regular intervals and share best practices of Scorecard use, challenges, and opportunities for expansion of the model. These meetings need not be held weekly or even monthly. Quarterly sessions with a consistent agenda should suffice. During these forums, a typical agenda may include:

- Achievements of each business unit or group in use of the Balanced Scorecard

- Lessons learned

- Challenges to future development, and any mitigating factors

- Key priorities in the months ahead

- Specific success stories to be shared widely among the employee population

If the crystal ball of Scorecard architects Kaplan and Norton is sharp enough, it may just be a matter of time before your team experiences a metamorphosis into what the authors termed a Strategic Management Office.[10] Just as the roles of Chief Information Officer and Chief Quality Officer have found their way onto corporate executive rolls, the strategic management office may emerge as the organizational custodian of the practice and management of strategy. This office of the future will recognize strategy as a necessary core competence of every organization and include strategy formulation and strategic planning, alignment, strategic communications, and Balanced Scorecard among a host of critical activities.

BALANCED SCORECARD TRAINING

Derek Bok, faculty chair of the Hauser Center for Nonprofit Organizations at Harvard University, once remarked: *"If you think education is expensive, try ignorance."*[11] A terrific quote, but not alone in the annals of training-related advice. For example I believe we've all heard these famous lines at some point in our lives, "Give a man a fish and you feed him for a day. Teach him how to fish and you feed him for a lifetime." Or as I read in *Reader's Digest*: "Give a man a fish and he eats for a day. Teach him how to fish and you get rid of him for the whole weekend!"[12] As full as the literature (both comic and business) is with references to the importance of training, it is all too often given short shrift in many Balanced Scorecard implementations. I pin this omission on the deceptive simplicity of the Scorecard model. Many newcomers approach the framework with unwarranted confidence, believing the Scorecard represents nothing more than a simple compilation of a few financial and nonfinancial measures, and think to themselves: how hard can that be to master? Weeks or months into the implementation, however, and they realize that perhaps it's not so simple after all. Yes, the fundamentals are quickly digestible, but the application of concepts, such as cause and effect, linkage to management processes, and use in governance of the organization, can prove challenging to even the most nimble of management minds.

The pitfalls of limited training were brought home to me in a recent engagement with a large public-sector client. They were, like many Balanced Scorecard adopters, extremely enthusiastic in embracing the tool and set forth an aggressive implementation schedule for the entire organization. A small team was convened to develop the high-level Corporate Scorecard, and within a few months that was to be cascaded throughout the entire organization. The team worked diligently in crafting an initial product and swiftly handed it off to their subordinates with the directions: "Okay, now you develop your own Scorecard." You can imagine the confusion, dismay, and frustration. Not only did most of the folks at the lower levels have no working knowledge of the Balanced Scorecard system, but many were barely even familiar with the term. Not surprisingly, despite the exuberant embrace of the Scorecard by senior leaders, the implementation skidded to a halt. I was brought in shortly thereafter to conduct training sessions throughout the organization on Balanced Scorecard fundamentals and the principles of cascading. To its credit, the organization was diligent in requesting that training participants complete evaluations of my sessions—a practice, incidentally, that all of you should follow. Virtually all of the evaluations formed a single theme: the training was helpful but should have been done months prior. One comment in particular sums up the sentiments of most employees charged with the responsibility of developing cascaded Scorecards: "It should have been delivered before we began; we have spent many months trying to 'break the code' on our own, and could have been a lot more efficient in developing our Scorecards."

The Initial Training Curriculum

Before you begin your training regimen, you must first decide who will form your class. My recommendation is to train as many people as logistically and financially possible. The Balanced Scorecard is primarily an agent of change, and acceptance of change is a direct by-product of understanding. Therefore, it is in your best interests to expose as many employees as you can to this new system. At the very least, trainees should include your executive leadership who will one day be expected to take the helm of this system, your Scorecard team, and other stakeholders, which could include members of your board of directors, select users, and even customers or suppliers.

Start your education efforts by preparing and distributing a comprehensive primer on the subjects of performance management and Balanced Scorecard. These topics are mature, and a rich and abundant supply of literature is available. I would suggest that you include the three seminal articles by Kaplan and Norton appearing in the *Harvard Business Review* from 1992 to 1996. Kaplan and Norton have subsequently written additional articles on the subject, containing more advanced theories, which may be used as your training progresses. There are literally hundreds of other articles and white papers to choose from, so narrow your search by including any documents that specifically reference your industry or implementation focus (corporate-wide versus business unit, for example). Several good-quality books have been published on these subjects as well, and you should consider providing at least one to each of your team members. Your team will also benefit from attending one of the many excellent conferences on performance management and the Balanced Scorecard. Again, you have the opportunity to tailor your training with your implementation by choosing an event focused on your industry type or implementation plan. These conferences provide a valuable exchange of ideas, challenges, and solutions.[13]

Ongoing Training

A Balanced Scorecard implementation is more akin to a lengthy and challenging, but ultimately rewarding, marathon than a sprint at breakneck speed. Accompanying the implementation at every juncture should be ongoing training, which quickly seals any voids in understanding and ensures that the process maintains its momentum throughout. In this regard, we can consider training in a similar vein to the concept of just-in-time inventory management, which suggests that raw materials should be delivered at the very moment they are required in the production process. The timing of Balanced Scorecard training should be considered with no less precision. At the outset of the implementation, training typically comprises the fundamentals: origins of the Scorecard, the four perspectives, implementation principles, and so on. At this point in your work, the utility of teaching Balanced Scorecard novices the nuances of, for example, a Scorecard–budgeting link is specious at best and may actually harm your efforts if your team feels inundated with information. Some learning experts suggest that we forget up to 50% of what we learn in a training session within the first 24 hours, so relevance is truly the name of the game.[14] However, as the Scorecard engine moves forward, your training should evolve in lockstep, providing insights into topics of immediate relevance.

As you trek the Balanced Scorecard landscape, you will encounter some fairly esoteric outcroppings along the way, including corporate governance, pay for performance, and strategic resource allocation. It's important to provide your team with the necessary context each requires before attempting to provide a linkage to the Balanced Scorecard. David Taran, CEO of Divco West Properties, understands the essential role of ongoing training in a Balanced Scorecard effort. His firm recently embarked on the development of a Balanced Scorecard system with a primary goal of forging a link between pay and performance using the Balanced Scorecard as the arbiter. David recently told me, *"It would have been extremely helpful to have training at each step in the process to clarify the Balanced Scorecard concepts and create buy-in along the way. In addition to ongoing communication, we recognize that training is an important component to creating change in our, and any, organization."*[15] The good news for everyone attempting to navigate their way through a Scorecard implementation is that the topic is one of much scrutiny and investigation. Every day, the field of knowledge surrounding the subject is growing, with researchers and practitioners alike providing new insights into even the most arcane of Scorecard derivatives. When you encounter a Balanced Scorecard–related topic for the first time, tap into this worldwide wellspring of know-how to craft a specific learning plan for your organization. Look for case studies documenting best practices, examples of implementations from within your industry, or even conferences devoted to the topic.

GETTING THE WORD OUT: COMMUNICATION PLANNING

Steve Kerr spent several years as the Chief Learning Officer at General Electric. This is an intriguing title, one vesting him with both the power and responsibility of introducing innovative new ideas of every conceivable shape and size into the venerable corporate giant. Along the way, Kerr learned much about the mechanics of acquainting people with ideas and suggested that the most transformational communication tool he ever used was $Q \times A = E$; Quality (Q) times Acceptance (A) equals Effectiveness (E). Many organizations have an abundance of the Q portion of the formula, but face a major deficiency in the A component. General Electric was not immune, as Kerr explains:

I said to executives, what if you guys build high-quality refrigerators nobody buys and you call them inventory? That's a bad thing. What if you produce high-quality strategies and everyone hates them? Why is that a good thing? Look how you market to your external clients. You wouldn't say to your customer "effective Monday, buy it!" Who would advertise that way? But, inside GE, executives were marketing their strategies that way.[16]

Does that sound at all familiar to you? It's certainly not uncommon for companies to unveil new ideas in a flash of promotion accompanied by virtually no concrete communication and expect employees to begin living the new idea immediately. The novel idea or change may be of the highest quality, but without acceptance from those charged with the responsibility of bringing it to life day in and day out, its potential value will never be realized.

The question for organizations large and small and of every type is how to effectively garner the acceptance of employees to new and innovative ideas, including the Balanced Scorecard. I believe the solution lies in what Stephen Covey would describe as "beginning with the end in mind."[17] In other words, if effectiveness in implementation is the ultimate goal, and acceptance unlocks the door to effectiveness, what penetrates the fortress of acceptance? The answer to that query is communication. Before employees in your organization can act on an idea, they must accept it, and in order to accept it, they must understand it fully. Consistent, well-timed, and adroitly delivered communication is the foundation for understanding, acceptance, and, ultimately, effectiveness.

Unfortunately, gold stars for communication are not in the immediate future for most companies. When it comes to sharing information, the rule of thumb for many organizations appears to be: too little, too late, and top down. In the era of scientific management at the turn of the 20th century, this oversight could be readily ignored, because employees of that epoch generally required little in the form of communication to perform their laborious and repetitive tasks. The knowledge economy of the 21st century, however, demands more from our leaders. If they expect to win both the hearts and minds of their staff, they must engage in virtually constant communication about the building blocks of success: mission, vision, values, strategy, and the necessity of change. The Balanced Scorecard is primarily a tool of change and, therefore, it can easily fall victim to the perils inevitably awaiting those who deprive their employees of communication. In the remainder of this section, we'll examine the critical elements of communicating your Balanced Scorecard, ensuring understanding, acceptance, and, ultimately, an effective implementation.

Objectives for Your Communication Plan

Before the fun work—yes, I did say fun!—of developing a Balanced Scorecard website, launching promotions, and kicking off all of the other elements of your communication plan, you should pause and reflect on exactly why you're engaging in this activity in the first place. What are your specific objectives for creating a communication campaign within the organization? To answer that question effectively, we must put ourselves in the shoes of our audience and attempt to anticipate their communication needs. Chances are that as murmurs begin to circulate through your corridors about the coming of this new measurement and management system, your employees are probably thinking:

- What is the Balanced Scorecard?
- Why have we chosen to use it now?
- Who is going to use it?
- What are the impacts likely to be from using the Scorecard?
- How is it different from what we've done in the past?
- What do you want me to do?
- What's in it for me to use the Balanced Scorecard?
- What tools will you offer to help me use the Balanced Scorecard?

Based on these foundational questions, you can begin to determine the objectives for your communication plan in the context of the unique culture of your company, past history in introducing agents of change, and the current level of knowledge among your population.[18]

One organization that has excelled in the art of communicating the Balanced Scorecard is Aliant, a leading information and communications technology company of 8,000 employees operating in Canada. Aliant was formed by the merger of four provincial telephone companies; therefore, unifying the new company under a common strategy was job one for CEO Jay Forbes. He chose the Balanced Scorecard as the harmonizing mechanism and began an ambitious rollout of the framework during the summer of 2002. Before creating a strategy map or measures, however, Forbes and his team focused on the critical task of introducing this new idea to staff throughout the geographically dispersed enterprise. A campaign was planned, with the first priority being the determination of goals and objectives for all future communications. After careful deliberation, the team crafted the following goals and objectives for their communication plan.[19]

Communications Goals

- Increase awareness of Aliant's strategic plan
- Increase awareness of Balanced Scorecard among Aliant employees
- Increase knowledge of the Balanced Scorecard and how it will be used to manage Aliant's strategy
- Ensure consistent and persistent communication about the Balanced Scorecard, its role, and eventual results

- Encourage employees to ask questions about how the Balanced Scorecard relates to them—how does it affect me?

Communications Objectives

- Attain understanding among employee base of the Balanced Scorecard and how it affects them
- Have the Balanced Scorecard be used as a key strategic management, communications, and measurement tool
- Ensure that the Balanced Scorecard remains in place in Aliant as a key strategic and measurement tool

With these goals and objectives forming the bedrock of the plan, the team was ready to embark on spreading their messages throughout the company.

Setting objectives for the communication plan will often lead you to the establishment of a theme or metaphor you can use to creatively trademark your implementation. Some people like slogans and themes, whereas others think they are hokey and convey little if any value. Whatever your opinion, there is little doubt that themes are colorful and often memorable, and memorability is a huge weapon in the arsenal of communication. For Bridgeport Hospital, the communication theme was "Destination to Journey 2005," using the analogy of a bus trip to the future. Highways represented the hospital's five strategic imperatives, landmarks represented the objectives, and mile markers represented the performance measures.[20] Whatever moniker you choose should reflect your organization, your culture, and your aspirations.[21]

Key Elements to Consider in Creating Your Communication Plan

A basic but proven technique to consider when developing your communication plan is the old W5 approach of who, what, when, where, and why. Beginning with the end in mind, the *why* represents our rationale for engaging in the task of communication, the goals and objectives for the plan as we discussed in the preceding section.

Who represents the target audience of your communication. The size of your enterprise and scope of your Balanced Scorecard engagement will influence your selection of audiences, but in general you should consider the following: senior leadership, your Balanced Scorecard team, employee base, board of directors, other stakeholders (customers, suppliers, etc.).

Next you'll determine the *what* of your plan—your key messages. A principle tenet of effective communication is the use of key messages to deliver a consistent and targeted story to your constituents, and the story you create should be based solidly on the objectives you've set for your plan. At Brother Industries (USA)—one of the world's premier providers of products for the home, home office, and office—a key message is the importance of customer satisfaction. Each month, at the company's Bartlett, Tennessee, facility, all employees gather to hear a discussion of results led by the company's president. Once he's provided an overview of performance, the president, Mr. Sugiura, ends each session with these words: "Thank you for your efforts, and let's continue to be part of a team that achieves customer satisfaction."[22] It's a simple message, but one that is used repeatedly to ensure that every employee recognizes the commitment the organization has made to its goal of satisfying customers.

When, not surprisingly, refers to the frequency of communication. This can prove to be a deceptively thorny issue, depending on your point of view. I err on the side of too much rather than too little communication and share that point of view with my clients, but I've learned the hard way that organizational cultures are like snowflakes—no two are alike. As a result, every company will possess different thresholds for the amount of communication it can tolerate. It's a dangerous tightrope to walk: On the one hand, provide too little communication and you risk losing acceptance because of a lack of understanding. Communicate too much, on the other hand, and the possibility of alienating your staff creeps in, along with disinterest as a result of the endless flow of seemingly trivial information.

Finally, *where* and *how* represent the communication vehicles. Remember I used the word "fun" at the beginning of the objectives section?; it was in reference to this part of the plan. The options are limited only to the bounds of your imagination, and based on what I've seen from clever and industrious clients, those bounds are constantly being stretched. From sophisticated internal websites, to games and trivia contests, to group presentations, to pay stub messages, the list of communication devices keeps growing. The best communicators employ several vehicles in their efforts and have made the vital recognition that effective communication works best when it is two-way in nature. Effective communicators provide ample opportunities for employees to engage in dialogue, comment on the direction of the implementation, outline their concerns, highlight possible barriers, and provide suggestions to ensure that the implementation maintains momentum. Dennis Madsen, CEO of outdoor gear store REI, understands the power of effective communication. He notes:

> I spend most of my time staying in front of employees, engaging them in dialogues. The executive team and I do quarterly "town hall meetings" with groups of 200 employees at a time, where forty minutes of the hour is devoted to questions and answers. Employees won't always tell you what's on their minds if they're forced to raise their hand in a public forum. So we leave three-by-five-inch index cards and pencils taped to every chair in the auditorium. Employees can write their questions, the cards are collected and brought up, and we answer them on the spot.[23]

Leaving the index cards for more reluctant employees is a simple gesture, but it connotes a strong commitment to ensuring that every employee's voice is heard.

Regardless of the communication method you choose, an important consideration is the effectiveness of your delivery. In other words, are your audiences receiving and comprehending your intended messages? Every communication plan should include tactics for evaluating the efficacy of the plan in delivering information to your constituents. This is frequently accomplished by employing simple survey devices to gauge how well your messages are being received. The following criteria may be used when evaluating the results of your survey efforts:[24]

- *No contact.* Has not heard of the Balanced Scorecard project.
- *Awareness.* Has heard about the project, but doesn't know what it is.
- *Conceptual understanding.* Understands the Balanced Scorecard and any individual effects.
- *Tactical understanding.* Understands both the personal and organizational effects of the Balanced Scorecard.
- *Acceptance.* Will support the Balanced Scorecard and the changes it will bring.

As a final thought on communication planning, I ask you to reflect on your career and conjure up images of the many change initiatives you've witnessed, or been a part of, during your tenure. I'm sure that many were accompanied by great initial fanfare, replete with passionate speeches from executives, glitzy presentations, and maybe even buttons or mouse pads to serve as a daily reminder of their importance. But what occurred beyond this initial splash of communication? As the initiative moved forward, was it ushered along each step of the way with reinforcing communication, answering the questions of what was coming next, why, and the likely impacts? Many organizations excel at the outset of a change but struggle in following up throughout the process. As mentioned earlier, the Balanced Scorecard is more similar to a marathon than a sprint, and thirst-quenching water along the route should be provided in the form of informative communication that serves as both an affirmation of the past and a guide for the future.

TERMINOLOGY AND THE BALANCED SCORECARD

One of the highlights of my Balanced Scorecard adventures of 2003 was a trip to Russia to deliver a series of workshops in Moscow and St. Petersburg. In preparation for the trip I researched my topics, developed my materials, and sent them off to my hosts for photocopying and distribution at the sessions. Being of North

American persuasion, it's probably not surprising that I used English as the sole language in all of my documents. I made the ethnocentric assumption that all participants in my workshops would speak English, which as it turns out was a mistaken one. Fortunately, my hosts were one step ahead of me and made sure my materials had been translated into Russian before my arrival. When I delivered the presentation, the language barrier was overcome thanks to the marvel of instantaneous translation. If you've ever watched proceedings from the United Nations, you're probably familiar with the process. I, along with all of the participants, wore headsets that facilitated this magical occurrence, and words had scarcely left my mouth when they were being translated and spoken in Russian for my audience. I was simply amazed at how adeptly the translators were able to keep a smooth flow of words moving from me to them, and ultimately to the participants.

At one point, however, our good fortune momentarily expired when we experienced a technical glitch and suddenly lost power in the system. I wasn't aware of the problem and kept right on trucking with my delivery, confident that every word I uttered was meeting the eager ears of my audience in their native tongue. To say we were set adrift in a sea of confusion would be an understatement. Just seconds after our translation system failed, what had been looks of interest and enthusiasm on the faces of my audience quickly transformed into frustration and confusion. We simply weren't speaking the same language at that point, and all hope of understanding and knowledge sharing had vanished. Say what you will about the power of nonverbal communication, but if you aren't using the same language to communicate, confusion is sure to reign supreme. Fortunately for me and the participants of my session, our technical problem was temporary and quickly overcome. For many organizations, however, the pain of miscommunication can linger, becoming a permanent thorn in the side of leading change.

Over the past years, the field of performance management, including the Balanced Scorecard, has spawned a new language on an already buzzword-laden public. Terms such as "key performance indicator," "objective," "critical success factor," "strategic imperative," and dozens of others fill the business pages and are expounded continuously by organizational pundits. Many of the words and phrases connote similar meanings (e.g., "metric" and "key performance indicator"), but depending on the organizational context and culture, they may have vastly different definitions. And that's when significant problems can begin to occur. As organizational learning expert Edgar Schein has noted,

> If several members of a group are using different category systems, they not only can not agree on what to do but will not even agree on their definition of what is real, what is a fact, when something is true or false, what is important, what needs attention, and so on. Most communication breakdowns between people result from their lack of awareness that in the first place they are making basically different assumptions about meaning categories.[25]

Some may read this and be reminded of the famous Shakespeare quote, "a rose by any other name," feeling minor differences in meaning are insignificant. My experience tells me otherwise. I've seen Balanced Scorecard implementations drag out for additional weeks based on differences of opinion over words such as *mission* versus *vision*. The first step on the road to Balanced Scorecard acceptance and use is ensuring that everyone is literally on the same page of word meanings.

A simple and proactive (there's a buzzword for you!) exercise that goes a long way toward unraveling the knot of confusion created by words is conducting a blueprint session. As the name implies, this session focuses on drafting the exact definitions of words and phrases that will undoubtedly surface during the implementation. In preparation for such a session, work with a subgroup of your Balanced Scorecard team in brainstorming a list of key words and terms. Distribute those to your larger team about one week before the session, and ask that each member provide a short definition to the champion at least two days before the event. The champion compiles all definitions, notes areas of similarity and difference, and then recirculates the broad list of proposed definitions to all team members. The document is then used as a discussion guide during the blueprint session, with changes and recommendations being captured by the meeting's note-taker. The tangible outcome of the blueprint session is a glossary that can be used throughout the implementation and shared with the entire organization. I've led several of these blueprint sessions and have yet to emerge without my head spinning! It's tough but incredibly valuable work that will produce dividends down the road as you take that first step toward shared understanding.

YOUR BALANCED SCORECARD IMPLEMENTATION PLAN

Back in 1997, a struggling country singer literally burst onto the national scene with a catchy song and shock of dark hair that sent the cowgirls a wailin'. The singer was Billy Ray Cyrus, and the song, a line-dancing favorite at weddings to this day, "Achy Breaky Heart." I'm sure you'll be cursing me for the rest of the day as you find yourself singing at a just barely audible level, "and if you take my heart, my achy, breaky heart." Despite the release of a compilation album a few years later (how can you put out a greatest hits album when you've only had one?), Billy Ray was relegated to the infamous ranks of the one-hit wonders. Like a shooting star, one-hit wonders appear out of nowhere, streak across the sky of public adoration at lightning speed, and vanish from sight just as quickly.

So what does all this have to do with the Balanced Scorecard, you ask? Some organizations' use of the Balanced Scorecard is tantamount to a one-hit wonder, making that initial splash and suddenly fading from view. These companies decide they must have a Balanced Scorecard immediately, so they swiftly assemble a team and instruct it to complete the task in record time. Once the questionable product is complete, the company considers it another project successfully completed, crosses it off the master list, and moves on to the next potential panacea. In many ways, this orientation dealt a death blow to the reengineering movement. As authors Davenport and Prusak note, *"The critical shortcoming of those who implemented reengineering was to treat it as a project rather than a way of life.... The most sophisticated organizations realize that they can never stop improving their business processes... if the need is there."*[26] In order for the Balanced Scorecard to reach its potential as a strategic management system, it must be nurtured along a steady implementation path and should evolve as your business inevitably does. Market forces, customer preferences, demographics, workplace changes, technology, and a host of other factors affecting your business are constantly shifting. Your Balanced Scorecard must never be considered a discrete response to your environment, but should instead be viewed as a dynamic navigation system capable of course adjustments as conditions warrant.

While the Scorecard should not be considered a one-time project, it must be implemented using the proven techniques and processes supplied by the discipline of project management. All Balanced Scorecard implementations should be accompanied by a comprehensive plan, guiding the development of the framework as its role grows and expands. For some enterprises, planning is a core competency that is carried out with ritualistic fervor regardless of the endeavor being pursued. I recently worked with a client that fit this description. Upon arriving at their offices on day one of our Balanced Scorecard work, I had barely been through introductions of team members when I was handed a phone book–sized Scorecard implementation plan. Others will take a more casual stance and use simple tracking mechanisms to ensure that the implementation is progressing at a respectable clip. Regardless of where you fall on the spectrum of project management, the key is simply to possess a plan for the Balanced Scorecard implementation.

Without a formal plan to guide your work, confusion is sure to creep into the process, as it did when I was called in to help turn around a troubled Scorecard implementation some time ago. Trouble can emanate from any number of sources, but in the case of this large nonprofit, the problem was a distinct lack of planning. This agency was as unprepared from a planning standpoint as it was enthusiastic about the Scorecard. Unfortunately, the interest and exuberance they felt for the tool failed to compensate for their lack of organization. Virtually every meeting slowed to a merciless crawl to discuss process questions. Team members and other stakeholders were naturally curious about the next steps in the process, but the leaders of the Scorecard implementation had barely thought through the current meeting, let alone the entire implementation journey.

Although Balanced Scorecard implementation plans will vary tremendously based on your planning proclivities and the size and scope of your implementation, in general they should share core characteristics. The first section of your implementation guide typically outlines what you plan to accomplish before actually developing any performance measures. Components of this section might include your rationale for using the Balanced Scorecard, where you'll be developing your first Scorecard, gaining sponsorship, forming your team, and crafting a communication plan. The second component of the implementation plan normally details the development phase of Balanced Scorecard creation. Here you chart the course you will take in building your Balanced Scorecard system by outlining the specific steps on your implementation journey, including gathering and reviewing background materials; developing or confirming mission, values, vision, and strategy; conducting executive interviews; creating a strategy map; translating the objectives on your map into performance measures complete with targets and initiatives; and drafting future expansion plans for the Scorecard (reporting, cascading, links to budgeting and compensation, etc.).

A potentially daunting variable in your planning efforts is the rate of speed at which you'd like to proceed along the implementation path. For some, there is little doubt that fast, faster, and fastest are the only ways to go, and the sooner you can reach the finish line the better. Handelman Company, a distributor of CDs to mass merchants worldwide, based in Troy, Michigan, believed that a high-velocity route was best. CEO Stephen Strome explains their rationale thus: *"We went for speed, creating the Scorecard in August 2002 and completing both divisions' Scorecard in January 2003 . . . the only way people embrace it is through exposure and time. They have to use the Scorecard enough to move it from the conceptual to the practical."*[27]

Mr. Strome's point regarding the transition from conceptual to practical being paved by use of the Scorecard is valid. Like anything else in the organizational orbit, the Balanced Scorecard can suffer from the enormous weight of inertia. Most organizations have lived this long without the Balanced Scorecard, and despite their sincere desire to create one, when push comes to shove, it can prove to be an enormous challenge to actually take the first step and begin using it. I see this with clients from time to time: They will work diligently to build a well-constructed strategy map and set of measures, only to have the work sit on the shelf for weeks or months. The rationale for this lethargy is typically, "we don't have data for all the measures," which may be 100% true, but it should not stop you from taking advantage of the many benefits you can derive from even a limited set of measures: an unrelenting focus on strategy, alignment throughout the organization, and the basis for more sound resource allocation decisions.

Ultimately, the rate at which you develop your Balanced Scorecard depends on several variables, including organizational readiness, the sense of urgency within the company, commitment of senior leadership to the tool, scope of the work (will you be developing a Corporate Balanced Scorecard or cascading throughout the enterprise?), and the availability of resources (both human and financial). Organizations facing a survival crisis will rightly focus on generating a few key metrics to right the ship as swiftly as possible, whereas others may approach the Balanced Scorecard at a more leisurely pace. While development time does vary on a case-by-case basis, a couple of rules of thumb are in order. First, your initial Balanced Scorecard, whether it is at the corporate level or for a business unit, should be completed within 16 weeks of commencing the work. Anything longer and you risk losing that most valued of organizational currency—momentum. Second, in keeping with the sage advice offered by Handelman's Strome that you must use the Balanced Scorecard to move it from conceptual to practical, you should make it a goal to hold your first review of Balanced Scorecard results within 60 days of the creation of your measure set. This is the case regardless of what percentage of data is currently collectible.

SELF-ASSESSMENT QUESTIONS

Balanced Scorecard Team

1. Have we formed a Balanced Scorecard team that includes the following characteristics:

- Is ceded with decision-making authority?
- Represents the different units/functions of our organization?
- Members possess different skill sets, problem-solving abilities, and personalities?
- Is comfortable operating in a climate of "creative conflict"?

2. Has our Balanced Scorecard team been provided with adequate resources (both human and financial) to ensure a successful implementation?

3. Have we appointed a Balanced Scorecard champion to provide both logistical and philosophical leadership to our implementation?

4. Do we have a plan in place to ensure that our Balanced Scorecard team convenes regularly once the initial phases of the implementation have taken place?

Balanced Scorecard Training

1. Has our team been provided with training in Balanced Scorecard fundamentals, including origins of the model, the four perspectives, strategy maps, and developing effective measures?

2. Have we circulated learning materials to our team in the form of articles, books, tapes, online learning sources, and conference proceedings?

3. Does our organization have an ongoing training plan for future Balanced Scorecard developments (e.g., cascading, linkages to budgeting and compensation)?

Communication Planning

1. Before rolling out a communication plan, did we create goals and objectives for the plan, taking into consideration our culture, demographics, and past history with change?

2. Have we developed a communication plan that includes the five elements of who, what, when, where, and why?

3. Do we regularly evaluate the effectiveness of our communication efforts?

Terminology

1. Have we held a blueprint session to ensure a shared understanding of commonly used performance management terms?

2. Has a glossary of performance management terms used by our organization been created and made available to employees?

Implementation Planning

1. Have we created an implementation plan for our Balanced Scorecard, one that includes both planning and development phases?

2. Did we hold our first Balanced Scorecard results meeting within 60 days of the creation of your measure set?

NOTES

1. Source: www.pbs.org/wnet/savageseas/weather-side-ice.html.
2. For more information on greyhound rescue, please visit www.adopt-a-greyhound.org.
3. Jon R. Katzenbach and Douglas K. Smith, *The Wisdom of Teams* (Boston, MA: Harvard Business School Press, 1993).
4. Jim Collins, *Good to Great* (New York: Harper Business, 2001).
5. Malcolm Gladwell, *The Tipping Point* (New York: Little Brown and Company, 2000).
6. Ibid., p. 56.
7. Leslie Perlow and Stephanie Williams, "Is Silence Killing Your Company?" *Harvard Business Review,* May 2003, p. 57.
8. Elspeth J. Murray and Peter R. Richardson, *Fast Forward: Organizational Change in 100 Days* (New York: Oxford University Press, 2002), p. 49.
9. Robert A. Baron and Donn Byrne, *Social Psychology; Understanding Human Interaction* (Boston, MA: Allyn and Bacon, 1984), p. 290.

10. Robert S. Kaplan and David P. Norton, "Strategic Management: An Emerging Profession," *Balanced Scorecard Report,* May–June 2004, pp. 1–5.

11. Quoted in: Jef Nance, *Conquering Deception* (Kansas City, MO: Irvin-Benham, 2000), p. 18.

12. Quoted in: "50 Funniest One Liners," *Reader's Digest,* September 2004, p. 108.

13. This paragraph is drawn from: Paul R. Niven, *Balanced Scorecard Step by Step: Maximizing Performance and Maintaining Results* (New York: John Wiley & Sons, 2002), p. 57.

14. Based on the work of Hermann Ebbinghaus (1850–1909).

15. From a telephone interview with David Taran, July 27, 2004.

16. Thomas H. Davenport and Laurence Prusak, with H. James Wilson, *What's the Big Idea?* (Boston, MA: Harvard Business School Press, 2003), p. 208.

17. Stephen R. Covey, *The 7 Habits of Highly Effective People* (New York: Fireside, 1989).

18. Selected questions from this list are drawn from: Andy Neely, Chris Adams, and Mike Kennerley, *The Performance Prism* (London: Prentice-Hall, 2002), p. 63.

19. From internal Aliant documents supplied to the author.

20. Andra Gumbus, Bridget Lyons, and Dorothy E. Bellhouse, "Journey to Destination 2005," *Strategic Finance,* August 2002.

21. Paul R. Niven, *Balanced Scorecard Step by Step for Government and Nonprofit Agencies* (New York: John Wiley & Sons, 2003), p. 93.

22. From telephone interview with Stan Romanoff of Brother Industries (USA), July 26, 2004.

23. "Gearing up at REI," *Harvard Business Review,* May 2003, p. 20.

24. See note 21.

25. Edgar H. Schein, *Organizational Culture and Leadership* (San Francisco: Jossey-Bass, 1992), p. 72.

26. See note 16, p. 174.

27. Lauren Keller Johnson, "Handelman Company Hits a High Strategic Note with the BSC," *Balanced Scorecard Report,* September–October 2003, p. 9.

CHAPTER 4

Strategy Maps

The success enjoyed by the Balanced Scorecard system over the past 15 years may be attributed to any number of contributing factors. First and foremost, it has been proven to drive breakthrough results for innumerable organizations representing every possible type and size of enterprise. In addition, at a time when the basis for competition in many industries is shifting from tangible assets to intellectual capital, the Scorecard has demonstrated its worth through an ability to document the transformation of intangible assets into tangible value. We could point to many other possible reasons for the success of the system, but underpinning them all may be the Balanced Scorecard's undeniable ability to grow and evolve.

When Kaplan and Norton introduced the concept to the world in 1990, they were simply trying to solve a measurement problem: How do we take the reliance off traditional financial metrics in recognition of the increasing prominence of knowledge-based assets? Their answer was the use of a balanced set of measures in four distinct, yet related, perspectives: Financial, Customer, Internal Processes, and Employee Learning and Growth. Early adopters flocked to the deceptively simple model and utilized it to drive much-needed alignment and focus around a core group of metrics throughout their companies. Having the entire company row in the same direction through the alignment and focus on a core block of measures is a wonderful thing, assuming you have the right measures in place. However, if those measures are leading to dysfunctional behaviors of some kind, that focused rowing could have you headed straight down a course of uncharted and rocky rapids that's sure to turn your cozy assumptions about measurement upside down.

Recognizing this potential hazard, Kaplan and Norton began prefacing the discussion of measures with one of objectives: What exactly were executives attempting to accomplish? Answering this fundamental question made the development of measures that much easier because a context was created for the deliberation. Additionally, if the measures chosen prove less than desirable, they could simply be replaced without altering the fundamental objectives derived from the strategy.[1] Such were the humble beginnings of an avalanche of activity in the Balanced Scorecard world. It soon became standard practice to begin a Balanced Scorecard implementation by articulating key objectives derived directly from the organization's strategy.

Have you ever been in any meeting on any subject in a room containing a white board and not had the board assaulted with a rainbow of colors and artistic renderings that would make Pablo Picasso proud? I doubt it. As Balanced Scorecard teams began developing objectives from their strategies, they instinctively began linking them together, using arrows to depict patterns of cause and effect. For example, items such as quality and training were no longer disparate elements of a strategy, but were linked together through a thick line on a flip chart or white board: "If we provide focused training to our employees, that will allow us to produce high-quality products with fewer defects." Drawing the relationships among objectives served several important purposes: It allowed Scorecard developers to quickly grasp important interdependencies, question assumptions, and simply create a better description of their unique strategies. The strategy map was born, and as Kaplan and Norton observed, *"(it) has turned out to be as important an innovation as the original Balanced Scorecard itself."*[2]

An old saying reminds us that "a picture tells a thousand words," and so it is with the strategy map. Most employees would blanch at the suggestion of poring over a 50- (if they're lucky) or 100-page strategy document, but give them a chance to review the strategy map and they are instantly captivated and ready to provide their two cents' worth on everything from the specifics of the objectives to the cause-and-effect linkages drawn throughout. Strategy maps provide a graphical representation of critical objectives, but do so in a plain and simple manner that is easily understood by every employee from top to bottom. In other words, they are powerful communication tools, signaling to all stakeholders what the organization is attempting to accomplish in a simple, coherent package. In this chapter you'll be provided with tools to cast a critical eye on your strategy map. We'll begin by examining how these maps are developed, including conducting workshops, key considerations for each of the four perspectives, how many objectives should appear on the map, writing objective statements, and the importance of cause-and-effect linkages. From there we'll consider how you should personalize your strategy map, ensuring that its content and design are consistent with the culture and norms of your company.

DEVELOPING THE STRATEGY MAP

Conducting Effective Strategy Map Workshops

In Chapter Two I noted that the Balanced Scorecard was well-suited to a team approach, drawing on various skills and talents to produce a stronger product than that which could be developed by any single individual. Most Scorecard teams will work together to craft their product in a workshop setting, and therefore, before we discuss the specifics of what your map might comprise, it's worthwhile to consider some fundamentals regarding the workshops.

My first rule for holding successful workshops is to conduct them off-site, away from your normal place of business. Unfortunately, no empirical data exists to back up this claim, but I firmly believe that Scorecards created in off-site locations are of a higher quality than those produced in an average conference room. The impetus for this bold suggestion is primarily focus. Getting away from the regular routine can literally offer a breath of fresh air to the harried executive, allowing him to clear his head, escape from the urgent daily issues, and focus on the strategically important business of crafting a Balanced Scorecard that tells the story of the organization's strategy. It's difficult to sustain the focus necessary to build a strategic management system when you know that right down the hall sits a ringing phone and a computer just bursting at the seams with unread e-mail messages, each of which promises an even greater workload tomorrow. Thoughtful reflection, careful analysis, and creativity are the ingredients leading to a powerful Balanced Scorecard system, and the best way to bring these attributes forward is to free participants from their normal operating environment. Fortunately, the choices abound; I've conducted Scorecard workshops in quaint country inns, summer homes belonging to executives, restored estate homes, and lots of hotel conference rooms as well.

That covers the "where," so now let's deal with the "what." Like any other meeting, your Balanced Scorecard workshops must include an agenda complete with topics, leaders, and suggested timing. While some may feel that creativity is cramped with such restrictive forces in place, the fact of the matter is that you've got a finite amount of time to work with and must generate the best product you can given that constraint. Groups that lack a formal agenda often spend the first hour or two of the day discussing process questions and contemplating the next steps in the Balanced Scorecard journey. Suddenly someone looks at a watch and realizes they have a scant four or five hours remaining to complete their entire charge for the day—not a simple task. The judicious use of time also forces you to keep the process moving along. If you attempt to reach complete consensus on every point relating to your Scorecard, you could be debating into the wee hours of the morning. At some point decisions must be made, abided by, and a conclusion to move on reached.

In Plato's *Republic,* the great philosopher remarked, "the beginning is the most important part of the work." Regardless of the endeavor, whether it's a Saturday morning tennis game, kicking off a new weight loss program, or engaging in some form of corporate change, we all know how important it is to get off to a good start. Strategy mapping workshops are no different, and if the taps of creativity and insight are to flow, you must ensure that your session begins strongly. There are many possibilities you might employ to gain this head start (e.g., reading inspirational quotes or outlining your "burning platform" for change). I was particularly impressed by the simple and compelling method chosen by the Scorecard team leader of my client, World Vision. John Wilcox, the director of Strategic Planning for this worldwide Christian humanitarian organization, began our strategy mapping workshop by asking each group member what he or she was hoping to get out of the day, and ultimately, the Balanced Scorecard. This simple exercise allowed all participants to openly and publicly affirm their belief in what the team was doing, why it was so important, and how they felt it would benefit the organization. John's sincere question helped set the tone for a day of sharing, learning, and insight as the team created its first-ever strategy map. Again, there are many ways to establish a strong opening, with some definitely less formal than others. Another client of mine began each meeting by spraying lavender in the air in the belief that the sweet aroma would clear a path for everyone to provide their best thinking throughout the day.

Every culture is different and will possess varying thresholds of tolerance for the multitude of communication and entertainment devices we've grown accustomed to in our daily lives. I'm speaking of those constant companions of the corporate warrior: cell phones, pagers, and personal digital assistants (PDAs). Many will argue in favor of the vital necessity of keeping these tools turned on; after all, it's not infrequent that at least one team member will be awaiting a critical call or page and must be ready to respond. Fair enough, but on the flip side, there is the distraction factor when a high-pitched ring pierces the energizing rhythm of a highly focused team on the verge of lighting a spark of creative insight.

I'm also convinced that the less engaged among workshop participants will seize on the ring of their phone to beat a hasty retreat from the session, if even for a moment. I can't tell you how many times I've heard the phone of a clearly disinterested participant ring and suddenly witnessed a remarkable transformation in their face from barely conscious to deeply concerned, as if this look of consternation provides a strong rationale for immediate departure. Ninety percent of the time it's not a mission-critical issue that brings them to this state, just a quick and sanctioned excuse to leave the room. Remember, the name of this game is focus, and you want to do everything in your power to ensure that your team remains focused and energized throughout the entire session.

Reviewing Your Strategy Map Objectives

Your ultimate aim in convening a strategy mapping session is the development of objectives in each of the four perspectives of the Balanced Scorecard. In this section we'll dissect the perspectives one by one, providing you with the ammunition you need to critically examine the objectives you've chosen.

Financial Perspective

When you watch television, do you find yourself reaching frantically for the remote control to turn down the volume as commercials come on? I do, but while in midstretch on one occasion recently I stopped suddenly, my attention drawn to the enticing graphics on the screen. The commercial was sponsored by a large bank and was touting the many innovations they were planning for their network of ATMs. In their version of the not-too-distant future, patrons can perform any number of currently impossible transactions, such as depositing currency directly into the machine, printing copies of checks just deposited, and many other similar feats of banking magic. It brought back fond memories of my earliest acquaintance with banking machines in the late 1970s, and I marveled at how far the technology has advanced. Of course, banking is not the exception; in every industry a tidal wave of innovation has swept our shores, improving productivity and making it simpler and more convenient for us to do everything from buy jeans to make our homes more comfortable with programmable thermostats.

While innovation and productivity in the world of commerce have flourished, as far as I know there are still only two ways for a business to make more money: sell more of their products and services, or spend less. Even as we dream up ever more creative ways to offer our means to the buying public, in the end our only methods of generating a healthier bottom line have remained the same as they were in the days the Hudson's Bay Company was selling beaver pelts on the Great Plains. All of this is good news for those developing objectives in the Financial perspective of their strategy maps because, unlike the remaining perspectives, the choices here are relatively limited. Kaplan and Norton rightly assert that a company's financial performance may be improved with two basic levers—revenue growth and productivity.[3]

Growing revenue is typically accomplished in one of two ways: by selling entirely new products and services to the market or by deepening relationships with existing customers, enhancing the value offered and generating additional profitability. Many organizations will attempt to do both, and in fact that is a strategy I pursue with my company. Many of my client engagements begin with a simple introductory training session on Balanced Scorecard fundamentals. These sessions will often generate further interest in the topic and frequently lead to consulting engagements, during which I assist the organization in implementing the Balanced Scorecard. In the process I am deepening my relationship with the client and improving my profitability. It's also critical for me to introduce new products to the marketplace as the Balanced Scorecard, and the business world, continue to evolve. In that vein, I am currently developing an online media product that will most likely be available as you read this book. This innovative offering will, I hope, position my firm for further growth in the years ahead as I introduce the concepts of the Balanced Scorecard to an ever-widening audience.

Productivity improvements are similarly achieved with a two-pronged approach. The first option available to organizations is simply reducing their direct and indirect costs by spending less on human resources, materials, and other business inputs. Virtually every client, in every industry, that I have ever worked with has included such an objective on their strategy maps. A second approach, one involving significantly greater sophistication, involves improving productivity by utilizing assets more efficiently, thereby requiring fewer dollars to support a given level of production.

The question when developing objectives for the Financial perspective is not one of either/or: either we must choose revenue growth or we must pursue productivity improvements. Ultimately, if yours is a for-profit business, increasing shareholder value is your goal, and it can only be accomplished through the shrewd management of *both* growth and productivity. The first, and perhaps most basic, choice you make when creating your strategy map involves balancing and managing the tension between these seemingly contradictory forces. In many ways, the Financial objectives you select represent the "end in mind" of your strategic journey, and as we'll see, the objectives in each of the three remaining perspectives will ensure you reach your destination.

Customer Perspective

Choosing objectives for the Customer perspective requires organizations to first answer two fundamental questions: (1) Who are our targeted customers? and (2) How do we propose to add value for those customers? Fundamental doesn't always equal easy, however, and these queries can prove challenging to corporate giants, public-sector agencies, and nonprofits alike.

Ask any CEO if he has a target customer group and he will most likely nod in the affirmative, but dig a little deeper by examining actual practices and you may witness another story altogether. Many companies pursue an all things to all customers strategy, failing to differentiate themselves from the pack and earning mediocre returns as a result. This herding behavior among competitors not only injures individual company profitability but also significantly weakens the profit margins of the industry as a whole. For example, from mid-1993 to 1998, margins in the German wireless telecommunications industry declined by roughly 50%. This precipitous drop occurred as the three main players in the field, Deutsche

Telekom, Mannesmann, and C–Tel, followed copy-cat strategies resulting in virtually identical product offerings, tariffs, and customer segments.[4] The objectives, and later measures, you choose for the Customer perspective will be of little value unless they are directed toward a specific group of targeted customers, allowing you to effectively measure the execution of your unique strategy.

It doesn't get any easier once you determine your target customer group. That simply leads to more questions, such as:[5]

- How do they buy the product or service?

- Why do they buy?

- What need is the product or service satisfying?

- How long will the need last?

- What is the competition doing?

Answering these brain teasers demands that you develop a specific value proposition, that unique mix of product, price, service, relationship, and image you offer to your targeted customers.[6] In Chapter One we briefly outlined the value propositions or disciplines offered by authors Treacy and Wiersema in *The Discipline of Market Leaders*:[7]

- *Operational excellence.* Organizations pursuing an operational excellence discipline focus on low price, convenience, and often no frills. McDonald's, a pioneering organization in the fast-food industry, represents an operationally excellent firm. Go into any of their restaurants from Boston to Beijing, and you can expect a similar experience, one punctuated by consistent menu offerings, low price, and quick service.

- *Product leadership.* Product leaders push the envelope of their firm's products. Constantly innovating, they strive to offer simply the best product in the market. I'm sure you can remember the first time you excitedly placed the headphones of a Sony Walkman over your head and were subsequently amazed by the clarity of the sound emanating from such a tiny device. Sony has a long and storied tradition of new product development and as such may be considered a product-leading company.

- *Customer intimacy.* Doing whatever it takes to provide solutions for customers' unique needs helps define customer-intimate companies. They don't look for one-time transactions but instead focus on long-term relationship building through their deep knowledge of customer needs. The Senalosa Group is a terrific example of a customer-intimate company, striving to meet the requirements of clients not only today, but growing with them and providing additional services as the need arises. Okay, that was a test. Did you know The Senalosa Group is the name of my consulting company? I pride myself on being customer intimate, but in case you want a more brand-name example, how about the Home Depot. In the growing home improvement market, they are a great illustration of a customer-intimate organization. Without sounding too much like a commercial, the Home Depot can help you with everything from finding a lamp for your first apartment to installing a fish pond in the backyard of your country estate, and while your needs as a homeowner will inevitably change, the Home Depot is there with you every step of the way.

The value proposition you select will greatly influence the objectives you choose to appear on your strategy map because each will entail a different emphasis. Consistency is key here, because you must ensure that your objectives accurately portray the story you're attempting to tell on the map. As an illustration, take the case of Wal-Mart, undoubtedly the paragon of operational excellence in a retail environment. Low prices and abundantly stocked shelves are testimony to their unrelenting drive to increase operational excellence and efficiency. Would you expect to see an objective such as "Attract the richest 1% of shoppers" in their Customer perspective? I doubt it. While they welcome the wealthier among us to shop at their ubiquitous stores, the rich don't represent Wal-Mart's target customer segment. Additionally, affluent consumers tend to purchase a higher percentage of leading-edge products and look for five-star service during their shopping experience. While Wal-Mart offers a broad selection of products and provides acceptable customer service, that is not what distinguishes them from their competition. More appropriate objectives for Wal-Mart's Customer perspective would include attributes of price, convenience, and selection. Exhibit 4.1 provides some key dimensions that may be considered when examining your objectives in the context of customer value propositions.

Internal Processes Perspective

When describing objectives for both the Financial and Customer perspectives of the strategy map, we have focused primarily on the "what" of strategy (i.e., what are we ultimately attempting to achieve in our pursuit of executing this strategy?). Revenue growth, productivity enhancements, customer satisfaction, and retention are all outcomes toward which we're striving. When we enter the realm of the Internal Processes perspective (and later Employee Learning and Growth), we veer sharply from the "what" to the "how" of value creation. Objectives in this perspective describe specifically how you will achieve the customer value proposition articulated in the Customer perspective and, ultimately, how you will enhance revenue and increase efficiency as measured in the Financial perspective.

Given that every organization is unique and relies on hundreds of processes, it is not surprising that the Internal Processes perspective will spawn the greatest

EXHIBIT 4.1   Key Dimensions to Consider when Developing Objectives for Each Customer Value Proposition

Operational Excellence	Product Leadership	Customer Intimacy
• *Price:* Offering low prices is at the heart of most operationally efficient organizations. • *Selection:* The products customers expect must be readily available. • *Convenience:* Transactions must be simple and swift, stripping away unnecessary elements. • *Zero defects:* There is no room for error in the lean, operationally excellent company; the highest standards of quality must be maintained.	• *High-performance product characteristics:* Customers expect the latest and greatest from product leaders. • *Entering new market spaces:* Product leaders push the envelope of design, using their ingenuity to move into new and nontraditional markets. • *Product and service introductions:* Product leading institutions must be the first to market to keep their customers coming back for more.	• *Customer knowledge:* To provide complete solutions, you must first know your customer (trends, demographics, buying patterns, etc.). • *Solutions offered:* Customers desire a total solution to their unique needs. • *"Share of wallet":* Customer-intimate organizations are attempting to deepen the bond between themselves and their customers. • *Retention:* Relationships for the long term are key to this discipline.

number of objectives in most strategy maps. For many organizations, the choices seem endless, sort of what I feel like any time I have to assist my wife in picking out carpeting or anything else for our home! Of course, if we make a poor decorating choice, the ramifications are relatively insignificant (my wife might disagree). The same is not so for organizations. The selection of Internal Processes objectives is critical in constructing a map that accurately weaves together the disparate pieces of strategy into a coherent whole.

In their extensive research on the topic, Balanced Scorecard architects Kaplan and Norton have simplified the task of Internal Processes objective selection by identifying four clusters of processes which are applicable to virtually any organization: Operations Management processes, Customer Management processes, Innovation processes, and Regulatory and Social Processes.[8] Each is discussed briefly in the following paragraphs.

Operations Management processes are the most basic of the four, covering the day-to-day routine processes necessary to first produce and ultimately deliver a product or service to the customer. Included in this spectrum of activities are sourcing of raw materials from suppliers (and, hence, achieving positive supplier relationships), producing the product or service, distribution, and risk management. Using popular and effective tools such as total quality management and reengineering, many organizations have sought to dramatically improve their Operations Management processes to achieve a competitive advantage, and in fact a significant number of companies achieved material results. Although this pursuit is undoubtedly worthwhile, it does not necessarily lead to a sustainable advantage because reliable and efficient operations have become almost baseline requirements for success in our modern economy.

Pontificating on the wildly successful Model T, Henry Ford once remarked of customers, *"They can have any color they want as long as it's black."* One can only imagine what his reaction might be in seeing the following phrase beckoning to potential customers on his company's website today, "Build and price your Ford." Okay, first we'd have to get his reaction to the whole Internet thing, but after that sunk in, we could focus on his thoughts of customer choice, and I'm sure he'd be shocked. We live in an era when the customer truly is king. With just a few keystrokes we can design anything from a new car to a personal computer to a pair of jeans. Technology, in particular the Internet, has forever transferred the balance of power from producer to consumer. As a result of this seismic shift, *Customer Management processes* have become of paramount importance to all organizations. A logical first Customer Management process is the selection of target customers. Stratifying the vast population of customers assists companies in identifying the subset that is most attractive to them. Once the targeted customers are selected, they must be brought on board through acquisition processes. Communicating and proactively marketing the value proposition will help turn prospects into paying customers. Next, the organization must retain customers by ensuring that it delivers a quality product or service and swiftly resolves any issues that arise. This is a vital step because estimates suggest that it can cost up to 10 times as much to acquire a new customer than to keep a current one.[9] Finally, the company attempts to grow its relationship with the customer, ensuring a profitable future.

The third member of our Internal Processes cluster is *Innovation*. Victor Hugo once remarked, *"There is one thing stronger than all the armies in the world, and that is an idea whose time has come."*[10] Organizations all over the world recognize this undeniable fact and have made ideas the fuel that drives our new economy. No company, despite any historical record of success, can rest on its laurels and continue offering the same menu of products and services year in and year out if it expects to thrive, or even survive, in our modern world. In the previous paragraph, we noted that the customer is king, and that monarch has a seemingly unquenchable thirst for innovative twists in everything from groceries to gravity boots. Organizations that are unwilling or unable to offer new products and services to an eagerly awaiting public are sure to be left behind.

Under the broad umbrella of innovation are a number of subprocesses, the first of which is the identification of opportunities for new products and services. Like a lifeguard constantly surveying her beach, companies must be perpetually on the lookout for the opportunity to introduce new products or services by working with key customers, applying new technology, or extending the capabilities of existing offerings. With opportunities located, organizations then must determine whether they will fund internally, work with joint ventures, or outsource entirely. The next step, one at the heart of the innovation process, is the development of the new product or service. Successful product development peaks with the introduction of a product or service well-matched to customer needs and able to be profitably manufactured. Finally, the nascent offering is delivered to the public— the result of a production process capable of ensuring consistent levels of quality and reliability.

In a paradoxical twist, our final core process requires us to look outward before we work inward. Organizations are increasingly being judged on their ability to act as good corporate citizens, contributing to the communities in which they operate and displaying responsibility in *regulatory, environmental,* and *social* concerns. While most jurisdictions impose certain conditions on the right to operate within their boundaries (e.g., through health and safety and employment practices), today's leading organizations wish to extend beyond simple compliance, demonstrating their commitment to a sustainable future through best practice environmental controls, health and safety standards, and community investment. Such acts are not entirely selfless because an increasing number of consumers are attracted to companies with strong track records of environmental and social performance, which ultimately leads to enhanced business for those on the leading edge of these practices.

Employee Learning and Growth Perspective

Whenever I work with clients on developing objectives for the Employee Learning and Growth perspective, I am reminded of that old saying, *"imitation is the purest form of flattery."* In fact, I find myself uttering those words frequently when work for this perspective rolls around. Most clients struggle with creating unique objectives that describe how they will transform their intangible assets into monetary value for the organization and rely on, for inspiration, the many examples I provide from previous engagements. This is somewhat ironic because the integration of an organization's unique intangible assets is what drives the transformation engine within the strategy map. David Norton goes even further in his criticism of organizations' work in this area, stating: *"The worst grades are reserved for... understanding of strategies for developing human capital.... The asset that is most important is the least understood, least prone to measurement, and, hence, least susceptible to management."*[11]

In a twist on the old saying, organizations must begin putting their mouth where their money is. Spending for intangible assets has ballooned. Just 25 years ago, American corporations spent about $49 billion on computers and other information-processing equipment, and it just kept growing from there. If you plot industrial age and information age spending on a graph, the two lines would intersect in 1991. That year, spending for production technology was $107 billion and information technology spending was $112 billion. Thus, 1991 may be considered year one of the Information Age. Since that time, companies have spent more money on equipment that gathers, processes, analyzes, and distributes information than on machines that stamp, cut, assemble, lift, and otherwise manipulate the physical world.[12] While spending on intangibles has grown immensely, attention to the effects of these expenditures has not. In the days ahead, it is absolutely critical for all organizations to assume the responsibility of creatively describing and measuring the effects of their intangible assets if they hope to realize the promise held by these building blocks of the knowledge economy.

The use of a simplifying framework can be a substantial aid in generating appropriate objectives for the Employee Learning and Growth perspective. Just as we used customer value propositions as a means of generating objectives in the Customer perspective and four overarching clusters of processes in the Internal Processes perspective, we will again turn to a method of classification that will significantly ease the burden as we pan for Employee Learning and Growth gold. Dividing the perspective into three distinct, yet interrelated, dimensions of capital will yield great insights into this challenging area of strategy map creation. The first is human capital, encompassing the skills and capabilities necessary to execute strategy and compete effectively in your marketplace. Information capital comprises the information infrastructure and support systems necessary to support the strategy. Finally, organization capital represents the intangibles providing for your ability to change and grow, including culture, leadership, and alignment.[13] We'll review each of these areas of capital in the following sections.

Human Capital

Business is probably the only field I know of that draws so heavily from, and welcomes, knowledge from other disciplines. Just look at some of the many book titles that aim to help you become a better leader: *Lincoln on Leadership, The Tao of Leadership*, and what library would be complete without *Jesus CEO*. Unlike those of us in the field of business who welcome input from every conceivable sphere of knowledge, I don't imagine other disciplines are so anxiously awaiting advice from outside their realms; for example, I can't imagine the medical field eagerly anticipating *Niven on Brain Surgery*. But business has benefited greatly from the contributions of others, and it is in that spirit that I offer this prescient quote from Pope John Paul II, first written 1991: *"Whereas at one time the decisive factor of production was the land, and later capital . . . today the decisive factor is increasingly man himself, that is, his knowledge."*[14] John Paul's words ring true regardless of whether we're discussing governments, nonprofit agencies, or businesses large and small; in today's economy intangible assets, chiefly knowledge, are the drivers of success. The corporate world has run with this undeniable evolution, investing heavily in knowledge development and sharing systems, and now the government is becoming aware that human capital is vital to its success as well. As part of the bill that created the new U.S. Department of Homeland Security, every federal agency must hire a Chief Human Capital Officer whose responsibility it is to ensure their agency's strategic alignment and maintenance and direction of Human Resources policies and programs.[15] Following are several possible objectives relating to human capital:

- *Human capital readiness.* The most fundamental objective relating to human capital is aimed simply at ensuring that your organization possesses the skills and knowledge you require to execute your strategy. Kaplan and Norton suggest that you begin this quest by documenting the competencies required to carry out the key processes as articulated in the Internal Processes perspective of the strategy map. This documentation will lead to the development of strategic job families, those clusters of high-value positions most critical to executing your strategy.[16] Once you've determined the job families and related competencies, you are tasked with measuring any gaps between future requirements and current realities. Closing the gap, or in some cases chasm, is typically accomplished through either training or recruitment of individuals possessing the requisite skills, each of which is discussed next.

- *Training.* Staying in a job for your entire career without acquiring any new skills is simply not an option in the new economy. A commitment to learning is a requirement of every employee regardless of the position held. Perhaps no one epitomizes the spirit of lifelong learning better than Sam Walton, founder of Wal-Mart. Here is a charming tale relating Walton's passionate desire to learn more about retailing:

  A Brazilian businessman sent a letter to the heads of 10 U.S. retailers in the 1980s, asking to visit and see how they ran a retail operation. Most didn't even bother replying, and those who did sent a polite "No, thank you." All except Sam Walton, that is. When the Brazilian and his colleagues landed in Bentonville, Arkansas, they were greeted by a white-haired man asking if he could help. "We're looking for Sam Walton," they said, to which he replied "that's me" and directed them into his pickup truck alongside his faithful canine companion, Roy. As they rumbled toward town, Walton pummeled the men with questions and it soon dawned on them: Walton had invited them to Bentonville so that he could learn about retailing in Brazil! Not long after, the Brazilians returned the favor by hosting Walton in São Paulo. Late one afternoon there was a phone call from the police. It seems Walton had been crawling around in stores on his hands and knees measuring aisle widths and had been arrested.[17]

  You don't have to have your permanent record blotted to demonstrate a commitment to learning, however. Simply constructing an appropriate objective on your strategy map and following up judiciously with a proper measurement will do the trick.

- *Recruitment and retention.* When you strip everything away from an organization—its products, services, machines, property, and processes—you're left with one thing, the one thing that really matters above all others: people. Historically, the role of the walking, talking, thinking machine known as a human was sometimes questioned; in fact, early 20th-century industrial engineers such as Frederick Winslow Taylor openly disregarded any possible contributions, other than pure physical toil, from the common human. How times have changed. Today we recognize and embrace the fact that employing the right people represents our best chance of reaching new heights. Jim Collins, author of the wildly popular *Good to Great,* found evidence for this in the study that inspired the book and notes: *"The executives who ignited the transformations from good to great did not first figure out where to drive the bus and then get people to take there. No, they first got the right people on the bus (and the wrong people off the bus) and then figured out where to drive it.*"[18] Collins' domain is principally the corporate world, but his advice holds regardless of the arena.

Speaking of General George C. Marshall, the great American soldier-statesman, Peter Drucker notes: *"With all of his political duties—holding together the entire civilian and military war effort—he spent half of his time on placing people, finding the right person for a particular job at a particular time."*[19] Recruiting and retaining the right people should undoubtedly have a place on your strategy map; however, an admonition is in order: Always exercise caution in the wording you employ to describe your intentions. I've had clients make such proclamations on their maps as "Recruit and retain "A" level performers." The impetus is sound, acquiring and keeping the best, but for many at lower levels of the organization, the subjective nature of just exactly what qualifies as being "A" level is both threatening and confusing. If you choose to use language like this, make sure you have carefully considered the exact characteristics you desire.

Information Capital

It's difficult to imagine an industry that hasn't been dramatically affected by technology over the last several years. So-called "disruptive" technologies have revolutionized the way we make, market, purchase, and use everything from household products to entertainment devices. In our modern economy, information capital serves as the raw material, driving the transformation of data into information and propelling the growth of individual companies and entire industries alike.

Given the pervasive influence of technology, virtually every organization should consider an information capital objective when forming its Employee Learning and Growth perspective. In my experience working with a wide array of organizations, these objectives typically resemble the following: "Improve technology infrastructure," "Leverage technology," "Increase knowledge management and information sharing," "Gather, share, and use information effectively." The first example relates to the infrastructure component of information capital, ensuring that you have the physical tools (e.g., mainframes, etc.) necessary to deliver information to users. The remaining examples center on the need to gather stored information, share it widely, and have employees harness it in their day-to-day actions.

As the previous examples illustrate, organizations hold a strong belief in the power of sharing information as the key that will unlock everything from enhanced creativity in the workplace to breakthrough gains in productivity. Backing up that belief is the fiscal commitment demonstrated; in 2003, U.S. companies spent $4.5 billion on software and other technologies that attempt to foster information sharing among employees.[20] Some critics suggest this pattern may be misguided because typical knowledge management and information sharing systems rely on the flawed paradigm of publishing: someone collects information, makes it available, and sits back to see what happens. This model is fraught with issues: (1) it's virtually impossible to catalogue all of the information swirling about a company; (2) it's often obsolete by the time it's captured; and (3) worst of all, many people don't share their most valuable information, choosing to give into a natural impulse to hoard what they perceive as the most critical information they possess.

A new way of thinking about information sharing proposes a brokering model in which those who have information and feel they can derive a benefit from sharing it are matched with others requiring it. Far from being a cynical approach, this model simply recognizes an innately human characteristic of keeping a close watch on what is most valuable to us. Software tools have been developed that aid in this task by sifting through the mountains of information pumping through a company at any given time and identifying common threads as they go. Without naming names, these systems alert people of shared interests, making a match possible.[21] Consider it an information dating service. With this as a backdrop, it may be appropriate to consider an objective such as "increase opportunities for information sharing" when contemplating the information capital component of Employee Learning and Growth. All organizations share the common desire of mobilizing information into action and must recognize that accessing information has both human and technological dimensions.

Organizational Capital

At what may have been the darkest hour for Great Britain during World War II, just before the Dunkirk deliverance, Prime Minister Winston Churchill stood before Parliament and issued these words: *"To sum up, our conclusion is that prima facie Germany has most of the cards; but the real test is whether the morale of our fighting personnel and civil population will counterbalance the numerical and material advantage which Germany enjoys. We believe it will."*[22] With those words, he ignited the passion and belief of an entire nation facing practically unbeatable odds, lifting the spirit and resolve of every person, in every corner of the nation. Such is the power of the human spirit. Regardless of the forum or field of endeavor, at the end of the day true success resides in the power manifested by hearts and minds.

Organizational capital represents our ability to evolve and grow as an organization, ensuring success today and sustaining that prosperity for the long term. Outlined as follows are elements that should be considered when developing this section of your strategy map:

- *Culture.* Talk about difficult things to define and measure; culture may be the granddaddy of them all. Let's deal with the definition part of the equation first. Organizational culture and leadership expert Edgar Schein defines culture as

> a pattern of shared basic assumptions that the group learned as it solved its problems of external adaptation and internal integration, that has worked well enough to be considered valid and, therefore, to be taught to new members as the correct way to perceive, think, and feel in relation to those problems.[23]

You're probably scratching your head thinking, "Okay, hmm, external adaptation and internal integration. I think I'll get a cup of coffee." At least that's what I'd be thinking. Schein's definition is undoubtedly accurate but a bit on the academic side. In more colloquial fashion we might simply consider culture as "the way we do things around here." I have yet to work with an organization that does not include a culture objective on its strategy map. Some examples include: "Create a culture in alignment with mission, values, and vision," "Foster a culture that encourages, recognizes, and celebrates both individual and team contribution," and "Strengthen knowledge-sharing culture." Choosing an appropriate objective here is a personal decision, because you must determine whether you wish to shape your current culture or develop an entirely new one. Only you can make that determination, but I will warn you that this objective entails a great amount of work.

First comes the challenge of measurement, which most organizations solve through surveys, and second comes the initiatives, in the possible form of new incentive and reporting systems among others, you'll need to put in place to accomplish this intimidating task. Finally, be cognizant that cultures are shaped over years of habitual and repetitive behavior and cannot be altered overnight. As mentioned earlier, to measure culture, and satisfaction in general, most companies will turn to employee surveys, an area of little experience for most. To help you get the most out of your employee surveys, follow the simple guidelines found in Exhibit 4.2.

- *Leadership.* Effective leadership is the common thread running through every facet of the organizational experience. From overseeing a transformational change effort to making tough day-to-day decisions to charting a new strategic course, strong leadership is an absolute must if you want to play to win in your markets. Your strategy map should acknowledge this fact by the appearance of an objective relating to leadership within your organization. In most cases these objectives will take one of two forms, either relating to the development of new leaders (ensuring a leadership "pipeline") or the characteristics, competencies, and behaviors you expect to be exhibited from effective leaders.

EXHIBIT 4.2   Creating Effective Surveys

Keep the following points in mind when creating employee surveys:

- Ask questions related to observable behavior, not thoughts or motives—Allows respondents to draw on firsthand experience and not inference.

- Measure only those behaviors that are linked to your organization's performance—Awareness of your new cafeteria hours may be interesting, but is it relevant to your results?

- About one-third of questions should lead to a negative response—This avoids our natural tendency to agree with things.

- Avoid questions that require rankings. We tend to remember the first and last things in a list, which may bias our answer to the question.

- Make sure the survey can be completed within 20 minutes—Recognize that everyone is busy, and taking an hour to complete a 100-question survey may elicit negative responses that show up in the respondents' answers.

Adapted from Palmer Morrel-Samuels, "Getting the Truth Into Workplace Surveys," *Harvard Business Review,* February, 2002, pp. 111–118.

- *Alignment.* The problems of misalignment are frequently and colorfully reflected by parents of youngsters participating in soccer leagues. If you've ever been to one of these matches, you know what I'm referring to: a blur of frenzied activity around the ball with not a single player venturing more than a few feet from that maelstrom of action. There is no coordination of activities, just a mad scramble covering a few square yards of the pitch. This is quite amusing if you're watching from the stands with your camcorder catching the moment for posterity, because the stakes are relatively minor, but for organizations, a lack of alignment can prove extremely hazardous to any hope of executing strategy. Employee actions must be aligned with mission, values, vision, and, most important, strategy if you wish to fully exploit the advantages of intangible assets such as culture and knowledge.

The first step on the road to an aligned organization is ensuring employee understanding of the building blocks of mission, values, vision, and strategy. Only through understanding will action follow. A simple and effective method of ensuring alignment is reviewing cascaded Balanced Scorecards from throughout your organization. While most Scorecards will rightly contain unique objectives and measures, they should be aligned toward a common strategy if you hope to have all oars rowing in a winning direction. We'll discuss the notion of alignment and cascading in greater depth in Chapter Six.

As I write these words, a new season is about to dawn in the National Football League (NFL) in the United States. Hope runs high amid the endless possibilities offered by a new campaign. From coast to coast, teams are readying themselves for the battles to come over the next 16 weeks. The accounts I've read in the sports pages and heard on the television are stirring, how various teams have jelled and the spirit of teamwork is sure to propel them to gridiron legend. Every team acknowledges that working together is their best hope of competing and ultimately succeeding in the forthcoming season.

It's a long way from the real and punishing tackles doled out on a football field to the intangible assets on your strategy map, but the ethic of teamwork stands the challenging comparison. In order to create value from the intangible assets appearing in the Employee Learning and Growth perspective of your strategy map, they must be aligned and working together as a team in support of your strategy. The objectives appearing here should not constitute disparate elements, but must form a coherent whole, the sum of which is greater than the individual parts. When selecting your objectives, ensure that they support the strategy you've chosen to pursue. For example, assuming for a moment you've chosen a strategy of customer intimacy, we would expect your Employee Learning and Growth objectives to mirror that selection. Within the human capital domain, you may then consider an objective centered on training in customer relationship skills. Information capital could be capably represented by an investment in customer relationship management (CRM) software, and within organizational capital, you may wish to pursue a culture of customer-centered behaviors. These objectives are aligned and fully support the strategy you've chosen.

The Number of Objectives on Your Strategy Map

I was just about to enter the conference room to begin a strategy mapping workshop for a client when I heard a whisper from behind me. It was the CEO of the company beckoning me to a secluded corner of the floor out of earshot and sight of the other participants. Perhaps he wants to give me a last-second pep talk, I thought to myself as we made our way down the brightly lit corridor, adorned on either side by the imposing portraits of past leaders. Once we stopped, he turned, looked directly in my eyes, and said with the most earnest of expressions: *"When we get in there I want you to keep us focused. My goal is to come out of this exercise with no more than ten objectives."* I assured him I would do my very best, balancing the need to tell the story of their strategy with his desire for brevity. With that we turned and headed for the conference room to kick off our session.

After my introduction of ground rules, a short primer on creating effective objectives, and an overview of our process, we got into gear by working on the Financial perspective. It couldn't have been more than 30 minutes into the session when the CEO insisted on the inclusion of at least six Financial objectives. The tide did not subside as we turned our attention to the other perspectives of the Scorecard; in fact, his appetite for objectives seemed to grow as the event wore on. By day's end, we had more than 40 objectives swelling the draft strategy map. Moral of the story: Despite your best intentions, the number of objectives on your strategy map can grow faster than weeds in an abandoned garden.

Fortunately, we were able to cull the objective herd in a subsequent session, but as the example illustrates, it is very easy to have the number of objectives forming your map balloon in no time at all. Several factors conspire to make this happen. First, some people will find it easier to offer a large number of mediocre objectives rather than expending the energy and cognitive horsepower required to create the right objectives for your strategy. I believe it was Mark Twain who, when corresponding with an acquaintance, once offered, *"I tried to write a short letter but it was too hard so I wrote a long one."* Maybe the CEO I alluded to earlier was a distant relative of Twain's. Objectives also tend to proliferate as cross-functional members of the team work to ensure that their group's interests are represented on the Balanced Scorecard. Finally, the work leads to expanding the ranks of objectives. After all, how often do you have the opportunity to carefully and thoughtfully reflect on the strategy of your organization and how you will effectively execute it? Not very often, I suspect, and as a result you want to leave no stone unturned in your efforts.

My database of client strategy maps reveals objectives numbering from a low of nine to a high of more than 30. Interestingly, the organization with only nine objectives on its map is one of my largest clients. The CEO was adamant that a strategy map is primarily a communication tool and as such should be a simple and pragmatic document. There is no magic number of objectives, but in my experience less is more. Never lose sight of the fact that a Balanced Scorecard is meant to provide focus to your organization, keeping you riveted to the most critical drivers of your success, and keeping peripheral items there, in the periphery. In their bestselling book *Execution,* authors Bossidy and Charan emphasize this point by noting, *"Leaders who execute focus on a very few priorities that everyone can grasp."*[24] If everything is a priority, then nothing is a priority.

The strategy map entails making difficult choices and trade-offs, but making such decisions is the essence of effective leadership. My final argument in defense of a relatively low number of objectives (say, between 10 and 15) is a pragmatic one. Each objective on your map will likely spawn at least one and sometimes two or more associated performance measures. Thirty objectives on a strategy map could easily escalate to more than 60 measures, and if you choose to cascade the Scorecard, in no time at all you may be flooded with hundreds of performance measures throughout the organization. If all else fails in your attempts to keep the number of objectives down to the critical few, remind your teammates of this quote from *Irrational Exuberance* author Robert J. Shiller, who suggests, *"The ability to focus attention on important things is a defining characteristic of intelligence."*[25]

Ensuring Understanding with Objective Statements

If you've already developed a strategy map, the following scenario will probably be familiar to you. After painstaking deliberation, your team has hammered out a strategy map that clearly and cogently describes your strategy. Performance measures are next on the agenda, but before embarking on that road, you decide to take a well-deserved break to recharge your Scorecard batteries. A couple of weeks later, the team reconvenes and is eager to begin creating measures for each of the objectives—and then it happens. You realize that you can't remember half of the stimulating and thought-provoking dialogue that led to the creation of the map you see before you today. Every objective on the page is a mystery, and while the general themes are evident, you can't recall any specifics. Of course, the job of translating these riddles into measures is rendered all the more difficult as a result.

To avoid situations like this, where your efforts are derailed and your sanity tested, you should write two- to three-sentence narratives for each objective as soon after the strategy mapping session as possible. I call these notes objective statements and have found them to serve multiple purposes. Primarily, they clearly articulate specifically what is meant by each objective on the map, which comes in handy if your map contains any nebulous objectives such as "increase productivity." That could translate to countless things and lead to any number of able measurements, thus the importance of outlining exactly what "increase productivity" entails in the context of your strategy map. The objective statements also answer the inevitable "what does that mean?" question you'll receive from curious readers of your map. Everything on the document may be second nature to you, but for a first-time reader who is new to the subject, it may resemble hieroglyphics scrawled on an ancient cave wall. A well-written objective statement should be brief (two to three sentences will suffice in most cases), clarify what is meant by the objective, outline why it is important, concisely describe how it will be accomplished, and describe how it links in a chain of cause-and-effect relationships among the objectives. Here is an example of a clearly written objective statement from a nonprofit client of mine:

Provide Timely Access to Accurate, Actionable, and Consistent Information

Good decisions from our staff depend on the right information being available at the right time, packaged in a way to meet both our and our clients' needs. Information is also critical to donors to demonstrate whether programs have achieved results. To achieve this objective we must identify what information is required to support decision-making, stop collecting information that does not add value, and create standardized information systems that ensure the availability of needed data.

Not surprisingly, the best time to write objective statements is immediately following the development of the map, while the information is still fresh in your mind. Exactly who writes the statements is open to debate and is a matter of personal preference, but I suggest you have small groups of two to three people complete the task. Having one person write a statement introduces the possibility of their biases and isolated points of view creeping into the process, whereas a small group can balance one another, ensuring an accurate depiction of the actual discussion that was held during the workshop.

Telling Your Strategic Story through Cause and Effect

Are you familiar with the name Robert McKee? Perhaps not, but I'm certain you'll recognize some of the works produced by his students: *Forrest Gump, The Color Purple, Toy Story,* and *Erin Brokovich,* just to name a few. McKee is arguably the world's greatest screenwriting coach, and the 18 Academy Awards, 109 Emmys, and 19 Writers Guild Awards won by his protégés are solid testimony to that assertion. In a recent interview, McKee discussed the real necessity of introducing the art of storytelling in a business context. As he puts it,

> A big part of a CEO's job is to motivate people to reach certain goals. To do that he or she must engage their emotions, and the key to their hearts is a story...if you can harness imagination and the principles of a well-told story, then you get people rising to their feet amid thunderous applause instead of yawning and ignoring you.[26]

The objectives and measures appearing on your strategy map should weave together through the four perspectives to tell your *strategic story.* All of the elements you need to create a compelling and dramatic story are present on the map: customers, processes, people, and finances. Your job is to creatively link the objectives in a manner that both tells a spellbinding story and allows you to garner additional insights about your business.

Consider for a moment two possible scenarios for presenting corporate objectives to your employee base. In the first case, your CEO goes to the front of the room, directs the audience's attention to a series of PowerPoint slides, and dutifully walks them through each chart with exacting precision and detail.

(My eyes are rolling back in my head as I write that.) Contrast that with your CEO telling the story of your company—the strategic destination of financial success, the customer outcomes that will fuel that success, the key processes driving results for customers, and the enabling infrastructure setting the foundation for it all. The linkages among the perspectives bring the story to life, demonstrating that your business is not a series of disparate elements but is actually a powerful and cohesive system that, if working seamlessly, is geared for success.

More than just an entertaining device to bring employees out of any organizationally imposed doldrums, cause and effect has a powerful business impetus. In effect, any strategy is simply a hypothesis offered by its authors, representing their best guess about an appropriate course of action in recognition of the operating environment, customer preferences and trends, macroeconomic forces, and so on. In order to execute the strategy, it must be tested in real time to validate assumptions and make necessary course corrections. For most organizations, strategy is a new destination, somewhere they haven't traveled to before. What is needed is a method to document and test the assumptions inherent in the strategy. The strategy map and Balanced Scorecard allow us to do just that. A well-designed strategy map should describe your strategy through the objectives you have chosen. These objectives should link together in a chain of cause-and-effect relationships from the performance drivers in the Employee Learning and Growth Perspective all the way through to improved financial outcomes as reflected in the Financial Perspective. We are attempting to document our strategy through measurement, making the relationships between the measures explicit so they can be monitored, managed, and validated. Only then can we begin learning about, and successfully implementing, our strategy.

Undoubtedly, a solid rationale for constructing cause-and-effect relationships among your objectives exists, but out in the real world, is it actually happening? The answer is largely no. In one recent study of performance measurement practices, the authors discovered that of 157 companies surveyed, only 23% consistently built and verified causal models.[27] I've seen cause and effect take many forms, with some organizations drawing links between practically every objective appearing on their map. I call these graphical nightmares "spaghetti diagrams" and am convinced that if I ever submitted some of the best examples of this culinary art to psychiatrists, they would be quickly knocking on the artist's door for a consultation. At the other end of the spectrum are maps with virtually no cause-and-effect relationships whatsoever. Investing the effort in creating these linkages may offer significant payoffs, as the authors in the aforementioned study discovered. They found that organizations that did create the linkages had, on average, return on assets figures 2.95% higher and return on equity of 5.14% higher than those organizations not using causal models.

Despite the potential rewards, there are strategy map creators among us who simply don't feel comfortable claiming relationships that may or may not exist, and that does not preclude them from enjoying great success from the Balanced Scorecard. Many leading Scorecard adopters exhibit limited cause and effect among objectives while still garnering tremendous focus, alignment, and improved resource allocation decisions from their work. In my opinion, the key linkages you should consider articulating on the map are between the Internal Processes and Customer perspectives. In many ways, the objectives appearing in the Employee Learning and Growth perspective are considered the enablers of everything you're attempting to achieve and thus may not warrant one-to-one connections with other sections of the map. However, the link between processes and customers is key, because it is here we signal two major transitions: from internal (employees, climate, processes) to external (customers) and from intangible (skills and knowledge, etc.) to tangible (customer outcomes and financial rewards). Customer outcomes signal the "what" of strategic execution and Internal processes supply the "how." All organizations should make an effort to explicitly document this equation, articulating specifically how they expect to transform their unique capabilities and infrastructure into revenue-producing results.

PERSONALIZING YOUR STRATEGY MAP

Most of us have experienced the joy of moving at least a few times in our lives, the word *joy* being used loosely. But once the initial pain and stress of the move is past, it's on to the exciting work of making our new house a home. Who among us has ever taken up residence in a new place and not made some changes? I would venture very few, because the personal touches make our new spaces comfortable; whether it's a fresh coat of paint, new light fixtures, curtains, or furniture, these individual touches reflect our taste and style, transforming a blank canvas into a living masterpiece.

While most people wouldn't dream of moving into a new house without adorning it with their personal touches, when it comes to strategy maps, they often do exactly that. New clients that have previously developed strategy maps often send them to me for comment, and one of the first things that jumps out is the fact that they all tend to look alike: full of business-speak terms and predictable objectives. After reviewing such a map replete with phrases such as "Integrate value-added technologies," and "Maximize economic value added," my first question to them is: "Do you really talk like that at your organization?" Usually the answer is a resounding no. Remember, the strategy map is a communication tool, and to fulfill that role it must use structure and language that reflects the norms, values, customs, and culture of your organization.

Your first decision in personalizing the strategy map is choosing the structure of the document. For example, in a for-profit enterprise, will you make the customary choice of placing the Financial perspective at the top of the map? Most organizations do so without really questioning whether that choice indicates their true beliefs and passion. Brother Industries (USA), however, is a fine example of a company that did take the time to ponder whether placing finances at the top of the strategy map was true to its strongest intentions. After careful consideration, they decided that customer satisfaction, a passionate belief held widely throughout the company, was most critical, and thus the Customer perspective should be placed at the top of the strategy map hierarchy. Interestingly, that led them to another question: "Does the hierarchical structure of the typical strategy map work for us?" Again, they chose the road less traveled and determined that the map was primarily a communication tool and thus should be both interesting and original, corresponding to the culture of the organization. The resulting strategy map, one that has proven to be remarkably successful in their communication and education efforts, is shown in Exhibit 4.3.

EXHIBIT 4.3   Strategy Map of Brother Industries (USA)

Reprinted with permission of the company.

Perhaps the most critical ingredient of the strategy map is the language you choose to represent your objectives. Terminology is vital, and as we all know, the right or wrong word in any given situation can have a powerful impact on results. Here is what organizational learning expert Peter Senge has to say about language:

> Words do matter. Language is messy by nature, which is why we must be careful in how we use it. As leaders, after all, we have little else to work with. We typically don't use hammers and saws, heavy equipment, or even computers to do our real work. The essence of leadership—what we do with 98 percent of our time—is communication. To master any management practice, we must start by bringing discipline to the domain in which we spend most of our time, the domain of words.[28]

Once again I implore you to recall the fact that a strategy map is a powerful communication tool, but to harness that power you must use language that can be understood and acted on by everyone who will look to the map for guidance, and my hope is that will be your entire employee population. If your organization is composed entirely of MBAs, PhDs, and other acronyms of erudition, that employee base will entail a certain choice of language. If, however, your employee base consists of everyone from interns to soccer moms bringing in a second income to young and ambitious executives on the rise, your language should reflect those demographics. My preference is for simple and comprehensible language because that will resonate with the vast majority of folks far more than the latest buzzwords from the *Wall Street Journal*. A great example of simple language comes to us from the Information Technology group of the Orange County Transportation Authority in Orange County, California. Their map is shown in Exhibit 4.4.

Granted, some of the language here borders on esoteric; for example, after working with them for months, I'm still not sure I know what a "proof of concept" is all about, but that's okay because they and their staff do, and that's all that matters. The overwhelming bulk of the language is clear and crisp, with a couple of objectives jumping off the page with real-world applicability. Which objectives did your eyes naturally gravitate toward? I've shown this map to audiences literally around the world encompassing different cultures, languages, and practices, yet I've never failed to have someone in the audience comment on "Get off the 3rd floor," and "Get more bang for our buck." You don't need to work for this organization to recognize that "getting off the third floor" means moving away from your normal routines and speaking to customers and users in other areas of the organization. Nor do you require an accounting designation to realize that "Get more bang for our buck" simply translates to exercising fiscal responsibility at every turn, always seeking to maximize value for dollars spent. To touch a personal chord with your employees, maximizing the benefits to be gained from the use of a strategy map, ensure that it accurately depicts your organization both in structure and language.

EXHIBIT 4.4 Strategy Map of the Orange County Transportation Authority IT Group

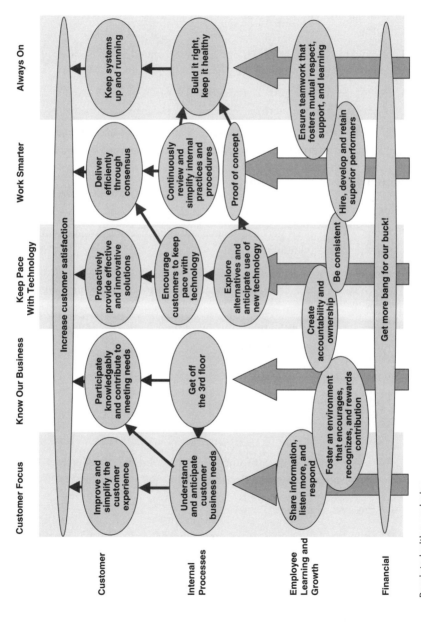

Reprinted with permission.

SELF-ASSESSMENT QUESTIONS

Developing the Strategy Map

Conducting Effective Strategy Map Workshops

1. Was our strategy map created at a location inspiring reflection, creativity, and insight?

2. During the session at which our map was created, did we adhere to a robust agenda, ensuring judicious use of our time?

3. Did we set the stage for a productive day of sharing and learning by engaging in an opening exercise affirming the Balanced Scorecard?

4. During the session, did we ensure that our participants remained active and present by limiting the use of cell phones, pagers, and PDAs?

Reviewing Your Strategy Map Objectives

Financial Perspective

1. Does our Financial perspective include objectives relating to both revenue growth and productivity?

2. When developing revenue growth, did we consider both the sale of entirely new products and services, and deepening relationships with current customers?

3. When creating productivity, did we discuss both cost reduction and asset utilization as possible objectives?

Customer Perspective

1. Have we defined our target customer segment(s)?

2. Do the objectives appearing in our Customer perspective reflect a core value proposition?

3. When we crafted our Customer objectives, did we ask ourselves what customers expect or demand from us?

Internal Processes Perspective

1. Do the objectives constituting our Internal Processes perspective answer the question of how we will achieve customer and financial outcomes?

2. When developing these objectives, did we consider the four key clusters of processes:
   ○ Operations management
   ○ Customer management

- Innovation
- Regulatory and social

Employee Learning and Growth Perspective

1. Does our strategy map address human capital within our organization, by including objectives relating to human capital readiness, training, or recruitment and retention?

2. When contemplating information capital, did our discussions include both infrastructure (mainframes, etc.) and support systems (software and information-sharing techniques)?

3. Have we considered organizational capital elements such as culture, leadership, and alignment in this perspective?

4. Do the objectives appearing in the Employee Learning and Growth perspective align with one another, reflecting our strategy?

The Number of Objectives on Your Strategy Map

1. Do we have an appropriate number of objectives on our map considering the following:

- Our size
- Culture
- Ability to execute
- Desired number of performance measures

Ensuring Understanding with Objective Statements

1. After creating our strategy map, did we convene small teams to write two- to three-sentence objective statements that further articulated what was meant by the objective?

Telling Your Strategic Story through Cause and Effect

1. Have we linked our objectives together in a pattern of cause-and-effect relationships that tells our strategic story?

2. Have we focused on demonstrating the linkages between the Internal Processes and Customer perspectives of the strategy map?

Personalizing Your Strategy Map

1. Does the structure of our strategy map (location of each of the four perspectives) reflect our culture and beliefs?

2. Have we used simple and understandable language and terminology throughout the map?

NOTES

1. Robert S. Kaplan and David P. Norton, *Strategy Maps* (Boston, MA: Harvard Business School Press, 2004), p. xii.
2. Ibid., p. xiii.
3. Ibid., p. 36.
4. Philipp M. Nattermann, "Best Practice Does Not Equal Best Strategy," *The McKinsey Quarterly,* September 2004.
5. Larry Bossidy and Ram Charan, *Execution* (New York: Crown Business, 2002), p. 239.
6. See note 1, p. 40.
7. Michael Treacy and Fred Wiersema, *The Discipline of Market Leaders* (Reading, MA: Perseus Books, 1995).
8. See note 1, p. 43.
9. Frederick Reicheld, *The Loyalty Effect* (Boston, MA: Harvard Business School Press, 1996).
10. Quoted in *The Forbes Book of Business Quotations* (New York: Black Dog and Leventhal, 1997).
11. As quoted in Brian E. Becker, Mark A. Huselid, and Dave Ulrich, *The HR Scorecard* (Boston: Harvard Business School Press, 2001).
12. Thomas A. Stewart, *Intellectual Capital* (New York: Currency Doubleday, 1999).
13. See note 1, p. 203.
14. See note 12, p. 12.
15. Reported in "In the News Briefs," *Balanced Scorecard Report,* September–October 2003, p. 5.
16. See note 1, p. 225.
17. Jim Collins, "The Ten Greatest CEOs of All Time," *Fortune,* July 21, 2003.
18. Jim Collins, *Good to Great* (New York: Harper Business, 2001).
19. Quoted in: Ken Jennings and John Stahl-Wert, *The Serving Leader* (San Francisco, CA: Berrett-Koehler, 2003).
20. David Gilmour, "How to Fix Knowledge Management," *Harvard Business Review,* October 2003, p. 16.
21. Ibid.
22. Winston S. Churchill, *Their Finest Hour* (Boston, MA: Houghton Mifflin, 1949).
23. Edgar H. Schein, *Organizational Culture and Leadership, Second Edition* (San Francisco, CA: Jossey-Bass, 1992).
24. See note 5, p. 69.
25. Robert J. Shiller, *Irrational Exuberance* (New York: Broadway Books, 2001).
26. Robert McKee, "Storytelling That Moves People," *Harvard Business Review,* June 2003, pp. 51–55.
27. Christopher D. Ittner and David F. Larcker, "Coming Up Short on Nonfinancial Performance Measurement," *Harvard Business Review,* November 2003, pp. 88–95.
28. Peter M. Senge. "The Practice of Innovation," *Leader to Leader,* 9 (Summer 1998), pp. 16–22.

CHAPTER 5

Measures, Targets, and Initiatives

PERFORMANCE MEASURES

Have you ever heard this line about men and their boats: "the happiest day of a man's life is the day he buys his boat, and the second happiest day is the day he sells it!"? Sailing is a passion for many people, and although I don't share their zeal, I must admit that on lazy weekend afternoons when I see sailboats drifting casually across a placid lake as smooth as the felt on a pool table, I'm envious of the vessel's passengers. But I'm sure that if I bought a sailboat, Murphy's Law would somehow coerce Mother Nature into withholding the favor of wind, leaving me sitting, frustrated, with nowhere to go. A strategy map without performance measures is a bit like a sailboat without wind—a pleasant diversion but far from being used to its maximum advantage.

The strategy map communicates our objectives, what we must do well, in order to execute our strategy. But how do we know that we are in fact performing well on our objectives? Performance measures are used to track and evaluate our progress on each of the objectives appearing on the strategy map. Just as a fresh wind breathes life into a sail, measures bring the strategy map alive by providing a means to gauge our success in implementing strategy. Measures form the core of the Balanced Scorecard system, driving desired action, providing all employees with guidance on how they may contribute to organizational success, and supplying management with a tool to determine overall progress on their strategic agenda. In this section of the chapter, we'll examine performance measures, specifically reviewing how they may be effectively developed, providing tests to critique your current measures, outlining why you must define the measures in a dictionary, considering how many measures you should have, and finally, discussing the importance of using measures to learn and not to punish.

Tips on Developing Performance Measures

In a business sense, I've been dwelling exclusively in the Balanced Scorecard world for almost 10 years, and as such words like *objective, strategy*, and *measure* are second nature at this point. I often have to remind myself that the same cannot be said for my clients, many of whom are brand new to the concepts underpinning the Balanced Scorecard and may feel both slightly confused and somewhat threatened by this new framework of measuring performance. You should make that same consideration. By reading this book you're making an investment in Balanced Scorecard knowledge, but your colleagues may not be required or inclined to engage so deeply, and as a result may require extra coaching when developing the Scorecard. In the paragraphs that follow, we'll review several ideas you can use that will enhance both the creativity and the end results of your measure development sessions.

Recognizing that some team members may be new to the concepts of measurement, it is a good idea to hold a measures primer session before actually attempting to develop measures in a workshop setting. During this event, which can be comfortably staged in two to three hours, you will outline your progress to date, introduce the concept of measurement, including definitions and characteristics of effective measures, and finally, use a case study to have the team develop mock measures. This is a nonthreatening way to introduce the topic and increase your team's level of sophistication at creating measures.

Once your team feels comfortable with the concepts of measurement, you're ready to hold your development workshop, during which you'll create the measures that will serve as faithful translations of the objectives appearing on your strategy map. Simplicity should be the guiding principle by which you operate during this event. I frequently encounter groups that have a strong proclivity toward overcomplicating these sessions by searching for perfect measures, grasping for metrics that will never be collectible because of data constraints, and overlooking the obvious. As an example of the latter, a colleague of mine told me the story of an insurance company client that included the objective of "increase conversion rates" on their strategy map, the goal of which was to convert prospects into actual paying policy holders. The team toiled for what seemed to be an eternity, exerting every drop of cognitive energy they possessed in an attempt to find just the right measure. Finally, my colleague said, "If you want to increase conversion rates, why not just measure conversion rates." A moment of stunned silence was quickly followed by proclamations of his brilliance at offering this gem of a measure. In reality it was there all the time, but they simply chose to ignore it in their quest for the *perfect* measure. I've found that in many cases the first measure that springs to your mind when contemplating an objective is often the best, and the search should end right there. In no way am I lobbying against robust and active dialogue on measurement, but I am simply suggesting that in some circumstances, endless debate is simply unnecessary, leading to more frustration and compromise than real value.

A starting point for your measurement efforts should be a basic question such as "What information do we need to run this business?" An open-ended query of that nature is sure to open the floodgates of creativity, with people offering a multitude of possibilities, many of which will likely match nicely to the objectives currently comprising your strategy map. If you find that you've unearthed a measure that does not have a corresponding objective on the map, but is indeed critical to navigating your enterprise, that diagnostic should lead to a reexamination of the map and the possible inclusion of a new objective.

Even the most ingenious and creative among us will occasionally run up against roadblocks in our attempts to develop performance measures for more challenging objectives on the strategy map. When that occurs, there are several intervention techniques you can use to get the group back on track. The first method is to simply define the terms comprising the objective in question. Say, for example, your team is struggling with an appropriate measure for the Employee Learning and Growth objective of "Support and empower people." Finding the right measure largely depends on specifically what is meant by "support" and "empower" in this context. A well-written objective statement, the importance of which we covered in Chapter Four, should provide the necessary details to help solve the mystery. Perhaps support in this circumstance equates to the provision of training in key skills, in which case measuring training would be the right choice. Empowerment may connote to lowering levels at which purchasing decisions can be made in the organization. With that as background, "number of purchase decisions requiring supervisor approval" may represent the best measurement choice.

Another method to unfreeze your measurement team's creativity is to use a form of visioning, during which the team contemplates the actual behaviors that may be produced as a result of the objective under question. As an example, consider the objective of "Increase efficiency and productivity," which may appear in many organizations' Internal Processes perspectives. Ask the team what they see people doing, or not doing, one year from now if you were to successfully achieve this objective. It could be that your company, like so many, is bogged down in a sea of paperwork, and when you cast your gaze to a future of "increased efficiency and productivity," you see people unencumbered by the necessity of filing endless reports and freed to serve customers and create real value for the organization. As a result of this visioning, you choose "reduction in required reports" as a performance measure for the objective. I particularly appreciate the visioning approach because it forces you to consider actual behaviors that will be encouraged as a result of instituting a measure, and driving behavior is really the core essence of measurement.

Articulating Your Measures in a Data Dictionary[1]

In Chapter Four we discussed the importance of clarifying the objectives appearing on your strategy map by writing two- or three-sentence narratives referred to as *objective statements*. They clearly define the objective, outline the rationale for selection, and briefly describe how it will be achieved. To ensure understanding throughout your company, measures should be subject to the same clarification process. This time, however, rather than composing a narrative, you'll use a template referred to as a *measure data dictionary* as the articulation device.

When you present your Balanced Scorecard to executives and employees alike, they will undoubtedly quiz you on the background of each measure: "Why did you choose this measure?" "Is it strategically significant?" "How do you calculate the measure?" "Who is responsible for results?" These and numerous other queries will greet your attempts to share your Scorecard with colleagues. The data dictionary provides the background you need to quickly defend your measure choices and answer any questions your audience has. Additionally, chronicling your measures in the data dictionary provides your team with one last opportunity to ensure a common understanding of measure details.

Exhibit 5.1 provides a template you can use to create your own measure dictionary. There are four basic sections of the template you must complete. In the first section, shown at the top, you provide essential background material on the measure. The second section lists specific measure characteristics. Calculation and data specifications are outlined in the third component of the dictionary. Finally, in the bottom section, you provide performance information relating to the measure. Let's examine each of these sections in some detail, using the example provided in Exhibit 5.1.

Measure Background

At a glance, readers should be able to determine what this measure is all about and why it's important for the organization to track.

- *Perspective.* Displays the perspective under which the measure falls.
- *Measure number/name.* All performance measures should be provided a number and name. The number is important if you later choose an automated reporting system. Many will require completely unique names for each measure, and because you may track the same measures at various locations or business units, a specific identifier should be supplied. The measure name should be brief but descriptive. Again, if you purchase software for your reporting needs, it may limit the number of characters you can use in the name field.
- *Owner.* Not only does the Balanced Scorecard transmit to the entire organization what your key strategies for success are, but it also creates a climate

EXHIBIT 5.1 Performance Measure Data Dictionary

Perspective: Customer	Measure Number / Name: C01 / Customer Loyalty Rating	Owner: David M.F. Webb, VP Marketing
Strategy: Revenue Growth	Objective: Increase Customer Loyalty	

Description: The Customer Loyalty Rating measures the percentage of surveyed customers stating they prefer our products to competitor offerings, and will purchase our products again. Our research indicates that loyal customers make more frequent purchases and tend to recommend our brands to others. Therefore, we believe increasing customer loyalty will help us achieve our strategy of revenue growth.

Lag/Lead: Lag	Frequency: Quarterly	Unit Type: Percentage	Polarity: High values are **good**

Formula: Number of quarterly survey respondents answering yes to survey questions #5: "Do you prefer our products compared to competitor offerings?" **and** #6:" Will you purchase our products again?" **divided** by the total number of surveys received.

Data Source: Data for this measure is provided by our survey company, "SST." Each quarter they perform a random survey of our customers and provide the results electronically to our marketing department. Data is contained in the form of MS Excel spreadsheets (MKT SURVEY.xls, lines 14 and 15). Data is available the 10th business day following the end of each quarter.

Data Quality: High - received automatically from third party vendor	Data Collector: A. Stroud, Marketing Analyst

Target: Q1 2001: 65%   Q2 2001: 68%   Q3 2001: 72%   Q4 2001: 75%

Initiatives:
1. Seasonal promotions
2. Customer Relationship Management project
3. Customer Service Training

Baseline: Our most recent data received from SST indicates a Customer Loyalty percentage of 59%

Target Rationale: Achieving customer loyalty is critical to our revenue growth strategy. The quarterly increases we're targeting are higher than in past years but reflect our increased focus on loyalty

Adapted from *Balanced Scorecard Step by Step* by Paul R. Niven.

of accountability for results. Central to the idea of accountability is the establishment of owners for each measure. Simply put, the owner is the individual responsible for results. Should the indicator's performance begin to decline, we look to the owner for answers and a plan to bring results back in line with expectations. In the example shown, I've listed a specific individual as the owner of the measure. However, some organizations feel more comfortable assigning ownership to a function and not a person. They rationalize that while people may come and go, functions tend to remain, and assigning the ownership to a function ensures that the responsibilities inherent in the task are not lost when a new person comes on board. This argument has merits, but I recommend you use actual names rather than functions. Not that people will hide behind their titles, but seeing your name associated with the performance of a key organizational measure will tend to promote more action and accountability than will a job function.

- *Strategy.* Displays the specific strategy you believe the measure will positively influence.

- *Objective.* Every measure was created as a translation of a specific objective. Use this space to identify the relevant objective.

- *Description.* After reading the measure name, most people will immediately jump to the measure description, and it is therefore possibly the most important piece of information on the entire template. Your challenge is to draft a description that concisely and accurately captures the essence of the measure so that anyone reading it will be able to quickly grasp why the measure is critical to the organization. In our example, we rapidly learn that customer loyalty is based on a percentage, what that percentage is derived from (survey questions), and why we believe the measure will help us achieve our strategy of revenue growth (loyal customers buy more and recommend our products).

Measure Characteristics

This section captures the "meat and potatoes" aspects of the measure you'll need when you begin reporting results.

- *Lag/Lead.* Outline whether the measure is a core outcome indicator or a performance driver. Remember that your Scorecard represents a hypothesis of your strategy implementation. When you begin analyzing your results over time, you'll want to test the relationships you believe exist between your lag and lead measures. We'll review lag and lead measures in greater depth in the next section of the chapter.

- *Frequency.* How often do you plan to report performance on this measure? Most organizations have measures that report performance on a daily, weekly, monthly, quarterly, semi-annual, or annual basis. However, I have seen unique time frames such as "school-year" for one government agency. Attempt to limit the number of semi-annual and annual measures you use on your Scorecard. A measure that is only updated once a year is of limited value when you use the Scorecard as a management tool to make adjustments based on performance results.

- *Unit type.* This characteristic identifies how the measure will be expressed. Commonly used unit types include numbers, dollars, and percentages.

- *Polarity.* When assessing the performance of a measure, you need to know whether high values reflect good or bad performance. In most cases, this is straightforward. We all know that higher income and customer loyalty is good, while a high value for complaints reflects performance that requires improvement. However, in some cases, the polarity issue can prove challenging. Take the example of a public health organization. If they choose to measure caseload of social workers, will high values be good or bad? A high number of cases per social worker may suggest great efficiency and effectiveness on the part of the individual workers. Conversely, it could mean the social workers are juggling far too many clients and providing mediocre service in an attempt to inflate their caseload numbers. In cases like this, you may want to institute a "dual polarity." For example, up to 25 cases per social worker may be considered good, but anything over 25 would be a cause for concern and necessitate action.

Calculation and Data Specifications

Information contained in this section of the dictionary may be the most important, yet most difficult to gather. To begin reporting your measures, precise formulas are necessary, and sources of data must be clearly identified.

- *Formula.* In the formula box you should provide the specific elements of the calculation for the performance measure.

- *Data source.* Every measure must be derived from somewhere: an existing management report, third-party vendor-supplied information, customer databases, the general ledger, and so on. In this section you should rigorously attempt to supply as detailed information as possible. If the information is sourced from a current report, what is the report titled and on what line number does the specific information reside? Also, when can you access the data? If it's based on your financial close process, what day of the month can you expect final numbers? This information is important to your Scorecard reporting cycle because you'll be relying on the schedules of others when producing your Scorecard. The more information you provide here, the easier it will be to begin actually producing Balanced Scorecard reports with real data. However, if you provide vague data sources, or no information at all, you will find it exceedingly difficult to report on the measure later. A warning: Spend the time you need to thoroughly complete this section. I have seen several Scorecards proceed swiftly through the development stage only to stall at the moment of reporting because the actual data could not be identified or easily collected.

- *Data quality.* Use this area of the template to comment on the condition of the data you expect to use when reporting Scorecard results. If the data is produced automatically from a source system and can be easily accessed, then it can be considered "high." If, however, you rely on an analyst's Word document that is in turn based on some other colleague's Access database numbers that emanate from an old legacy system, then you may consider the quality "low." Assessing data quality is important for a couple of reasons. Pragmatically, you need to know which performance measures may present an issue when you begin reporting your results. Knowing in advance what to expect will help you develop strategies to ensure that the data you need is produced in a timely and accurate fashion. Data quality issues may also help direct resource questions at your organization.

- *Data collector.* In the first section of the template, we identified the owner of the measure as that individual who is accountable for results. Often, this is not the person we would expect to provide the actual performance data. In our example, D. F. Webb, the VP of Marketing, is accountable for the performance of the measure, but Marketing Analyst A. Stroud serves as the actual data contact.

Performance Information

In the final section of the template, we note our current level of performance, suggest targets for the future, and outline specific initiatives we'll use to achieve those targets.

- *Baseline.* Users of the Balanced Scorecard will be interested in the current level of performance for all measures. For those owning the challenge of developing targets, the baseline is critical in their work.

- *Target.* Some of your measures may already have targets. Perhaps a goal of 15% return on equity is clearly outlined in your latest analyst reports or lowering emission levels at your plants by 5% is legislated by your state government. Wherever targets exist, use them now. For those measures that don't currently have targets, you can leave this section blank and complete it once the targets have been finalized. For those of you who do have at least some targets, list them based on the frequency of the measure. In this example, I've shown quarterly customer loyalty targets. Some organizations may find it difficult to establish monthly or quarterly targets and instead opt for an annual target, but track performance toward that end on a monthly or quarterly basis.

- *Target rationale.* As in the previous item, this will only apply to those measures for which you currently have a performance target. The rationale provides users with background on how you arrived at the particular target(s). Did it come from an executive planning retreat? Is it an incremental improvement based on historical results? Was it based on a government mandate? For people to galvanize around the achievement of a target, they need to know how it was developed and that while it may represent a stretch, it isn't merely wishful thinking on the part of overzealous executives.

- *Initiatives.* At any given time, most organizations will have dozens of initiatives or projects underway. Often, only those closest to the project know anything about it, and any possible synergies among initiatives are never realized. The Scorecard provides you with a wonderful opportunity to evaluate your initiatives in the context of their strategic significance. If an initiative or project cannot be linked to the successful accomplishment of your strategy, then you have to ask yourself why it is being funded and pursued. Use this section of the template to map current or anticipated initiatives to specific performance measures. We'll return to the topic of initiatives later in the chapter.

Testing Your Current Performance Measures

As a Balanced Scorecard practitioner, you're well aware of the difficult choices you face at various points in the process. Choosing among competing objectives is your first challenge, and once you've completed that task, the work becomes even more daunting as you attempt to create a reasonably sized set of performance measures, choosing from a broad universe of possible contenders. The choices here are of paramount importance to the ultimate success of your Balanced Scorecard system because performance measures are at the core of the system, drawing the attention of your entire workforce and directing behavior toward the achievement of your strategy. To ensure that you've chosen effective performance measures, test them against the following criteria:

- *Quantitative.* Your aim in creating and using measures is an objective view of performance, and thus subjectivity should be avoided at all costs. Not that numbers cannot be manipulated wildly for nefarious purposes, as the recent spate of accounting scandals plaguing the corporate world will clearly attest. Despite this potential drawback, for the vast majority of ethical, law-abiding corporate citizens, numbers provide an objective reality check on their current performance. The chief issue with subjective performance measures is the possibility of personal biases creeping into the process. Let's say you decide to rate supplier performance as either "good," "fair," or "poor." Your definition of good may be miles away from mine, and although we're viewing the same event (supplier performance), we're doing so from two completely unique worldviews, which are bound to influence our perceptions. However, if the same supplier were rated based on the number of on-time deliveries, the opportunity for personal biases slips from view. We can all agree that 10% on time is poor and 90% on time is good.

- *Isolating the true event.*[2] Do your measures track specifically what you set out to measure when you developed them (i.e., do they isolate the crucial event?). Take customer loyalty as an example: Many companies will gauge their success on this metric by the number of repeat customers, but is this really measuring loyalty or simply customer retention? Loyalty consists of more than simply coming back and making repeated purchases; it also contains elements of satisfaction and advocacy (to learn more about customer satisfaction, see Exhibit 5.2). Based on repeat purchases, my bank probably feels I'm extremely loyal to them, because I started with just a checking account, soon added credit cards, eventually a mortgage and savings account, and on and on. I'd score off the charts if they measured loyalty on repeat purchases, but what I really am is lazy, and in this context we're probably all a little on the indolent side. Can you imagine how much of a hassle it would be to extricate yourself from a longtime banking relationship? I have more secret codes, passwords, and PINs than the U.S. Army has manuals! At this point my bank would basically have to throw my paltry holdings from their rooftop to have me leave them. However, if they asked me if I were 100% satisfied or would recommend them to friends and associates, they may get another answer completely. When creating your measures, ensure that you have isolated the single event that truly encapsulates what you are attempting to gauge; otherwise you risk including random measurement "noise" and nonessential dimensions of performance.

- *Accessible.* The term *cost-benefit analysis* is familiar to most of us working in the organizational realm. It suggests that every action must be weighed in terms of both anticipated benefits and likely costs to ensure that the outcomes are worth the effort. This exercise readily applies to the capture of performance measures, as you'll quickly determine some are decidedly easier and more cost effective to capture than others. New and missing measures are often the differentiators of a successful Balanced Scorecard, those distinctive metrics you haven't captured in the past that shed new light on value-creating processes within your company. However, you should avoid selecting "wish list" measures that will force you to incur significant costs in time and infrastructure to farm out the data necessary to track the measure on a consistent basis because the attendant costs, both in financial and frustration terms, will most likely not warrant the potential benefits. And measurement can prove costly; just ask police forces throughout the United

EXHIBIT 5.2   A Closer Look at Customer Satisfaction

Customer satisfaction may be the most popular measure appearing in the Customer perspectives of Balanced Scorecards around the world. In one recent study, 70% of respondents noted it appeared on their Scorecard.[a] Popularity, however, is not always tantamount to effectiveness, and many pundits have begun to question the efficacy of this venerable indicator. A chief complaint of many skeptics is the specious link between satisfaction and growth. As a glaring example of this possible deficiency, detractors point to K-Mart, which reported a significant increase of satisfaction scores in the American Customer Satisfaction Index (ACSI) while simultaneously experiencing sharp declines in sales and tumbling into bankruptcy.[b] Others question the unrelenting drive exhibited by companies attempting to reach the pinnacle of 100% satisfaction. One recent study debunked the value of reaching 100 percent satisfaction, noting that customers who were only 80% satisfied spent as much as those who were reportedly 100% satisfied. It seems getting that extra 20% requires significant investments with little payback.[c]

Despite these drawbacks, most companies will continue to include customer satisfaction on their Balanced Scorecards in attempt to discover the driving forces behind the purchase decision, and how they can retain their customers for the long term. Because most companies will turn to surveys as the primary means of data collection, the following tips should be kept in mind when developing and administering these tools:

1. *Survey a variety of customers.* Your current customers know you the best and are most likely to provide positive responses when asked about their experiences with your firm. To balance this bias, survey past customers, those you know have left, and also competitors' customers to learn more about their buying habits.

2. *Ask about the specifics of their experience.* To know if a customer is generally satisfied or not satisfied is directionally helpful, but to really ascertain what makes them tick, dig deeper to get their reaction to the many specific attributes of your products and services.

3. *Ask about competitors.* Henry Ford's objections notwithstanding, customers have a choice—plenty of choices, in fact. Satisfaction with your products is part of an overall spectrum of relative satisfaction based on their use of your and competing products and services.

4. *Ensure that the survey is administered by the head office or a third party.* There can be a lot riding on the results of these surveys, including financial incentives and resource perks. As a result, unscrupulous employees may be tempted to deliberately manipulate results in their favor. Eliminate that possibility by using either head office staff or a third party to administer your survey.

5. *Keep it simple.* The longer and more complicated the survey, the lower the response rate.

[a]Performance Measurement Survey by the American Institute of Certified Public Accountants and Lawrence S. Maisel, 2001.
[b]Frederick F. Reicheld, "The One Number You Need to Grow," *Harvard Business Review*, December 2003, p. 49.
[c]Christopher D. Ittner and David F. Larcker, "Coming Up Short On Nonfinancial Performance Measurement," *Harvard Business Review*, November 2003, p. 90.

Kingdom. The Best Value program in that country is said to have added £29 million a year to the cost of running the police force because of extra effort involved in reporting against government-imposed metrics. The jury is still out on the effects of this program.[3]

- *Frequently updated.* When developing measures for the Employee Learning and Growth perspective, it's not uncommon for my clients to propose a measure of employee satisfaction in an attempt to keep their fingers on the pulse of the organizational climate. When I ask how they'll actually measure satisfaction, they invariably suggest an annual survey. The problem with this approach is that our calendar is made up of 365 days, and they're tapping into employee feelings on one of those days. What happens the other 364 days of the year? Maximum benefit is derived from a Balanced Scorecard when you utilize measures that can be updated frequently, providing fresh insights into the realities of your business. Aim for measures that can be updated at least quarterly, if not monthly.

- *Mixed-message measures.* Measure results should be self-evident, allowing little room for ambiguity. With that in mind, how would you feel about the measure of turnover? Is high turnover good or bad? It depends largely on who is leaving and why. Underperforming employees being led hastily to the door is one thing, whereas the loss of high-performing potential corporate stars is another matter entirely. All performance measures must be clearly defined, eliminating any possibility of ambiguity in the interpretation of results. In the previous example, perhaps the company could track the "Number of employees voluntarily leaving the company" or "Number of involuntary departures," a decline in the latter possibly signaling improved recruiting processes.

- *Easily understood.* My earliest Balanced Scorecard work took place at an electrical utility company in Canada. As with all utilities, this organization was concerned with environmental performance, and they sought not only to comply with, but exceed, local standards. To help us judge environmental performance, we enlisted the company's director of environmental affairs to assist in crafting just the right metric. After meticulous study on the matter, he concocted a truly brilliant index of 13 environmental indicators all wrapped neatly into one measurement package. Brilliant though it may have been, when it came time to report results, the measure did little more than elicit head scratches from confused executives and employees alike. To put it simply, no one had a clue what the measure meant. Because deciphering the measure's meaning was akin to cracking some ancient code, it promoted virtually no response from anyone in the organization. Your ultimate goal in building a Balanced Scorecard is motivating action toward the achievement of your strategy. That is rendered virtually impossible if people do not understand either the operational or strategic significance of your measures. While robust measures—capturing the essence of the activity under consideration—are critical, they must be conceptually simple enough for the majority of your employee population to understand them.

- *Relevant.* The measures appearing on your Scorecard should accurately depict the process or objective you're attempting to evaluate. A good test is whether measure results are actionable. If some aspect of performance failed, you should be able to recognize the significance of the problem and fix it. This issue is demonstrated through the use of performance indices, which many organizations will use on their Scorecards. An index is a combination of several individual measures combined in some way to result in a single overall indicator of performance. Employee satisfaction may appear on your Scorecard as an index of the weighted-average performance of turnover, absenteeism, complaints, and survey results. Indices are a great way to quickly depict performance variables in a single indicator, but they have some inherent weaknesses. First, they may obscure results and limit action. If turnover at your organization was at an all-time high but was given a low weight in your employee satisfaction index, you may never know there are issues because the overall index could appear to be on target. If key staff members are among those leaving the firm and you haven't mounted a response, you may soon pay a heavy price in other areas of performance as reflected on the Scorecard. Indices also frequently fail to pass the "easily understood" criterion discussed previously. A "logistics" index appearing in the Internal Process perspective may contain valuable information but be baffling to those outside of the supply chain side of the organization. Again, indices can provide useful information, especially when you have several measures you'd like to include but wish to keep your total Scorecard count limited. Based on the previous arguments, however, you should limit their use to only a handful of your total at most.[4]

- *Mix of lag and lead.* When learning that I've written books, people often ask me how many have been sold. To be honest, I really don't know for sure, but could find out easily by contacting my publisher. I do, however, follow my book rankings at online booksellers such as Amazon.com quite closely. In doing so, I've discovered that if my book sales suddenly spike, there is a strong possibility I'll receive additional training and consulting inquiries in the weeks following that jump in sales. In other words, the book sales on Amazon are a predictor, or leading indicator, of consulting and training engagements. That is the essence of the lead/lag relationship: any measure that correlates, predicts, or drives another is said to be a leading indicator of that measure. A traditional example would be a company's sales, which may be considered a classic lagging indicator. All organizations are interested in boosting sales revenue, and as a result must determine what drives or predicts sales and begin measuring that event. Perhaps it's "Time spent with customers," or "Number of customer visits"; the answer will depend on the organization, but the key is to find that variable and begin measuring it. A Balanced Scorecard should contain a mix of lead and lag indicators. A Scorecard containing only lagging measures clearly defines where the company wishes to go but leaves them guessing about how they'll get there. Conversely, choosing only leading indicators will provide interesting insights but will yield precious little information regarding whether those measures are leading to their intended results of driving core outcomes such as sales. The lag/lead relationship can show up in almost any organizational setting. An interesting example comes from the Department of Corrections in New York City.[5] Using their performance measurement system, this department tracks commissary sales in its jails. They've determined that if sales of cigarettes and candy suddenly increase, a riot may be in the planning stages. Inmates realize that they'll be confined to their cells immediately after any kind of uprising, and therefore stock up on supplies. A spike in candy and cigarette sales in this case is a leading indicator of the number of prison riots. Knowing this relationship exists allows prison officials to take action and attempt to avert a potentially dangerous confrontation.

- *Control.* When selecting performance measures, it's important to question whether you can truly control the measure under consideration. Tracking a metric you cannot control may provide useful information, but your ability to influence future results is limited, thereby reducing the overall effectiveness of the indicator. When discussing lag and lead measures earlier, I cited the example of sudden spikes in my book sales leading to greater consulting opportunities. I've also noted a similar relationship between the sales of Kaplan and Norton's first book *The Balanced Scorecard*[6] and sales of my books. Many people initially turn to the Scorecard architects to receive a grounding in the principles of the framework and then purchase my books in an attempt to garner information about effective implementation techniques. This is interesting for me, but because there is little I can do to control the sales of Kaplan and Norton's texts, the metric is of questionable utility.

- *Driving the right behavior.* At several junctures in the preceding paragraphs, I've noted the importance of using measures to drive behavior, suggesting that is the core purpose of this process. Therefore, as a final test of your crop of measures, I challenge you to critically examine them in light of the behavior they drive from people throughout your organization. Are they leading people to act in ways that will lead to the implementation of your strategy or are they in fact unwittingly leading to suboptimization of your efforts? One consultant I know tells the story of a client in the fast-food industry that, despite the best of intentions, chose a measure that led to disastrous results. It seems this organization found that its restaurants were throwing away a lot of cooked food at closing time, and obviously that was draining profits. To put a halt to such a debilitating practice, the company instituted an efficiency measure for each outlet, charting the quantity of food that was disposed of each day. Clever managers, not wishing to be demonized by poor performance, quickly devised a method to ensure great scores on the measure. If their restaurant closed at midnight, they would not cook any food between eleven and midnight until a customer entered and ordered. That way there was little chance of having any refuse at the end of the day. Of course, customers did not share the zeal of "chicken efficiency" and soon began staying away in droves once they learned this restaurant had effectively taken the fast out of fast food. The measure was devised with noble motives but drove a behavior that proved to be completely counterproductive. What about your measures? Are they leading to the right behavior from your employees?

As a word of caution, don't feel that every measure populating your Balanced Scorecard has to measure up to each of the criteria outlined on the preceding pages. In fact, if you can find a single one that does meet every element listed, it should probably be exhibited in a museum somewhere. You can search endlessly for, and never find, the perfect measures, consuming valuable time and effort that could otherwise be directed at extracting value from the measures you do have that adhere to a majority of the characteristics described above.

How Many Measures on a Balanced Scorecard?

Most modern organizations are up to their necks and sinking quickly in a sea of performance information, a fact supported by recent research from a Hackett Benchmarking study, which found the typical monthly performance report to contain 140 different measures.[7] One has to wonder about the strategic nature of these measures, considering that strategy is inextricably linked with making choices and trade-offs resulting in more focused behavior. A focus on strategy should lead to a reduction in the number of performance measures used to monitor our businesses, not contribute to the increases we're currently witnessing.

The Balanced Scorecard was originally conceived and designed to assist organizations in effectively executing their unique strategies, and as a result the measures appearing on a Scorecard should serve as faithful translations of that strategy. The exact number will vary, depending on the individual organization, but in keeping with the focus inherent in strategy, the set of measures should be limited to just those necessary to determine success in execution. Most pundits have settled on a number of between 20 and 25 measures spanning the four perspectives of the Scorecard as being applicable to most organizations. It's not a requirement to have an equal number of measures within each of the perspectives, however, and in fact you may necessarily "overweight" one of the perspectives in telling your strategic story. Having said that, the term is Balanced Scorecard, and you should ensure adequate representation across the perspectives to guarantee the chosen indicators weave together to form a coherent whole.

The term "dashboard" is sometimes used as a synonym for the Balanced Scorecard, and while it has shortcomings, in relation to the number of measures you choose the metaphor is appropriate. When driving your car, you monitor critical variables such as speed, fuel consumption, and engine heat. There are literally hundreds of things occurring under the hood as you drive, but we needn't be provided with updates unless something falls out of an acceptable range. It's the same within our organizations; there are hundreds of activities taking place every day, but the task of leadership is to monitor the critical and strategic indicators of success, guiding the overall direction of the firm, not intervening in tasks and decisions three or four levels below. Maintaining this level of focus is facilitated by the use of a small set of performance measures linked directly to strategy.

Social philosopher, management scholar, and best-selling author Charles Handy once remarked, *"Measuring more is easy, measuring better is hard."*[8] In keeping with his words, there are those among us who will find it simpler to brainstorm 50 to 100 mediocre measures than to work through the pain of finding the right 20 to 25 that provide true strategic value. But as with our discussion of objectives in Chapter Four, "less is more," and the benefit of searching deeply for the most appropriate measures will yield benefits in the form of increased understanding, focus, and alignment throughout the organization. Your quest in creating performance measures is the generation of a precise set of interrelated indicators that tell your strategic story in as concise yet compelling a fashion as possible.

Measurement Is About Learning, Not Punishment

There are a lot of words I could use to describe leaders who terrorize employees for making mistakes, belittling and humiliating them for even the slightest of transgressions, but many of those words are unprintable in this book! Recently I read a new and colorful description of this particularly debilitating managerial practice. The authors called it "Pigeon Management," and described it thus: *"You dump all over people, fly away, wait for them to make a mistake, and come back and dump on them again."*[9] So does that mean every statue in every park in the world represents a bad manager? We've all witnessed executives or managers who have exhibited this behavior, leaving a sordid trail of disenfranchised and jaded employees in their menacing wake. I'll bet you're thinking of someone from your past—or heaven forbid, your present—right now. I know I am, and the pictures those memories conjure up are not happy ones. In my case, picture Mr. Dithers from the Blondie cartoons on negativity steroids and you'll know the type of person to whom I'm referring. We can all take a few chuckles from Dagwood Bumstead's plight and move on, but in the real world, the consequences of constant punishment are just that—real and extremely damaging.

Many organizations will turn to the use of performance measures in an attempt to introduce accountability for results, holding people responsible for their actions. While performance measurement, when implemented carefully, can fulfill this goal, sloppy application of its principles can lead to disastrous outcomes. Such was the case with a large airline in the United States. This company instituted a strict set of measures to monitor key variables such as flight delays, a common complaint of many weary travelers. Results gleaned from measuring delays were not used to learn about their root cause, however; far from it in fact, as harsh penalties awaited those who scored badly. This system produced the unintended effect of encouraging employees to look out for number one, often cheating, rather than focusing on any shared goals of achieving high-quality outcomes for passengers. One gate agent aptly described the cancerous environment: *"If a delay occurred on a flight scheduled to make connections elsewhere, he (the CEO) wants to see the corpse . . . it's management by intimidation."*[10]

Once your Balanced Scorecard is up and running, you as leaders have a choice to make: "Do we punish measure owners for poor performance or take the opportunity to learn from those results and recalibrate for an improved future?" Your employees will be waiting for the answer, and if you choose the former you can expect, as we saw in the previous example, people walking on egg shells, avoiding responsibility, refusing to take sensible risks, playing the blame game, and generally doing whatever it takes to cover their backs. Great leaders recognize and embrace the fact that making mistakes is a natural part of the learning process.

There is a terrific old story, possibly apocryphal, about Tom Watson, Jr. of IBM, that illustrates the point of learning from mistakes. Apparently a young executive had made some poor decisions that had cost the company several million dollars. He was summoned to Watson's office, fully expecting to be summarily dismissed. Upon entering the office, the young executive pointedly declared, "I suppose after that set of mistakes you will be wanting to fire me." In a most casual tone, Watson replied, "Not at all young man, we have just spent a couple of million dollars educating you."[11] The next time you lose that big account or miss a key deadline, remind your boss of this icon of business and his unique approach to employee education.

Mobil North American Marketing and Refining was one of the early adopters of the Balanced Scorecard system, working closely with Kaplan and Norton in the early 1990s. By 1995 they were well established as one of the pioneering success stories of the Balanced Scorecard world. A significant piece of that success resulted from a paradigm shift at the top of the organization, a transition from using measures to punish to using measures to learn. As the story goes, the first quarter of 1995 had been unusually warm in North America, and as a result sales of home heating oil and natural gas were below normal, thus translating to Mobil's revenues falling short of budget. In April of that year, Chief Executive Bob McCool convened a meeting at headquarters to review first-quarter results. It's not too much of an exaggeration to say that people were actually quaking in their boots as they entered the room. Everyone knew they were well below plan, and in the past such results had actually resulted in people losing their jobs. McCool opened the meeting by acknowledging the financial shortfall, and people were thinking "oh no, here it comes," but he continued in a way nobody expected. He went on to say that he understood the financial results were largely a result of the warmer weather and noted that this was the first quarter they began using the Balanced Scorecard. He told the group that the Scorecard allowed him to view performance across a wider set of indicators and from that view he could see that market share in key customer segments were up, refinery expenses were down, and employee satisfaction was up. As he put it, *"In all the areas under our control we did a great job, let's keep up the good work."*

Needless to say the audience was stunned. But McCool was able to see beyond the financial numbers, which resulted primarily from something beyond their control and focus on the drivers of their strategy. He knew that if they stayed the course on those indicators, financial results would follow, and that's precisely what happened. By the end of the year, Mobil had become the most profitable company in the industry.[12] Unlike so many executives, McCool was not blinded by the near-term shortcomings reflected by a few indicators in the Balanced Scorecard, but instead used those results as a way to learn about the business and hypothesize about the future, and in so doing demonstrated his commitment to a new way of managing, one that was embraced throughout the organization.

ADDING MEANING TO MEASUREMENT THROUGH THE USE OF TARGETS

On a bright and crisp autumn day about 10 years ago, my wife and I went for a walk in a cozy city park in our then-hometown of Halifax, Nova Scotia. We've always had some of our best talks as a couple when we're out enjoying nature, and the conditions that day were perfect—a full palette of fall colors displayed proudly by the trees overhead, a light breeze off the ocean to keep us cool while we walked, and the rhythmic cracking of leaves underfoot. The topic that day, a lofty one, was a discussion of our goals for the next five years. Like most couples we had occasionally spent time talking about the next phase of our lives—what better way to spend a rainy Saturday or pass the hours on a long car trip. But on this quintessential autumn day, things were distinctly different. For the first time in our married life, we made a commitment to achieving our shared goals and soon after took the unprecedented step of writing them down and applying our signatures to the pledge of working together to create our own destiny. The motivation supplied by simply articulating our goals on paper was among the most powerful acts I've ever borne witness to in my adult life; what was once idle talk was transformed into a beacon of inspiration that compelled us both to work our hardest in making our dreams a reality. I'm proud to report that within five years we achieved virtually all of our goals. As we learned that day, clearly defined targets and goals, whether in our personal or professional lives, impart meaning and context to the data and experiences that surround us.

The poet Robert Browning recognized, *"A man's reach should exceed his grasp, or what's heaven for?"*[13] In both life and in business, we must constantly pursue improvement or risk being left behind. The Balanced Scorecard is a powerful measurement device, translating a strategy into the concrete indicators that will be used to gauge success, but without targets, the desired result of a measure, what does that performance information tell us? How does it ensure we're improving and not being left behind? For example, let's say your company decides to measure manufacturing defects and discovers that your defect rate this month is 5%. Like a shipwrecked sailor stranded on a deserted island, this information is isolated and alone. Only by considering our performance in light of desired results is meaningful information produced. If we learn that average defect rates in the industry are 1%, and our closest competitor is approaching near defect-free performance, then our data point of 5% becomes far more relevant. With this information as ammunition, we see that significant improvements are necessary, and thus we may create an initial target of slicing our defect rate to 2%. With a target firmly entrenched, the performance data we collect is imbued with meaning that can be used to guide decision making, facilitate resource allocation decisions, and rally employees around a worthy challenge. Targets truly bring Balanced Scorecard measure data to life, and as a result have become part and parcel of the vast majority of implementations, with one study suggesting that 93% of organizations utilize quantitative goals.[14] More than simply firing up the troops, targets have also been demonstrated to hold tangible benefits for companies making them a standard practice. In fact, another study found that performance increases an average of 16% in companies that establish targets.[15] In the following sections, we'll dig deeper into this underutilized element of Balanced Scorecard value, discussing sources of target information for your measures, and reviewing elements to keep in mind when setting targets.

Sources of Target Information[16]

As challenging as the development of measures can prove, for many organizations establishing meaningful targets frequently represents an even more arduous task.

Choosing the right target, one that maintains the delicate balance between a motivating challenge and practical reality, is often more art than science and not a core competence of typical businesses. Even when targets are established, it is not uncommon for the less inspired among us to refuse to be held accountable to new standards of performance, preferring the safety and predictability of the status quo. Thus the choice is a critical one in generating commitment to the use of performance measures in an attempt to improve performance. Often, the difficulty in setting targets arises from a lack of knowledge regarding potential sources of information: Are the targets picked from thin air, out of a hat? Several potential sources of information, both internal to and outside the confines of the organization, that will assist you in creating meaningful performance targets, are outlined in the following sections.

Internal Sources

The most logical sources of target information are probably sitting in corner offices scattered throughout your building right now. I'm referring, of course, to your *executive team*. When developing measures you canvassed your leadership, asking them what information they needed to make effective decisions and steer the organizational ship, so it makes perfect and consistent sense to follow up that query with what represents an acceptable level of performance for the measures. Karen Harrington of Dakota County government in Minnesota took it one step further when enlisting leaders in the development of targets by asking them: "What level of performance would keep you up at night?" or "At what level do you wish to see an alert?" These provocative questions introduce pragmatism to the process, which is sure to transform target setting from a mere academic exercise to a real-world issue that must be solved.

Moving down the organizational ladder, all *employees* are potentially potent sources of target data. After all, they're on the front lines of commerce, working with customers, engaging in processes, and dealing with suppliers and other stakeholders in an effort to create positive results. These encounters shouldn't be wasted, like the best parts of a movie that may be left on the cutting room floor, but should be used to inform the process, bringing real-world experience to bear on the target-setting effort. Practical benefits aside, employee involvement in the process also increases their understanding of and commitment to the use of performance measures. In my experience, regardless of the change initiative, people are far more likely to respond to the intervention if they have a legitimate say in the actions that will ultimately affect them.

A final source of internal information to be mined when creating targets is *baseline and trend data* you currently possess on existing performance measures. The past is often a meaningful guide to the future, and recent trends and baselines can be used to project future performance on critical indicators of success. The caveat here relates to the level of volatility within your industry. If it is evolving, with the rules of the game changing rapidly, then repeats of, or minor improvements on, past performance may not be enough to sustain profitable performance.

External Sources

Every business has a wide breadth of *stakeholders, including customers and suppliers*, who will possess expectations about your organization, whether explicitly stated or implicitly implied. Customers are an obvious source of valuable information and are typically pleased to provide it when asked. I've even had clients invite key customers to their strategy mapping and measures development workshops, ensuring their voice is heard, and valuable feedback and input elicited.

Whenever an important purchase is to be made, many households turn to the pages of *Consumer Reports* for the latest information on products and providers in an attempt to gain insight used in the purchase decision. In addition to general services such as those provided by *Consumer Reports, industry rating agencies* exist for virtually every organization type known to modern enterprise. Surveying these agencies provides a glimpse into your performance as assessed from an external point of view and can go a long way toward providing valuable target information for key metrics.

Another resource for target information comes in the form of *benchmarking* studies and results. At any given time, there is a decent chance that your organization, if it is of sufficient size, is benchmarking its performance on some dimension against the best practices of your industry (or, increasingly, outside of your industry). Whether it's call center performance, month-end close time, or invoice processing, benchmarking provides insights you can swiftly put to work in emulating star performers. Realism must be applied in liberal doses when attempting to re-create the best practices of those you study, however. They most likely ascended to those soaring heights because the practice under the microscope is critical to their survival, or it may even represent what Jim Collins refers to as their "hedgehog concept," the intersection of what they feel they can be the best in the world at doing, what drives their economic engine, and what fuels their passion.[17] Realizing that the level of competence best performers have achieved is simply not attainable given your current resources, attempting to imitate their performance may in some cases prove at a minimum to be unrealistic and at worst demoralizing.

Other Target-Setting Elements to Consider

You've recognized the necessity of targets as an indispensable component of any Balanced Scorecard, and have explored every territory available in your quest to create the right targets, so what's left? In this final section of our discussion, I will provide several elements of the target equation you should consider both when setting and later when assessing the targets you've established:

- *Different circumstances may call for different types of targets.* If your goal is to introduce breathtaking change in your organization, an ultra-ambitious target may be just the thing to start you on your lofty trajectory. Some organizations refer to such leviathan-sized targets as *Big Hairy Audacious Goals or BHAGs.*[18] As seemingly outrageous goals that could take anywhere from 10 to 30 years to achieve, BHAGs stretch the organization, ripping it from the clutches of a business-as-usual mindset and introducing the possibility of monumental change. A famous political BHAG was President Kennedy's 1961 proclamation of sending a man to the moon before the end of the decade, but BHAGs come in all shapes and sizes. Take, for example, the case of Granite Rock, a California rock-crushing company that set as its BHAG the achievement of customer service exceeding Nordstrom, the department store famous for its exemplary treatment of customers.[19]

  If the single, unifying focal point of a BHAG is not what you require, perhaps you should consider the use of *stretch targets.* Targets of this nature, set three to five years in the future, are normally applied to a wider range of organizational activities, and while not as dramatic as BHAGs, do promise discontinuous performance. Increasing market share from 20% to 50% within three years could represent a stretch target.

  Finally, the most common type of targets are of the short-term *incremental* variety. These are the annual (typically) targets established in association with the measures appearing on the Balanced Scorecard that have been designed to ensure improved performance leading to successful execution of the strategy. As noted previously, most companies assign annual targets to their Scorecard metrics, but increased value is derived from matching the target to the reporting frequency. If, for example, you capture data monthly, having a monthly target enhances the information value of the result, allowing you to generate improved dialogue and plan with greater efficiency for the future.

- *Consider the use of target ranges.* As discussed earlier, choosing targets may be more art than science, particularly for those who are new to the performance measurement arena. The targets you select must be robust enough to encourage performance beyond the ordinary but not so outlandish as to engender disbelief and scorn from the people you hope to inspire—not a simple act. For that reason, many organizations turn to the use of target ranges when computing values. In addition to a single discrete numerical value, designated ranges are created reflecting various levels of performance. For example, let's say you're measuring the "Number of new customers acquired" for the first time and are struggling with the right target. After strenuous discussion and debate, you arrive at a target of 100 new customers each quarter as your target, but are uncertain as to how appropriate this goal is given your inexperience. As a result you assign ranges as follows: should new customers acquired reach 90 or above, performance is considered good, or "green," if you choose to use the popular traffic light metaphor. Performance suggesting that caution is in order, "yellow" in other words, might fall between 70 and 90 new customers a quarter. Finally, below-target performance, or "red," is anything under the acquisition of 70 new customers per quarter. Hilton Hotels, a committed proponent of the Balanced Scorecard, has followed the color-coded range approach to target setting and found it to be very beneficial:

> The simple visual feature helps indicate a sense of direction. Team members can easily see how well their property is performing…by communicating results visually to show strengths and weaknesses, the color coding system leaves little doubt in anyone's mind regarding how a particular unit is performing on its specific objectives.… Moreover, the system provides a margin of error, in case the original targets turn out to be inappropriate.[20]

- *Targets must be updated to reflect changing conditions.* Targets are not meant to be carved in stone, standing the test of time regardless of changing conditions, but must reflect the environment you face. You should expect to update your performance targets at least annually in light of actual business results and your desired future direction. However, several circumstances may dictate an in-year change to a target, including:

  ○ *A change in strategy.* Should you deem that your current strategy is inappropriate or simply not working and you decide to alter it, performance measures and targets should shift accordingly.

  ○ *Rapidly changing customer trends or preferences.* New fads and crazes are constantly sweeping this and all nations, and organizations must be ready to capitalize when the tide of customer preferences washes up on their shores. Take the case of that venerable American brand, Hush Puppies. Sales were down to 30,000 pairs a year when suddenly the brushed suede classics became all the rage in New York City in the early 1990s. This "epidemic" soon spread, and by 1995, thanks to a new generation of customers from coast to coast, sales had skyrocketed to 430,000 pairs and the year after more than 1 million![21] A target of 30,000 pairs of shoes may have seemed perfectly acceptable in 1992, but by 1995 that target would appear ludicrous.

  ○ *Extenuating circumstances may also lead to a midyear target course correction.* As I write this, a series of devastating hurricanes have just cut a path of destruction from the Caribbean to the United States. Obviously, businesses have been dramatically affected by these powerful acts of nature and must necessarily reconsider their performance commitments for the rest of the year. What seemed like a logical target only a few weeks ago may be rendered impossible by these frightening events. It doesn't have to be a dramatic act of God that triggers a reevaluation; anything that has a major impact on your business should lead you to examine the targets you've set in light of the best available current information.

○ *Keep it real.* At other junctures in this discussion, I've noted the need to develop targets that offer a stimulating challenge while remaining grounded in reality, or as others have more plainly expressed it: *"While goals can be useful in forcing people to break old rules and do things better, they're worse than useless if they're totally unrealistic."*[22] Taking this to an even higher plane of pragmatism, when setting targets you must be cognizant of the actual limits of any process or activity you're undertaking. Using tools such as statistical process control (SPC), you may be able to determine the outer limits of what is possible with any process you currently engage in regularly and thus set targets that are within its capability.[23] Setting targets that extend beyond what is physically possible as documented using SPC techniques can prove to be a demoralizing waste of time.

MAPPING AND PRIORITIZING ORGANIZATIONAL INITIATIVES

Initiatives represent the specific programs, activities, projects, or actions you will engage in to meet, and hopefully exceed, your performance targets. Depending on the size of your operation, there may be anywhere from dozens to hundreds to even thousands of organizational initiatives taking place within your business today, with their nature and scope varying widely. Initiatives may include anything from developing a new website to launching a new leadership development program or redesigning your financial management system to hosting a booth at a local trade show.

The prevailing view among most pundits is that organizations are suffering through far too many initiatives, many of which are merely pet projects of an eager executive that add precious little value for the firm. The answer, according to these experts, is to narrow down your initiatives to the critical few that lead to breakthrough results. As the authors of one study note,

> We examined the strategy implementation rate among a sample of twenty companies and made an interesting discovery. Organizations, even large corporations, that attempted to drive more than four or five major strategic initiatives at any one time were far less successful than those that focused on a maximum of three or four. One executive we interviewed told us: We take the touch decisions as to which two, three, or four initiatives to do in the next six, twelve, or eighteen months. We over-resource them, if anything. We drive them hard and fast, nail them down, and then move on to the next set of priorities. Does this mean we do nothing else? Not at all, but these are the ones that each executive and

every employee knows have to be given our absolute top priority, even at the expense of their own pet projects.[24]

My experiences as an employee of organizations large and small leads me to agree with this supposition. My work as a Balanced Scorecard consultant, however, takes me to a slightly different conclusion: Many organizations will simultaneously have too many and too few initiatives.[25] There is no shortage of initiatives swirling about the typical company, but frequently there is a dearth of strategic initiatives launched in support of new measures comprising the firm's Balanced Scorecard. A tremendous benefit of embarking on the Scorecard path is the creation of new and missing measures, those differentiating yardsticks that keep you constantly apprised on the road to strategy execution. Chances are if the measures are new, there are no supporting processes or initiatives to ensure that targets are being achieved and the strategy advanced, hence the argument of too few initiatives in many circumstances.

Once you've developed a Balanced Scorecard, your immediate challenge is to carefully screen initiatives, ensuring those currently in place are contributing to strategy, while simultaneously introducing new initiatives in support of critical strategic objectives and measures. Outlined next is a four-step process you can use to assess the strategic capability and value of your initiatives:

1. *Develop an inventory of current initiatives.* Before we determine which initiatives are strategic contributors, we must first compose a list of all projects currently underway throughout the organization. To make this step meaningful, that search should be exhaustive. Initiatives will be ongoing in every nook and cranny of your business, and you must document them all if you hope to make an informed decision about which projects are simply wasting valuable and scarce resources and which are catapulting you toward the achievement of your goals. Logical stops on this sleuthing tour include your budgeting office, which may possess a master roster of projects, and your strategic planning department, because they have a vested interest in key organizational projects.

2. *Map initiatives to your strategic objectives.* To competently complete this step, you'll need to conduct significant due diligence on each of the initiatives you've catalogued, ensuring that you understand the strategic significance, purpose, scope, duration, anticipated benefits, and costs of each. Using that knowledge as raw material, you must then examine each initiative in the context of your strategy map, determining which provide critical supporting links to the objectives housed on the map and which are simply occupying valuable organizational space. A simple rationalizing tool is the insistence that a project adequately document the prerequisites noted earlier (i.e., strategic significance, scope, purpose, anticipated benefits, costs). It will be difficult to avoid having a little subjectivity creep into your analysis, but as we know, strategy is messy business and often considered as much an art as a science. Exhibit 5.3 displays a template that will assist you in

EXHIBIT 5.3 Mapping Initiatives to Objectives

Perspective	Objectives	Benchmarking	Maintenance Overhaul	ISO 9002	Frequent Purchase Program	IT Tools & Training	360 Feedback	Critical skills training	Partner Program	Just in Time Mfg.	Decision Training	Facility makeover	New Pricing Programs
Financial	Enhance revenue streams												●
	Improve utilization of assets	●								●			
Customer	Find new partners								●				
	Increase customer loyalty				●								
	Grow Market Share				●								
Internal Process	Develop customer profiles					●							
	Eliminate defects		●	●									
Employee Learning & Growth	Close our skills gap							●					
	Increase empowerment						●				●		

Adapted from *Balanced Scorecard Step by Step: Maximizing Performance and Maintaining Results* by Paul R. Niven.

identifying which initiatives map to specific objectives. On the left side of the document, you will list your strategic objectives as they appear on your Balanced Scorecard. The upper portion of the template provides space to record your initiatives. In our example, only one initiative, "facility makeover," cannot be directly linked to a strategic objective on the Balanced Scorecard.

3. *Eliminate nonstrategic initiatives and propose missing initiatives.* This is perhaps the most politically explosive of the steps, because it is highly unlikely that any project sponsor will take lightly the news of their initiative being labeled as "nonstrategic" or "redundant." The diplomatic skills of your Balanced Scorecard executive sponsor will be tested here as he attempts to communicate the greater good toward which you're striving in this exercise. Bruised egos aside, this is also the step with the potential to generate a quick economic payback for embarking on the development of a Balanced Scorecard, as the funneling of funds and talent from nonstrategic initiatives to projects that enhance the organization's value contributes quickly to your bottom line. When Crown Castle International, a leading provider of leased towers, antenna space, and broadcast transmission services, engaged in this exercise they were able to pare their overall list of initiatives from 180 down to 12! CEO John Kelly even suggested the process wasn't overly difficult: *"Actually, it was pretty easy to cut our list down from 180 to 12 because people had a very clear understanding of what our strategic priorities were. We racked and stacked all initiatives, and looked at which ones were most important relative to the four elements of our strategy."*[26] This step also entails the establishment of new initiatives to capture the value-creating mechanisms discovered as a result of building your Balanced Scorecard. To ensure these initiatives are crisply documented, consider using a strategic initiative template such as that displayed in Exhibit 5.4.

4. *Prioritize strategic initiatives.*[27] Assuming you don't have unlimited financial resources at your disposal, you should, as a final step in our process, prioritize your initiatives in order to assist in resource allocation decisions. The key is basing the decision on a common set of criteria that will determine the most appropriate initiatives given your unique priorities. Obviously, the initiative's effect on driving strategy is the chief concern, but you can't ignore investment fundamentals such as cost, net present value, and projected time to complete. Essentially, every initiative should have a valid business case to support its claim as being necessary to achieve your strategy. Once you've drafted business cases for each of the initiatives, you can use a template similar to that shown in Exhibit 5.5 to assist in making the prioritization decision. Each criterion you choose is assigned a weight depending on its importance within your company. The assignments are subjective; however, strategic importance should always carry the greatest

EXHIBIT 5.4   Strategic Initiative Template

Date: [   ]

This template is intended as an enterprise-wide tool to enable the Executive to quantify, assess and prioritize proposed strategic initiatives based on their impact on strategic objectives.

Please limit input and commentary to the space provided and use minimum 10 pt. font.

Line of Business / Business Unit: [   ]

Strategic Initiative Name [   ]

Executive Owner: [   ]   Initiative Leader [   ]

Anticipated Start Date: [   ]   Anticipated End Date: [   ]

Initiative Description/ Scope:

[   ]

Strategic Impact	Strategic Impact (H,M,L)
Describe Strategic Impact:	
Financial:	
Customer:	
Internal Process:	
Employee Learning & Growth	

Resource Allocation Requirements

Capital & Operating Budget ($000)	2002	2003	2004	2005
Capital Spending Profile	$0	$0	$0	$0
Operating Budget Spending	$0	$0	$0	$0

Economic Fit	
NPV: Net Present Value	
IRR% : Internal Rate of Return	
Payback Period	

Investment Summary ($000)	2002	2003	2004	2005
Revenue (incremental)	$0	$0	$0	$0
Revenue (retained)	$0	$0	$0	$0
Expense Savings	$0	$0	$0	$0

Net FTE Impact (+/- FTE's)				

Key Dependencies

[   ]

Key Risks to Successful Implementation and Mitigation Activities

[   ]

Describe Internal Impact (employees / processes) of this Initiative

[   ]

Describe External Impact (customers / suppliers / shareholders) of this Initiative

[   ]

EXHIBIT 5.4 Strategic Initiative Template *(Continued)*

Please limit input and commentary to the space provided and use minimum 10 pt. font.

Milestones, Deliverables, & Corresponding Due Dates

Key Milestone	Deliverables	Due Date

Key Initiative Resources (Top 5 Involvement)

Name	Time Allocation (%)	Explanation of Time Allocation

weight in the decision. Next, each initiative must be scored on the specific criteria listed in the chart. You may use ratings of between 0 and 10, or if you prefer a wider scale, use 0 to 100. I've used 0 to 10 in my example. Before assigning points to each, you must develop an appropriate scale. For example, a net present value (NPV) of greater than $2 million may translate to 10 points, NPV of $1.75 million yields 9 points, and so on. Involving more than one executive on a full-time basis may translate to a score of 2 points in the resource requirements section because their involvement could impose a heavy burden on the organization. Develop scales that work for you; however, to ensure mathematical integrity, a high value should

EXHIBIT 5.5 Prioritizing Balanced Scorecard Initiatives

Criteria	Weight	Description	Initiative #1		#2		#3		#4	
			Points	Score	Points	Score	Points	Score	Points	Score
Linkage to Strategy	45%	Ability of the initiative to positively impact a strategic objective	7	3.2	1	.45				
Net Present Value	15%	Present value of initiative benefits discounted 5 years	5	.75	10	1.5				
Total Cost	10%	Total dollar cost including labor and materials	5	.50	10	1.0				
Resource Requirements (Key personnel)	10%	Key personnel needed for the initiative including time requirements	8	.80	10	1.0				
Time to Complete	10%	Total anticipated time to complete the initiative	8	.80	10	1.0				
Dependencies	10%	Impact of other initiatives on the successful outcomes anticipated with this initiative	3	.30	10	1.0				
				6.4		6.0				

From *Balanced Scorecard Step by Step: Maximizing Performance and Maintaining Results* by Paul R. Niven.

always represent preferred performance. Those initiatives generating the highest scores should be approved and provided with budgets to ensure their timely completion. Notice in our example that Initiative One generates a higher total score than Initiative Two despite the latter's impressive scores on five of the six criteria. The reason for the discrepancy is the critical variable of strategic linkage. Initiative One demonstrates a strong linkage to strategy, whereas Initiative Two is missing that connection.

Initiatives are a universal way of organizational life that are not likely to vanish from the radar screens of most executives any time soon. Given their pervasive impact, it is simply common sense to ensure that these investments in time, energy, and money are leading you toward the achievement of your strategy. The results of mapping and prioritizing initiatives, in the form of economic payback for the Scorecard, increased accountability, and a link between budgeting and strategy (which we'll explore further in Chapter Seven), will prove to be well worth the effort necessary to work through the four steps discussed.

SELF-ASSESSMENT QUESTIONS

Performance Measures

1. Did we hold a measures primer session to introduce the topic of developing measures to our team?
2. Do our measures reflect the information we need to run our business?
3. Have we articulated all of our measures in a data dictionary?
4. How do our measures stack up against the following characteristics of effective measurement:
   - Quantitative
   - Ability to isolate the true event
   - Accessible
   - Frequently updated
   - Mixed messages
   - Easily understood
   - Relevant
   - Mix of lag and lead
   - Control
   - Ability to drive the right behavior

5. How many measures do we have on our Balanced Scorecard? In light of our strategy, and strategy map, is that too many or too few?

6. At our organization, do we use measures to punish or do we learn from our results?

Targets

1. When establishing targets for our Balanced Scorecard measures, did we consider the following potential sources of information:
   - Our executive team
   - Employees
   - Baseline and trend data
   - Stakeholders (customers, suppliers, etc.)
   - Industry rating agencies
   - Benchmarking

2. Do we use BHAGs, stretch targets, and incremental targets?

3. After considering our level of experience with performance measurement, have we utilized target ranges or relied exclusively on a single number for each target?

4. Have we updated our targets each year, and when appropriate, made in-year alterations?

5. Do the targets we've set balance an inspiring challenge with practical reality?

Initiatives

1. Have we mapped our initiatives to our strategy map?

2. Based on that mapping exercise, have we eliminated or reduced the scope of initiatives not deemed as contributing to our strategy?

3. Do we use a tool to screen and prioritize new initiatives?

NOTES

1. The bulk of this section has been drawn from my first book *Balanced Scorecard Step by Step: Maximizing Performance and Maintaining Results.* Minor modifications have been made. Any organization developing a Balanced Scorecard should expend the energy necessary to document their performance measures in order to

crystallize shared understanding and ensure the measures are in fact measurable. I felt it was important to include this material for those who have not read one of my earlier books.

2. Based on work by Andy Neely, Chris Adams, and Mike Kennerley, *The Performance Prism* (London, FT Prentice Hall, 2002), p. 38.

3. Ibid.

4. Paul R. Niven, *Balanced Scorecard Step by Step: Maximizing Performance and Maintaining Results* (New York, NY, John Wiley & Sons Inc., 2002), p. 148.

5. Rudolph W. Giuliani, *Leadership* (New York, NY, Hyperion, 2002), p. 87.

6. Robert S. Kaplan and David P. Norton, *The Balanced Scorecard* (Boston, MA, Harvard Business School Press, 1996).

7. Institute of Management and Administration, "20 Best Practice Budgeting Insights: How Controllers Promote Faster, Better Decisions," 2001.

8. Andy Neely, Chris Adams, and Mike Kennerley, *The Performance Prism* (London, FT Prentice Hall, 2002), p. 158

9. Stephen C. Lundin, John Christensen, and Harry Paul, *Fish Tales* (New York, NY, Hyperion, 2002), p. 126.

10. Jody Hoffer Gittell, *The Southwest Airlines Way* (New York, NY, McGraw-Hill, 2003), p. 146.

11. As told in: Edgar H. Schein, *Organizational Culture and Leadership* (San Francisco, CA., Jossey-Bass, 1992), p. 238.

12. Robert S. Kaplan and David P. Norton, *The Strategy Focused Organization* (Boston, MA, Harvard Business School Press, 2001), p. 59.

13. Ted Goodman (editor), *The Forbes Book of Business Quotations* (New York, NY, Black Dog and Leventhal, 1997).

14. Best Practices Benchmarking Report, *Developing the Balanced Scorecard* (Chapel Hill, NC, Best Practices LLC, 1999).

15. Edwin A. Locke, "Motivation by Goal Setting," *Harvard Business Review,* November 2001.

16. Adapted from Paul R. Niven, *Balanced Scorecard Step by Step: Maximizing Performance and Maintaining Results* (New York, NY, John Wiley & Sons Inc., 2002).

17. Jim Collins, *Good to Great* (New York, NY Harper Business, 2001).

18. James C. Collins and Jerry I. Porras, *Built to Last* (New York, NY, Harper Business, 1997).

19. James C. Collins, "Turning Goals into Results: The Power of Catalytic Mechanisms," *Harvard Business Review,* July, 1999.

20. Robert Duboff, "Hilton Hotels: A Comprehensive Approach to Delivering Value for All Stakeholders," *Cornell Hotel and Restaurant Administration Quarterly,* August, 1999.

21. Malcolm Gladwell, *The Tipping Point* (New York, NY, Little Brown and Company, 2000), p. 4.

22. Larry Bossidy and Ram Charan, *Execution* (New York, NY, Crown Business, 2002), p. 38.

23. Harper A. Roehm, Joseph F. Castellano, and Saul Young, "The Seven Fatal Flaws of Performance Measurement," *CPA Journal,* June 1, 2004.

24. Elspeth J. Murray and Peter R. Richardson, *Fast Forward* (New York, NY, Oxford University Press, 2002), p. 46.

25. Robert S. Kaplan and David P. Norton, *The Balanced Scorecard* (Boston, MA, Harvard Business School Press, 1996).

26. Janice Koch, "The Challenges of Strategic Alignment: Crown Castle's CEO Shares His Perspectives," *Balanced Scorecard Report,* July–August, 2004, p. 11.

27. Adapted from Paul R. Niven, *Balanced Scorecard Step by Step: Maximizing Performance and Maintaining Results* (New York, NY, John Wiley & Sons Inc., 2002).

CHAPTER 6

Cascading the Balanced Scorecard to Drive Organizational Alignment

Church bells rang in a melancholy tone, names were solemnly read aloud, and people around the globe took part in quiet reflection on the third anniversary of September 11, 2001. My memories of that day consist mostly of shock, confusion, sorrow, and disbelief at the enormity of the events playing out in New York City. In the days ahead, as the literal and metaphorical dust slowly began to clear, the sadness remained, but it was replaced in a small way with the feeling of sheer awe at the dedication displayed by those working at Ground Zero. A more powerful demonstration of alignment of purpose is barely imaginable. If ever a situation called for people of disparate backgrounds to work together for a common cause, this was it, and work together they did: police officers, firefighters, health and human service personnel, and thousands of volunteers all united in the common cause of saving as many lives as possible. The results accomplished by those willing to sacrifice everything at Ground Zero are a powerful testament to the power of alignment, of what can be achieved when we work together toward a common purpose.

Although most of us don't face life-and-death situations when we enter our offices in the morning, the power of alignment is nonetheless critical to the success of every organization. As romantically compelling as it may be, the myth of a Corporate Lone Ranger, with fabled powers of leaping tall cubicles in a single bound and unjamming copy machines while still finding time to lead the company to greatness is just that—a myth. In our modern world of immense challenges, everyone from top to bottom in the organization must have their eye on the ball, understand the company's goals, and be working in tangible ways to further them. Not only is this an organizational imperative, but employees, in an effort to derive meaning and contribution from their work, are demanding knowledge of overall strategy and objectives as well. Knowledge workers, those of us who work primarily with intangible assets to create value, demand more from a job than the collection of a paycheck. Increasingly, employees expect work to be intellectually stimulating, supply an outlet for creativity, and provide them with the opportunity to make a meaningful contribution to results.

During our discussion of strategy in Chapter One, I noted the grim statistic of only 5% of the typical workforce understanding their company's strategy. Motivated action stems from a deep understanding of strategy, an ability to translate that knowledge into meaningful day-to-day behaviors directed toward goal achievement. Sounds a little clinical I know, so I'll simplify it for you. If you don't understand your company's overall strategy and objectives, it will prove exceedingly difficult for you to determine how to make a meaningful individual contribution. As Balanced Scorecard users, we know the tool is very much up to the task of translating and communicating strategy throughout the vast expanse of your enterprise, thereby propelling knowledge and understanding of strategy in its broadest sense. But to really kick-start individual contribution engines throughout your organization, people must have the ability to demonstrate how their everyday actions are making a difference and assisting the company in fulfilling its strategic objectives. Cascading the Balanced Scorecard is a proven technique to make that happen.

Cascading refers to the process of developing Balanced Scorecards at ever lower levels of your business. These Scorecards align with your organization's highest-level Scorecard by identifying the strategic objectives and measures lower-level business units, departments, and groups will use to track their progress in contributing to overall company goals. While some of the measures used may be the same throughout the entire organization, in most cases the lower-level Scorecards will include measures reflecting the specific opportunities and challenges faced at that level.[1] Just as pulling back the curtains in a dark room exposes every crevice to the brilliance of the sun, cascading pulls back the shades on strategy, transforming it from a poorly understood edict imposed by senior management to a set of simple objectives and measures that clarify how I, as an employee, am making a direct contribution to the success of the organization.

In the pages ahead we'll dive deeply into what will prove to be the refreshing waters of cascading, examining both how to effectively cascade and what to look for when reviewing cascaded Balanced Scorecards. While this process can prove challenging, as you'll see there are many considerations and decisions to be made, the rewards are well worth the efforts. In fact, Kaplan and Norton have discovered that the greatest gap between Hall of Fame organizations (those deemed to have excelled in the art and practice of the Balanced Scorecard as judged by Kaplan and Norton through their firm, the Balanced Scorecard Collaborative) and all others occurs in aligning the organization to the strategy. *"This demonstrates that effective organizational alignment, while difficult to achieve, has probably the biggest payoff of any management practice."*[2] Not surprising really, when you consider that through alignment you're harnessing the greatest resource known to humankind: the minds and hearts of your employees.

DEVELOPING IMPLEMENTATION PRINCIPLES FOR CASCADING SUCCESS

Over the years I've learned the hard way that I'm not the handiest of people. To illustrate that point, there is one famous incident of Niven lore in which my brother and I were attempting to replace a brake light on his car and one of us (I won't mention who) ended up with stitches! To my knowledge the car was subsequently sold for a reduced price sans brake light. If only we'd read the instructions and done some preliminary planning, the bloodbath could have been averted. Before embarking on any project, there must be sufficient planning to guide the work. The same can be said of your cascading efforts: the work must first be carefully planned in order to be adeptly executed.

You most likely developed your highest-level Balanced Scorecard through the services of a cross-functional team working together and adding diverse viewpoints in an effort to craft a product that reflects the entire organization. When you begin cascading, the likelihood of having the entire team work on every cascaded Scorecard is slim, if not nonexistent. It wouldn't be logistically possible to begin with and could take an immense amount of time to complete. More likely is the scenario under which your team fans out throughout the company, and each member leads cascading sessions within his or her respective groups. This approach is vastly more efficient but does introduce the possibility of varied techniques being employed in each location, a major no-no in Balanced Scorecard development. Consistent implementation practices throughout the organization are an absolute must if you hope to gain the benefits offered by true strategic alignment. If each group develops a Scorecard based on its individual interpretation of the framework, it stands to reason that many of those created will bear little resemblance to your highest-level Scorecard, resulting in confusion, frustration, and most important, a lack of goal alignment. To ensure that doesn't happen, outlined as follows are several elements you should consider when developing your cascading plan:

- *Balanced Scorecard perspectives.* Will all groups be required to use the four perspectives of the Balanced Scorecard: Financial, Customer, Internal Processes, and Employee Learning and Growth? Or will individual groups have the liberty to develop their own perspectives and perspective names?

Personalizing the Balanced Scorecard may produce benefits in the form of enhanced buy-in and local understanding, but dissimilar terms scattered throughout the company may lead to confusion.

- *Number of objectives and measures.* Will you impose a limit on the number of objectives and measures any group may have as part of its Balanced Scorecard? Keep in mind that as you begin cascading the Scorecard, you could quickly generate dozens if not hundreds of performance measures throughout the organization.

- *Use of corporate objectives.* When developing their Scorecards, will groups be required to use certain corporate objectives or have carte blanche in developing unique objectives that tell their story? Some organizations will ask business units and departments to use the same objectives (whenever possible) as those used in the Corporate Scorecard. The goal is to encourage uniformity and consistency throughout the company. A possible disadvantage is limiting the creativity of groups as they determine how they can best influence Corporate objectives and measures. As a compromise, organizations will sometimes impose a limited number of required objectives on all groups, while also including shared objectives between interdependent groups and allowing unique objectives.

UNDERSTANDING THE HIGHEST-LEVEL BALANCED SCORECARD

Understanding the highest-level Scorecard's (frequently the Corporate Balanced Scorecard) core elements forms the foundation of effective cascading efforts. Lacking a solid knowledge of the objectives and measures that compose your story, employees will be groping in the dark in their attempts to create meaningful cascaded Scorecards that articulate how they will contribute to the organization's success. Picture a cascading session in which the group sits around a table eager to begin crafting their Scorecard, when they are directed to an objective such as "Delight our customers" appearing on the Corporate Balanced Scorecard. Without the necessary context surrounding why and how this objective was developed, they are left wondering what it means to them and how, if at all, they may contribute to its achievement.

I've noted the Balanced Scorecard's formidable communication power throughout the text, yet despite the best efforts of Scorecard architects, the knowledge contained in the tool is not always self-evident to those viewing it. Communication and education efforts are of paramount importance as you share the Scorecard with your employees, discussing what the objectives and measures mean, why they were selected, and how they advance the company's strategic agenda. Informing your staff can be done in many ways, including executive briefings during which your senior leadership outlines the Scorecard, videos, intranet pages devoted to the Scorecard, or presentations by the Scorecard development team. How you accomplish the task is secondary to the notion of simply doing it, getting out there and sharing your story with all employees in an effort to ensure that they understand the elements your Balanced Scorecard comprises. Once they've grasped the foundational dimensions of your highest-level Scorecard, they're able to translate it into a Scorecard that outlines how they will influence the execution of corporate strategy, demonstrating how their day-to-day activities are contributing to strategic objectives.

CASCADING IS BASED ON INFLUENCE[3]

The ultimate goal of cascading is the demonstration by all groups within your organization of how their actions lead to overall strategic success. To make this contribution, each group must ask the question of how they might influence the objectives and measures appearing on higher-level Balanced Scorecards. We can use Exhibit 6.1 to illustrate the concept.

It all begins with your highest-level Scorecard, what some would refer to as the corporate-level or organization-wide Scorecard. The objectives and measures appearing on this Scorecard represent what you consider to be the critical variables driving your success. Therefore, every Scorecard subsequently created, at all levels of the organization, should link back to this document.

The first level of cascading occurs as business units (as described in Exhibit 6.1; your terminology may differ) examine the high-level Scorecard and ask, "Which of these objectives can we influence?" The answers to that question will form the basis for their own Balanced Scorecards. Chances are they won't be able to exert an impact on every objective appearing on the high-level Scorecard. After all, organizations build value by combining the disparate skills of all employees within every function. Therefore, each group should rightly focus on the objectives and measures over which it may exert an influence. However, if a group is unable to demonstrate a link to any objectives, you would have to seriously consider what value it is adding to the whole. The business unit may choose to use the language shown in the high-level Scorecard or create objectives and measures that more accurately reflect the true essence of how it adds value to the organization.

Once business units have developed Balanced Scorecards, the groups below them are ready to take part in the process. Individual departments will now review the Scorecard of the business unit to which they report and determine which of the objectives they can influence. This is a key distinction; departments reporting to business units look to that business unit's Scorecard when cascading, not the highest-level Corporate Balanced Scorecard. To create alignment, their focus must be on the strategically relevant objectives and measures within their busi-

EXHIBIT 6.1   The Cascading Process

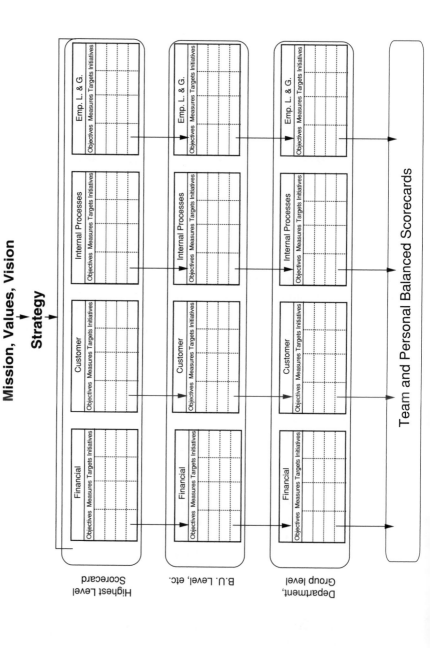

Mission, Values, Vision

Strategy

Team and Personal Balanced Scorecards

ness unit. Once again, they may use similarly termed objectives and measures or develop unique names for their Scorecard elements.

Let's look at an example of cascading using a fictional taxi company. Exhibit 6.2 provides excerpts from Scorecards at three levels of this organization, which will demonstrate the principles of cascading just discussed.

Within the customer perspective, the company has chosen an objective of providing safe, convenient transportation to its customers. To gauge effectiveness on this objective, they will measure the increase in the number of passengers carried. A 10% increase for the year is the target to which they aspire.

Fleet Services is one of several business units within the company. When developing their own Balanced Scorecard, they began by closely inspecting the Corporate Scorecard to determine which of the objectives appearing on that Scorecard they could influence. As is the case with all business units, Fleet Services is anxious to show how their important work links to the company's overall goals. When reviewing the company's customer perspective, they see the objective of providing safe, convenient transportation to customers and feel they have a strong impact on this objective. They too have a goal of providing safe and convenient transportation, so they carry the objective forward to their own Scorecard. However, the measure of increased number of passengers carried is not considered appropriate for them. It's a critical indicator, but they would like to develop a measure that indicates how they *influence* the number of passengers carried. They conclude that by ensuring the company's entire fleet of cabs is available every day, they can help the company increase the number of passengers carried. Hence, they measure the percentage of the taxi fleet that is available.

Fleet Services comprises several groups, one of which is the Maintenance Department. Among their many responsibilities is ensuring that the company's fleet of taxis is serviced efficiently. When developing their Balanced Scorecard, they begin by reviewing the Scorecard of the business unit to which they report, Fleet Services. Upon review they see the objective of providing safe and convenient transportation. They feel they can impact this objective, and thus choose it for their own customer perspective. They ask themselves how they might influence the measure of taxi fleet availability and realize that if they're able to complete vehicle repairs in a timely fashion, the company will have more vehicles at its disposal, and customers won't have to wait for cabs. They strive to complete at least 75% of vehicle repairs within 24 hours.

While each of the three Scorecards profiled in this example share a common objective, the measure chosen at each level represents what is necessary for the group to contribute to overall success. Those linked performance measures are the key to ensuring alignment throughout the company. Employees in the Maintenance Department are now able to conclusively demonstrate how their activities link back to a key goal for the company. Likewise, senior executives can rest assured that Fleet Services personnel are focused on the necessary elements to drive value for the company's customers.

EXHIBIT 6.2 Cascading the Balanced Scorecard

Corporate Scorecard

Perspective	Objective	Measure	Target
Customer	Provide safe, convenient transportation to our customers	Increase in number of passengers carried	10%

Fleet Services Scorecard

Perspective	Objective	Measure	Target
Customer	Provide safe, convenient transportation to our customers	Percentage of taxi fleet available	90%

Maintenance Department Scorecard

Perspective	Objective	Measure	Target
Customer	Provide safe, convenient transportation to our customers	Percentage of vehicle repairs completed within 24 hours	75%

REVIEWING CASCADED BALANCED SCORECARDS

As with Balanced Scorecard development in the broad sense, cascading can be accomplished in either a matter of weeks or it may require months, depending on the size of your organization and scope of the Balanced Scorecard implementation. I'm all for the momentum generated with a swift implementation timeline, because the frenzied level of activity often unites people in a desire to achieve a common purpose. However, rapidly cascading the Scorecard poses significant downside risks as well. In their haste to drive alignment as quickly as possible, some organizations will forgo the necessary task of reviewing the cascaded Scorecards to determine if in fact they are aligned with overall strategy and have everyone rowing in the same direction. Skipping this requisite task can often lead to cascading efforts that produce an ad hoc mix of Balanced Scorecards scattered throughout the company, which do little in uniting employees toward a common strategic goal, and in fact may even drive wedges between cooperative efforts, jeopardize effective resource allocation decisions, and generate confusion and hostility toward the process.

Just as a simple checkup with your doctor can alleviate the possibility of severe pain and suffering down the road, reviewing cascaded Scorecards is a diagnostic exercise that is sure to pay benefits in enhanced focus, alignment, and understanding of corporate strategy. As a starting point in your review efforts, recruit your Balanced Scorecard team to audit the Scorecards produced by their respective business units or departments. Your team members' deep functional knowledge combined with Scorecard subject matter expertise arm them with the skills necessary to supply an informed critique on the Scorecards produced within their groups. To assist your team in their efforts, you could look for the following elements when reviewing cascaded Scorecards:

- *Adherence to cascading principles.* A simple first diagnostic is ensuring that the Scorecards are following the rules you developed when creating cascading principles. For example, do they consistently use agreed-upon terminology and include any required objectives.

- *Look for influencing objectives.* Creating alignment is the chief goal of cascading, and therefore all cascaded Scorecards should contain objectives and measures that will influence those appearing on the next Scorecard in the chain. Any cascaded Balanced Scorecard containing highly esoteric objectives and measures that display no linkage to those composing the Scorecard one level up should be viewed with extreme caution. While some of the indicators on the Scorecard in question may be critical to the unit's success, if they are not contributing to the overall direction of the organization, what is their true strategic value?

- *A suitable number of objectives and measures.* Especially for large organizations, cascading can quickly spawn hundreds or, thanks to the advent of sophisticated software systems, even thousands of performance measures. Recall the essence of the Balanced Scorecard—focus. As Charles Handy reminded us in our discussion of measures, "Measuring more is easy, measuring better is hard." Difficult, yes, but worth the exertion because a limited set of performance indicators derived directly from strategy will prove far more valuable in navigating your course than a large number of operational metrics with loose connections to strategy.

- *Appropriate targets.* As we noted in Chapter Five, target setting is not an area of highly honed competence for many companies. Setting appropriate targets requires careful judgment considering the environment, current performance, future expectations, and so on. Ensure that the targets appearing on cascaded Scorecards reflect a healthy balance between inspiring challenge and practical reality. Targets must also be mathematically verified for measures that aggregate to a corporate total. For example, at the corporate level, your Balanced Scorecard may contain a measure centered on cost reductions with a target of $1 million this year. Targets from cascaded Scorecards must total to at least $1 million if you hope to achieve this target at the corporate level.

- *Ensure coverage of objectives.* The Corporate Scorecard contains the objectives and measures, directly translated from your strategy, that you'll use to judge your success. They were chosen after vigorous debate and discussion, representing your best thinking on the subject. Given their obvious importance in executing strategy, it's imperative that cascaded Scorecards, when examined at a macro level, provide coverage to all objectives. If, after reviewing your cascaded Scorecards, you determine there are corporate-level objectives with no representation at lower levels, that is a strong signal that those below the corporate level don't consider the objective crucial to success. At this point you either reevaluate the necessity of the objective or engage in education efforts about why it is vital to the success of your enterprise.

- *A mix of lag and lead indicators.* Cascaded Scorecards must not rely exclusively on either lagging or leading indicators, but provide a robust mix of the two that when blended together will assist in the unit achieving its goals.

Have you ever participated in any type of team building event that featured a rough-and-tumble tug-of-war competition? If you have, I sincerely hope you've never experienced the messy misfortune of ending up on the muddy end of the rope. To stay clean and dry in that competition, you need a strong anchor, someone with the strength to keep your side out of the mire. But even someone with prodigious strength can't beat a whole team of people pulling in unison at the other end of the rope. It's the same with cascading. Your anchor is the high-level Corporate Balanced Scorecard that tells the overall strategic story of the enterprise, but as compelling as its tale may be, it requires the dedication and effort of every employee working in concert throughout the company to transform it into a tangible success. Cascading the Scorecard binds people to the anchor, adding strength and knowledge along the way, ultimately leading to an organization aligned in purpose and united in the determination to effectively execute their strategy.

SELF-ASSESSMENT QUESTIONS

1. Before cascading the Balanced Scorecard, did we develop implementation principles addressing the following:

   ○ Perspective terminology

   ○ The number of objectives and measures

   ○ Use of corporate objectives

2. Have we sufficiently communicated the contents of our highest-level Balanced Scorecard to employees, ensuring they understand its contents before attempting the development of cascaded Scorecards?

3. Have we instituted a review process for cascaded Balanced Scorecards, keeping the following elements in mind:

   ○ Adherence to agreed-upon cascading principles

   ○ Contributory objectives on lower-level Balanced Scorecards

   ○ An appropriate number of objectives and measures

   ○ Appropriate targets

   ○ Suitable coverage of corporate-level objectives

   ○ A mix of lag and lead indicators

NOTES

1. Paul R. Niven, *Balanced Scorecard Step by Step: Maximizing Performance and Maintaining Results* (New York: John Wiley & Sons, Inc, 2002).

2. David P. Norton and Randall H. Russell, "Best Practices in Managing the Execution of Strategy," Balanced Scorecard Report, July–August 2004, p. 3.

3. Portions of this section are adapted from Paul R. Niven, *Balanced Scorecard Step by Step for Government and Nonprofit Agencies* (New York: John Wiley & Sons, Inc, 2003).

CHAPTER 7

Key Balanced Scorecard Process Linkages: Budgeting, Compensation, and Corporate Governance

In an era when quality products are merely the ante to get you a seat at the competitive table, increasingly it's the conception and execution of differentiating strategies that elevate certain companies above the pack. Learning from the measures in a Balanced Scorecard has provided the boost to new heights of competitive advantage for many of these winning companies. Using the Balanced Scorecard as a measurement system undoubtedly provides substantial benefits, but leading Scorecard practitioners recognize the vast potential in linking the tool to key processes throughout the organization, forging a bond between short-term actions and long-term strategy. In this chapter we'll examine three critical organizational processes: budgeting, compensation, and corporate governance, and consider how the Scorecard serves as the thread that bonds all three to corporate strategy.

STRATEGIC RESOURCE ALLOCATION: THE BALANCED SCORECARD AND BUDGETING

As I write these words in early September 2004, the days are getting a little shorter, the nights feel a little nippier, and the inventory of leaves on our neighborhood sidewalks is ever-increasing. To me this signals the coming of autumn, my favorite season, a crisp and fresh time of year full of exciting changes. For those of you in the corporate world, these images may conjure up the thought of another new beginning, one that is far less bucolic—the annual budget process. Just as Christmas supplies and merchandise seem to arrive in stores earlier every year, the annual budget exercise also creeps up on us before we know it. If yours is like most companies, you and your family will probably be knee deep in yuletide boxes and bows before your budget for next year is finalized. At this time of year, the bane of budgeting can swallow up to 30% of management's time and cost an enormous amount of money. In fact, Ford is reported to have determined its total planning and performance measurement cost amounts to about $1.2 billion per year![1]

The excessive time and money demanded from planning and budgeting might be considered tolerable if the significant toil yielded real benefits for the organization. However, the converse may be true, as organizations and management pundits around the world have united in their vitriolic diatribes on our antiquated budgeting systems, suggesting they are a waste of time in the hypercompetitive landscape of modern business, which renders budgets out of date before the ink on the paper used to print them has dried.

A key shortcoming of budgets, one we noted in Chapter One, is the sad fact that about 60% of organizations are unwilling or unable to link the process to their strategy. In today's short-term-focused world, executives and managers are under immense pressure to deliver "expected" numbers to placate fickle analysts and investors just waiting to pounce on the poor company falling a penny or two short on revenue or profit projections. This myopic viewpoint comes at the expense of strategy, because leaders are hesitant to spend precious resources on strategic initiatives that promise to possibly add value three or four years down the road. Why take such a risk when the same capital could be used to prop up current earnings, satisfying Wall Street and keeping everyone on an identical road to mediocrity.

It has been suggested that in extreme cases, the use of budgets may provide a root cause for the massive collapse of corporate ethics witnessed in the past several years. For example, at WorldCom, miscreant leader Bernard Ebbers's rigid demands were legendary throughout the company. As one staffer put it, *"You would have a budget and he would mandate that you had to be two percent under budget ... nothing else was acceptable."*[2] Operating in such stifling, pressure-cooker environments eventually causes some normally moral and responsible people to make errors in judgment that can ultimately lead to ethical landslides of mistrust, crime, and frequently, bankruptcy.

Fortunately for most of us, the budgeting process doesn't lead to a jail cell, but it probably does send the sales of pain relievers and antacids through the roof as the pain of preparation—and the inevitable game playing that accompany the task—are enough to test the wits of just about anyone. There is a light at the end of this painful and time-consuming tunnel, however, and that radiant beam is provided by the Balanced Scorecard. Rather than completely exiling the budgeting process, many organizations have aligned it with the strategy execution characteristics inherent in the Scorecard and have thereby forged a powerful bond between resource allocation and strategy. In the pages ahead, we'll examine the steps employed in driving the Balanced Scorecard and budgeting linkage.

An Overview of the Process

Exhibit 7.1 presents a graphical view of the linkage between budgeting and the Balanced Scorecard. At the far left we see mission, values, and vision, which serve as the starting point in any discussion of the Balanced Scorecard. A strategy is derived from these fundamental building blocks, one in concert with their core essence and also reflecting trends, assumptions, key variables, and environmental elements. The Balanced Scorecard translates the strategy, bringing it to life through the use of objectives, measures, targets, and, most important for the discussion to follow, initiatives. Quantifying initiatives as they appear in cascaded Scorecards throughout the company will form the basis for operating and capital budget requests. The arrow in the background of Exhibit 7.1 reflects the dynamic nature of the task. Not a single one of the elements comprising the chart should be considered static and immovable objects to corporate prosperity, but must be viewed as malleable inputs to success, capable of change as conditions inevitably alter. Let's review the specific steps in our process.

Step One: Plan for Success

Strategically allocating resources using the Balanced Scorecard represents a radical alteration to the budgeting exercise for most organizations, and therefore will not be without challenges. As we've seen throughout the Balanced Scorecard implementation, communication will prove to be a tremendous ally in generating momentum for the change. Your planning and communication efforts should be focused on outlining the rationale for the switch in tactics, guiding individuals through the logistics of the effort, and demonstrating the benefits of the process. The team you convened to create the Balanced Scorecard can once again be called on to assist you in these efforts, but to maximize the effectiveness of this process, that group should be supplemented with what some of you might call a planning council. This squad, composed primarily of Finance types from representative business units and departments, works with the Balanced Scorecard team to both lend credibility to the effort and add subject matter expertise in the area of budgeting. The planning council may be called on to develop training materials, create budgeting templates, and work with budget preparers throughout the organization to ensure a smooth transition to this new method of budget generation.

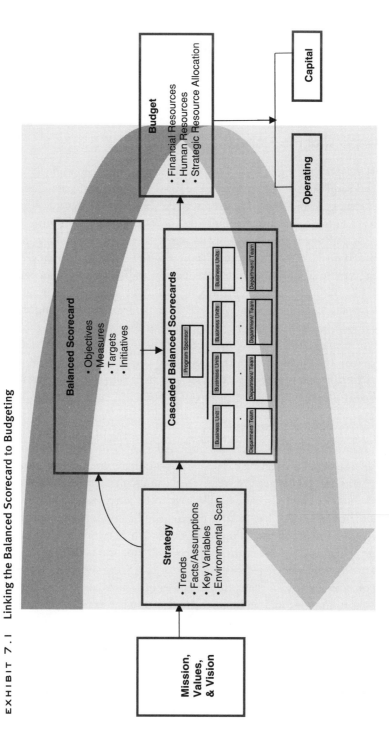

EXHIBIT 7.1 Linking the Balanced Scorecard to Budgeting

Step Two: Develop or Refine Your Highest-Level Balanced Scorecard

The method of Scorecard and budget linkage described here relies heavily on the development of cascaded Balanced Scorecards. Therefore, a high-level organizational Scorecard, clearly spelling out the key objectives, measures, and targets for the organization, must be in place as the foundation for cascading efforts.

Step Three: Create Aligned Scorecards Through Cascading

As the old saying goes, this is "where the rubber meets the road." We described cascading in Chapter Six as the process by which all business units, departments, and groups within the organization are able to clearly demonstrate how their everyday actions contribute to the execution of strategy. The objectives in these Scorecards provide the desired future state, the measures supply the yardsticks of performance, targets supply inspiration and challenge, and finally, initiatives furnish the projects and actions to turn these dreams into reality by closing any gaps between current and desired performance. The link to budgeting is formed when we calculate the monetary investments necessary to launch and sustain initiatives appearing in cascaded Balanced Scorecards. Whether small (e.g., staffing a trade booth at a local convention) or large (e.g., implementing an enterprise resource planning system), every initiative entails the allocation of resources, both human and financial. The cost of these resources should form the basis of budget submissions from all groups populating your organization.

Sounds simple enough, but a complicating wrench is thrown into the works when you consider the many standard operating budget line items, such as utilities and maintenance, that are required to keep things up and running. Should a forced linkage be made between these day-to-day facts or organizational life and the initiatives making up a Balanced Scorecard? Differences of opinion exist on the subject. Scorecard architects Kaplan and Norton have advocated the use of so-called *dynamic budgeting*, which represents an amalgam of operational and strategic budgeting.[3] They suggest that an operational budget be used to allocate resources necessary for typical, recurring operations. Given the large volume of current service offerings, most of an organization's spending would be dictated by the operational budget. The strategic budget is reserved for spending designed to close any significant gaps that exist between current and desired performance on critical performance indicators.

Another school of thought suggests that only one budget be used, and it should contain the entire mix of operational and strategic elements necessary to reflect a true picture of the organization. Following this advice forces an organization to consider every possible line item on the budget in light of strategy, which could be a Herculean task. Financial innovations such as activity-based costing, which provide input on cost drivers, are helpful in this regard, but will not eliminate the specter of subjectivity from creeping into the analysis. Proponents of this school also suggest, with some merit, that challenging managers to relate strategy to even the most mundane of activities will bring the concept to the forefront and promote learning through the exchange of ideas around the company.[4] The Scorecard and budget linkage process described here will work with either budget school. Your choice will depend on how accurately you can attach costs to strategic initiatives and the depth of your commitment in instituting a change of this magnitude.

Step Four: Compile Resource Requests

I don't know about you, but I definitely haven't heard as much hype about the paperless office recently. The idea was in vogue a few years ago as prognosticators envisioned an ultra-efficient office with information whizzing through the airwaves in e-mails and other electronic documents, keeping creative minds filled and formerly messy desks clear. Interestingly, some researchers—yes, there are paperless office researchers—consider the idea a myth and suggest that paper actually encourages important organizational dynamics.[5] Regardless of where you fall on the paperless spectrum, chances are your budgeting process never has satisfied its seemingly unquenchable thirst for paper and has been stuffing binders and filling photocopiers as long as you've been engaging in the process. Our process requires a little paper, because you must create easy-to-complete templates for distribution to all budget preparers within your company. An example is found in Exhibit 7.2.

Picking up on our taxi company example used in Chapter Six, we find an excerpt of the Fleet Services business unit's budget template. In the example, they have proposed two initiatives they feel are crucial in helping them achieve 90% fleet availability. The first represents an investment in state-of-the-art diagnostics equipment, consisting of both machinery and software. This equipment will allow them to swiftly determine the source of mechanical problems, returning cars to the street and generating revenues much quicker than in the past. Fleet Services would also like to expand their service bay. Currently, many cars awaiting repairs must sit in an adjacent alley until an opening arises in the tight quarters of the current service bay. Automobiles are the company's most valuable asset, and having them sit idle while waiting for repairs is an expensive waste. Keep in mind this is just one measure. You'll require documents such as this for all measures (no wonder budgets produce so much paper!). Each initiative must be accompanied by supporting documentation as well (e.g., costs, timing, dependencies, key milestones, payback periods).

Spending requests such as those outlined in Exhibit 7.2 must be gathered throughout the company and summarized in relation to their corresponding Balanced Scorecard objective. Exhibit 7.3 provides another example from our fictitious taxi company. Unlike any taxi company I've ever encountered, this rev-

EXHIBIT 7.2 Condensed Budget Submission Form

Business Unit: Fleet Services				
			Resource Requirements	
Measure	**Target**	**Initiatives**	**Operating**	**Capital**
Percentage of taxi fleet available	90%	Diagnostics equipment (machinery & software)	$100,000	$250,000
		Service bay expansion	$150,000	$300,000

olutionary outfit has determined its strategy as making customers its first priority. It has created three objectives to translate this truly differentiating strategy into a reality: "Provide safe, convenient transportation," "Increase market share," and, based on the popular Ken Blanchard book, "Create raving fans." So who knows, the next time passengers cautiously cast their glance beyond the scratched and warped divider and onto the front seat, instead of a half-eaten gyro and a pile of receipts, they may find a copy of this business best-seller!

In making resource allocation decisions, it's important for leaders to be aware of the current status of corporate objectives. The column labeled "current scorecard status" fulfills that purpose using a simple traffic light metaphor to illustrate the objective's performance. Green is synonymous with meeting or achieving the target, yellow represents a situation in which caution and attention are in order, and red indicates performance requiring improvement. In this example, the company is performing well (green) on its objective of providing safe, convenient

EXHIBIT 7.3 Aggregated Budget Requests by Objective and Strategy

Objective	Current Scorecard Status	Budget Request Operating $000's	Budget Request Capital $000's
Provide safe, convenient transportation	Green	$XXM	$XXM
Increase market share	Yellow	$XXM	$XXM
Create raving fans	Red	$XXM	$XXM
Percentage of Total Spending		46%	42%

transportation, while market share is in the caution zone (yellow), and the creation of raving fans leaves something to be desired (red).

The template is completed by columns detailing the proposed amount of spending, in both operating and capital dollars, on each of the three customer objectives. Additionally, we see what percentage that amount constitutes of the total budget requests from across the company. For example, our taxi company is proposing that 46% of its total operating budget be used to advance the three customer objectives shown on the page; 42% of the corporate total is directed at capital budget items in support of those same objectives. Although these percentages appear high, we must remember the organization's overarching strategy of making customers their number-one priority. As such, it is not surprising they will be overweighting their customer-based expenditures. In addition to providing raw information, this template is designed to stimulate discussion and generate questions regarding the proposed spending levels. How much is the company willing to spend to sustain its green light performance on the provision of safe, convenient transportation? Is that a differentiating objective in the minds of customers? Alternatively, will significant spending on the creation of raving fans really manifest in repeat business, leading to greater market share? These and other questions must be contested before any budget becomes final.

Step Five: Finalize the Budget

During Chapter Five, I spoke of the inspirational power of a compelling target in driving people toward breakthrough performance. Challenging targets may require expensive initiatives, and thus it is likely that your ability to fund will be outstripped by the sheer volume and cost of budget requests streaming in from all parts of your company. Closing the gap between requested and available funds is the focus of this, our final step in the Balanced Scorecard and budgeting link.

Group leaders from throughout the company should attempt to be at their silver-tongued best as they guide the senior leadership team through their unit's budget requests in formal presentations, outlining the strategic significance of the initiatives included, and how they will positively impact Balanced Scorecard targets. At this point the process becomes iterative in nature, with executives reviewing and questioning the proposals, attempting to determine which are worthy of inclusion in the budget. To ease the decision-making process somewhat, you may wish to develop an internal ranking system for the initiatives you propose. A simplified rating system may be devised to represent the potential impact of removing a specific initiative on the Balanced Scorecard. For example, a 1 might indicate an initiative that could be eliminated and have minimal impact on the ability of the group to achieve its target. A 2 may translate to an initiative that could be cut, but with a definite effect on the group's chances of meeting targeted expectations. Finally, initiatives awarded a 3 could represent projects that are deemed as crucial to the successful achievement of Scorecard targets. The ratings will be necessarily subjective, but they will serve as a powerful impetus for conversations centered on establishing spending priorities.[6]

Step Six: Bask in Your Time and Dollar Savings

Okay, this isn't really an official step in the process. Nobody wants to see you or your finance team dancing gleefully through your building basking in the glow of an abbreviated budget season. There are significant benefits to be derived from linking the Balanced Scorecard to budgeting in the manner suggested previously. First, in answer to a chorus of critics who decry the complexity of modern budgeting exercises, the technique outlined is relatively simple and acts in accordance with the basic principles of the Balanced Scorecard. It also reinforces your strategy by ensuring that budget dollars are tied directly to objectives that will lead to the fulfillment of your strategic agenda and are not simply dreamed up by over—or underzealous managers looking to benefit from their formidable budget gaming skills. Collaboration may also be enhanced from following this procedure, as disparate business units compare Scorecard targets and initiatives in an attempt to rationalize spending while still finding the appropriate resources to complete synergistic initiatives. Considering all those benefits, maybe you should be dancing.

LINKING PAY WITH PERFORMANCE: THE BALANCED SCORECARD AND COMPENSATION

Does Money Really Make the World Go Round?

During our discussion of cascading in Chapter Six—and elsewhere in the book—I've mentioned the ever-increasing importance employees place on finding meaning and contribution in the work they perform. Twenty-first-century knowledge workers expect vocations to provide opportunities to flex creative muscles, apply analytical tools, and work with others in generating solutions. Makes work sound so noble a pursuit, doesn't it? And certainly it is. However, gently brushing aside this dignified rhetoric for a moment leaves us with some pragmatic elements to consider. You may have a mortgage that must be paid every 30 days, children who today are craving the latest X-Box game and tomorrow will be ready for college, and, time permitting, perhaps you even have a hobby or two you enjoy pursuing in your spare time. The common denominator is money, and in some cases, depending on your house, kids, and hobbies, the need for lots of it. A steady paycheck is a necessity to make ends meet.

The ubiquitous presence of incentive compensation systems in place at companies around the world is a testament to the power of money as an extrinsic motivator of human behavior. Always seeking more of a good thing, most organizations have instituted some form of these programs, which attempt to focus employee actions on specific goals, the achievement of which leads to monetary rewards in the form of bonuses for workers and enhanced revenue and profitability for the firm. But do they actually work? Many researchers believe they do provide significant value to both employer and employee. In one study of "What really works" within successful organizations, the authors bluntly asserted, *"It should be obvious that the best way to hold people to high standards is to directly reward achievement. Ninety percent of the winning companies in our study tightly linked pay to performance, while only fifteen percent of the losers did."*[7] Similarly, it has been suggested that effective implementation of a strategic plan is greatly enhanced when reward and recognition systems gear employee attention and focus toward the key dimensions of the new direction.[8] You know companies must be on to something when the U.S. federal government starts to take notice and get in the act. Last year, when lawmakers passed the fiscal 2004 Defense Authorization Bill, they included a provision to create a $500 million fund managers can use to reward high-performing employees. Supporters have suggested: *"This is a critical step that will enable agencies to reward their best employees and will instill a culture of achievement in the civil service system."*[9]

Given the benefits noted previously and the positive experiences of organizations worldwide, it appears that pay for performance is here to stay. In the pages ahead, we'll examine how Balanced Scorecard practitioners have taken advantage of incentive compensation trends and discuss key principles that must be considered when linking the Scorecard and compensation.

The Balanced Scorecard and Compensation

One of the greatest attributes of the Balanced Scorecard framework is its applicability to virtually any organization operating in any arena. During my consulting career, I've had the pleasure of assisting organizations in fields as diverse as financial services, utilities, health and human services, manufacturing, local and federal governments, and law enforcement, just to name a few. Although every engagement is unique, I do ask some standard questions when our work commences, one of which is: *"What will it take to make the Balanced Scorecard 'real' at your organization? In other words, how do we transform it from an interesting academic exercise to something people live and breathe everyday?"* Without question, the number-one response to that question is, *"Link it to people's pay."*

The Scorecard is a powerful communication device signaling the key objectives of the organization, and through cascading the line of sight between individual contribution and overall goals can become 20-20, but for many people it simply doesn't hit their radar screen until it lands in the middle of what Stephen Covey terms their "rice bowl," more commonly referred to as their paychecks. In many ways the Balanced Scorecard and compensation is a match made in pay-for-performance heaven because the Scorecard contains the key metrics, exclusively derived from strategy, that set a trajectory of future growth and profitability, while the pay component of the equation keeps everyone committed to doing whatever it takes to achieve Scorecard targets.

Most senior executives recognize the compatibility of the two and are anxious to form a quick bond between Scorecard indicators and rewards. Jack Welch, who even in this era of rock star status being conferred on CEOs, may be the most well known and respected CEO of all time, has put it in his own simple and inimitable way, *"By not aligning measurements and rewards, you often get what you're not looking for."*[10] In other words, why would you not link rewards to the most crucial of your performance measures? This sentiment is appropriate coming from an executive, because the responsibility of matching deeds to words falls squarely on their well-compensated shoulders. If leaders expect all employees to embrace the principles embodied in the Balanced Scorecard, they must ensure that the reward systems over which they ultimately preside are in concert with those doctrines. Offering bonuses based on financial and nonfinancial indicators of performance not only cements this consistency but also conveys a strong belief on the part of senior management that the hypothesis embodied by the Balanced Scorecard (i.e., that nonfinancial metrics are the driving forces behind future financial success), is an accurate one worth vigorously pursuing.

Forging an Effective Pay-for-Performance Link: Balanced Scorecard and Incentive Compensation Principles

Pop quiz: What do these two things have in common: (1) The price paid for an airline ticket by passengers on the same flight, and (2) The answers you get when calling your wireless company and inquiring about your rate plan? Answer: No two are alike. With all of the fare categories, loyalty programs, and intense competition among carriers, the chance of two passengers paying the same price for an airline ticket is virtually nil. Similarly, have you ever called your wireless company to inquire about your calling plan or tried to have them explain the convoluted bill you receive each month? I have yet to get a straight (or consistent) answer to any of my queries on this subject. The same can be said for linking the Balanced Scorecard to incentive compensation systems; no two organizations will do it in precisely the same manner. There are innumerable variables to consider, rendering a "one size fits all" program impossible to find. Rather than describing any quintessential method, because none exists, in the pages that follow I've outlined several key principles you must consider when forging the critical pay-for-performance link:

- *Communicate the incentive compensation plan.* It's an undeniable fact of modern organizational life that we are constantly bombarded with information:

corporate memos, e-mails, telephone calls, reports, press clippings, and so on. To function effectively in this chaotic world, we increasingly call on our powers of filtering: ignoring noncritical stimuli, focusing on the essential information we need to process our daily tasks. One of those essentials, something sure to have our antennae at full attention, is the subject of compensation. Reward systems, and incentive compensation in particular, always hold the potential to ruffle feathers, and thus before launching any plan it's imperative that you first communicate your intentions widely. The purpose of the incentive compensation plan must be shared: why it's the right step in this stage of your Scorecard implementation and how it advances not only the Scorecard, but the organization's strategic agenda as well. When it comes to incentive compensation, perceived fairness is as important as the actual monetary awards. Therefore, the plan's design must be carefully communicated, allowing participants to quickly determine how it works and what it will take to be successful within the confines of this new system.

- *Who participates in the plan?* The first hurdle to cross in making this link is determining exactly who will participate in the incentive compensation plan you're creating. Will you limit involvement in the plan to select employee categories or open it up to everyone currently drawing a paycheck? Creating an effective incentive compensation plan is somewhat analogous to walking a tightrope without a net—one false step spells big trouble in a big hurry. Should you have the wrong measures or targets in place, for example, the plan could lead to dysfunctional decision making and behavior, which ultimately costs you a fortune while failing to move you any closer to the execution of your strategy.

  Because of the risks inherent in the process, some organizations choose to pilot the Scorecard and compensation link at the executive level of the company. While this doesn't completely mitigate the risks, it does offer a certain measure of security because many of the measures employed at this level have been battle tested over several years. Conversely, in order for the Scorecard to be accepted and used throughout the organization, employees must pay attention to and understand it. For that reason, many companies choose to make the plan available to all employees in an attempt to drive focus and energy toward the key metrics embodied in the Balanced Scorecard. The choice is not philosophical, and in fact should rest on the confidence you place in the measures you've chosen to include in the Balanced Scorecard and compensation link. If you feel comfortable in their ability to drive behavior, leading toward the execution of your strategy, making the plan available to all employees signals your confidence in the Scorecard and their ability to influence results, leading to a win-win proposition for all.

- *Are rewards based on individual or group efforts?* Should individual or group performance be the ultimate arbiter of incentives? Pundits and practical experience tell us that most work in modern organizations has a cross-functional component and, therefore, rewards should represent this reality. However, the vexing "free rider" problem first posed by economists suggests the possibility of some less-motivated employees earning a reward on the backs of their fellow workers who are bearing most of the burden, thereby alienating the larger group and possibly depressing performance. The structure and reality of work flow tend to outweigh economic constructs in most organizations, but with the majority leaning toward group incentives in an effort to foster team spirit and encourage the achievement of stretch targets.

  There is a third alternative: providing both group and individual incentives, which is the approach adopted by Charles Schwab, the leader in the U.S. private brokerage market. In the mid-1990s, as Schwab encouraged customers to migrate toward their online channels, many branch employees were understandably threatened by the change, fearing for their jobs. This presented a unique challenge to Schwab leadership, who somehow had to convince the group feeling under siege to support customers in their transition from bricks and mortar to the Internet. Part of the solution lay in the use of a balanced incentive program designed to ensure that all employees, both branch and online, would share in the rewards of both channels. Schwab devised a system that provided both individual rewards for outstanding performance along with group awards based on overall branch performance.[11]

- *Perspectives to include in the incentive compensation plan.* A well-constructed Balanced Scorecard represents a coherent portrait of the organization demonstrating that the whole is greater than the sum of the parts. When you designed your Scorecard, you were attempting to tell a story, combining seemingly disparate elements across perspectives into a compelling tale of strategic success. Rewarding performance on just one of the perspectives, therefore, seems contradictory to the entire set of principles on which the Balanced Scorecard is constructed. Incentives should be spread across the four perspectives, thereby inspiring your team to grasp the greater significance of individual performance metrics as they work together to spell success. Having said that, practical reality dictates that many organizations must apply weights to perspectives in an attempt to focus employee attention on critical drivers of performance. In one study on the topic, researchers found that most respondents applied a heavier weight to financial measures, which averaged about 40% of potential rewards. The Customer, Internal Processes, and Employee Learning and Growth perspectives were weighted approximately 20% each.[12]

- *Measures to be used.* While each measure appearing on the Scorecard is important—otherwise, it would not have been chosen—every business will have some metrics it feels are the most critical to success in the near term or are most representative of the differentiating features of the particular value proposition. These indicators should be included in the incentive compensation plan. As an example, consider Harrah's Entertainment, operator of 26 casinos in 13 states with more than $4 billion in revenue and $235 million in net income in 2002. Relying heavily on deep data mining and decision-science marketing applications, this innovative enterprise has determined that visitors to their casinos expect fast service and friendly, helpful attention. Thus, customer satisfaction scores have become an obsession throughout the company, with everyone from chefs to valets to slot attendants receiving training on the subject. As a differentiator of success, improved customer satisfaction scores are a major component of the bonus plan at Harrah's. Since the program's inception, the company has paid out a whopping $43 million in bonuses to nonmanagement employees based on customer satisfaction scores.[13] It's nice to know that at least a portion of our casino losses is going to deserving employees!

As the Harrah's example demonstrates, great results can await organizations with the insight to link performance drivers to paychecks; however, the dangers of selecting the wrong measures can send results spiraling in the opposite direction. I've spoken of Peter Drucker glowingly throughout this book, but as this next story illustrates, even the best can make near-fatal mistakes: Drucker was once charged with developing a new compensation system for General Electric (GE). Because he had considerable experience on the topic from consulting work with Sears, he based the new plan on the Sears system in which store managers had their pay linked to one-year sales results. At GE that translated into linking business unit leader pay with the return on investment (ROI) of their division. As it happens, GE was reorganizing at the time, and giving business units responsibility for innovation was one outcome of the change. You can probably imagine what happened next. As Drucker puts it:

> What we did—in retrospect, it's obvious—was absolutely a mistake. Innovation requires investment today without any return for a long time. Under the new compensation plan for a general manager to spend a penny on innovation meant taking money not just out of his own pocket but also away from his people. So for ten years GE didn't innovate. It became apparent very soon that we had created an enormous disincentive to innovation.[14]

One of the first actions of GE's new chief executive at that time, Reg Jones, was to change the severely flawed compensation plan.

- *Lead and lag indicators.* This just in from the "You're probably not going to believe this" file: There are researchers who actually spend time analyzing the amount and nature of humor (you know, jokes) used by senior executives and how that practice correlates to their performance. In case you're interested, the authors of the hilarity study found executives that ranked as outstanding used humor twice as often as those rated as average.[15] I bring this topic up because it represents in the extreme a case of lead and lag: the number of jokes told by your boss may be a leading indicator of performance. So does that mean you should link the number and quality of one-liners uttered by your stand-up CEO to his pay? I don't think so. Using leading indicators in the calculation of incentive compensation can be problematic because these drivers of future performance frequently focus more on activities than outcomes. Let's say you hypothesize that *appearances at trade shows* is a leading indicator of *sales to new customers,* and thus link it to compensation. Your sales staff may rack up hundreds of thousands of miles going from show to show just to make an appearance, all the while paying only scant attention to customers. Remember that you're attempting to reward results by bonding the Scorecard to compensation, and as such you must focus your efforts on the lagging indicators of performance. Again, the key is balance. A healthy and appropriate mix of lead and lag indicators in the compensation pot ensures that your staff is focusing both on results today and the determinants of sustaining that success.

- *Thresholds and targets.* Linking incentive compensation to a variety of Balanced Scorecard metrics opens the door to the possibility of distributing awards although your company's financial performance has been subpar. For that reason, many organizations pursuing pay for performance will institute a threshold that must be met before any rewards are distributed. In most cases, this yardstick comes in the form of a financial metric, typically return on equity or return on investment. The idea is simple: Keep all employees riveted on the notion that meeting financial targets is of paramount importance and must be achieved before any incentives will be shared. All measures forming part of the compensation plan must have targets, and standard practice for most companies is the use of multiple target bands, with each exemplifying increasing degrees of stretch. Threshold performance equates to a minimum standard, while midpoint suggests greater effort, but promises enhanced rewards. Finally, stretch performance normally represents best-in-class performance and results in significant upside awards for employees if the goal is achieved. Using these strata of achievement ensures that employees are not satisfied with the status quo but instead focus on ever-greater levels of effort, which results in enhanced performance for the company and fatter pocketbooks for them.

- *Different types of rewards.* The wealthy among us have always enjoyed the extravagance that comes in the form of custom-made products. Now, though, personalized goods and services are increasingly within the budgets of all. Computers, the Internet, DNA research, and other technologies are creating a whole new paradigm that makes possible the delivery of custom-designed products to the masses, at ever lower prices. Microsoft founder Bill Gates has described the phenomenon of mass customization this way: *"Once you know exactly what you want, you'll be able to get it just that way. . . . Computers will enable goods that today are mass-produced to be both mass-produced and custom-made for particular customers."*[16] While the drive is on for companies to offer customized solutions to ever more discerning customers, they frequently hold this innovative spirit in check when designing incentive plans, launching mass programs for all employees despite individual wishes or preferences.

  This certainly doesn't have to be the case, because financial rewards may be seamlessly supplemented with intangible awards, which can provide an equally powerful dose of pride and satisfaction for employees. I have a friend whose company rewards outstanding performance with tickets to sold-out events such as concerts and plays. Others allow star performers to choose their own perks, which may range from attending the lecture of a famous speaker to sitting on the 50-yard line of next year's Super Bowl. Offering such out-of-the-box rewards isn't really breakthrough thinking on behalf of organizations; it is simply recognition that employees, like customers, are individuals possessing unique desires and preferences that must be met.

- *Frequent reporting of results.* Employers engage in pay-for-performance schemes because they want their people focused with laser-like precision on the metrics that will propel the business forward. Of course, in our modern world, attention spans are shorter than sunny January days in Anchorage, Alaska, so it's imperative to report results frequently if you expect to keep employee focus riding in high gear. Linking incentives to metrics that are calculated once a year—employee satisfaction is a possible example—will hardly galvanize employee actions because the results are so far in the future as to seem an eternity away. Your team needs swift performance information it can act on now to determine where it stands and what must be done to earn the promised rewards. In Chapter Two, I introduced the dramatic turnaround at Continental Airlines, which resulted in part from their use of key performance measures as a means to maintain focus. Continental also relied heavily on monthly incentives during their reinvention. During each month when the airline ranked among the top five in on-time departures, every member of its 35,000 nonmanagerial personnel received a cash bonus of $65. The program was so successful that the company soon raised the bar, challenging employees to vault on-time departure percentages to the ranks of the top three in the industry. Again, management's faith was rewarded as employees enthusiastically rose to the challenge, ultimately helping the company avert bankruptcy and climb to profits of $385 million just two years later.[17]

Despite the many challenges appearing in the preceding pages, a Scorecard and compensation bond can offer a legitimate win-win proposition to the organization and employees alike. Companies benefit from the enhanced focus and motivation leading to the achievement of Scorecard targets, while employees' wallets have the potential to swell up thanks to a well-deserved windfall. But is it worth the significant effort necessary to craft an effective program? Fortunately, research is beginning to catch up to the gut instinct that tells us this union of Balanced Scorecard and incentive compensation is a worthwhile endeavor. In one study sponsored by Mercer Human Resources Consulting, 88% of respondents considered the use of Balanced Scorecard measures linked to reward systems to be effective.[18] Money may or may not make the world go round, but it certainly can grease the wheel of your Balanced Scorecard, making it far more appealing and potentially profitable to the employees whose support you count on when implementing the system.

THE BALANCED SCORECARD AND CORPORATE GOVERNANCE

The Call for Change

"I don't sense an enthusiastic pursuit of the fundamental principles of corporate governance even today. . . . I see a reluctant minimalist approach, staying one step ahead of the regulators more than anything else."[19] So says Intel CEO Andrew Grove, reflecting the deep skepticism that casts a suspicious shadow over the corporate governance practices in place at most corporations today. While cries for governance reform are not new—since the 1970s, for example, there has been concern over the independence of directors—recent highly publicized corporate failures such as those at Enron, WorldCom, and elsewhere have heightened the hysteria and significantly increased the sense of urgency surrounding governance reforms.

Specifics vary from company to company, but the role of corporate Boards may be summarized with the following three key responsibilities:[20]

1. *Oversight of the company's strategic direction and risk management.* Challenging strategic direction, providing insight, and identifying, monitoring, and managing risk.

2. *Ensuring accountability.* Making certain ethical behavior is displayed, ensuring compliance, and providing internal and external stakeholders with reliable information for decision making.

3. *Evaluating performance and senior-level staffing.* Evaluating corporate, CEO, and Board performance, and selecting a qualified chief executive.

A failure to competently perform these vital tasks can wreak havoc on individual companies and economies alike, as a glance at the business pages on most mornings will attest. At Enron the failing took place principally within the audit committee of the Board, while at WorldCom the willingness of directors to approve lavish loans and compensation proved to be the weak link that would result in the company's undoing. Bankruptcy proceedings typically follow these ignominious lapses, and while such events are devastating at any company, regardless of their size and scope of operations, when you're talking hundreds of billions of dollars and the loss of thousands of jobs, the results can often be cataclysmic for those affected.

What Boards of Directors Really Need

In the wake of the debilitating scandals plaguing the corporate world, the U.S. government has enacted some of the toughest securities and governance legislation to hit businesses since the 1930s. The headliner of this wave of government intervention is the much-discussed and debated Sarbanes-Oxley Act of 2002. Undoubtedly, the Act has our best interests at heart, but the law of unintended consequences being ever-present, it has also spawned many significant challenges for organizations attempting to comply with its prodigious sections and subsections. The primary challenge is simply finding the time and resources to complete the tasks mandated by Sarbanes-Oxley, with some organizations suggesting that thousands of hours must be dedicated to the task annually.

It's too early to tell whether these reforms are directly leading to a reduction in corporate malfeasance, but at the very least it would be comforting to learn that perceptions were changing. Sadly, that is not necessarily the case, as a recent study indicates. In conjunction with the Directorship Search Group and the Institutional Investors Institute, consulting giant McKinsey surveyed 150 U.S. corporate directors serving as members of Boards of more than 300 public companies across all economic sectors and 44 U.S.-based fund managers with a total of $3 trillion in assets under management, on the topic of Board governance. Asking "To what extent recent reforms have improved Board governance?" 63%

of the directors and 83% of the fund managers replied "a little or moderately."[21] Considering the thousands of staff-hours and millions of dollars dedicated to compliance with these new standards, this finding is somewhat discouraging to say the least.

Perhaps the heavy hand of the law is not all that is required in implementing the massive changes necessary to restore trust and confidence in corporate governance. A root-cause analysis of the shortcomings affecting Boards of Directors may reveal a more fundamental issue—the lack of in-depth knowledge about their business's strategy and operations. Recent studies have suggested that upwards of 40% of directors don't sufficiently understand their firm's value-creation process.[22] This is not surprising when you consider that the average Board member spends just 90 hours per year on Board business, much of which is spent sitting in meetings for which the preparation amounts to a cursory glance at a thick binder handed to the unsuspecting Board member as she walks through the door.

To fulfill their significant, and now highly regulated, responsibilities, Board members require information that goes beyond high-level graphs and abstractions and provides a penetrating view inside the organization's strategy and value-creating mechanisms. Going a step further, management professor and governance catalyst Edward Lawler has suggested that Boards need a Balanced Scorecard to illuminate corporate performance: *"Boards need indicators of how customers and employees feel they are being treated...how the company operates...about the culture of the organization."*[23] In retrospect it seems as plain as the nose on my face—of course, the Balanced Scorecard should be utilized to advantage by time- and information-starved Board members. After all, it reflects the translation of the organization's strategy, providing a complete map of landmarks on the journey to strategic success, and supplying a concise tale explaining how the seemingly disparate elements comprising the tool weave together to create the firm's competitive advantage. It's all there: financial yardsticks craved by public markets, the customer value proposition feeding the economic engine, the key internal processes that resolutely chug along in creating value day in and day out, and finally, the human, information, and organizational capital awaiting transformation into tangible results. This is the information of substance Boards can use as raw materials for meaningful dialogue and debate on strategy and operations, as they work to fulfill their sacrosanct obligations.

The Next Frontier: Board of Directors Balanced Scorecards

The corporate Balanced Scorecard significantly enhances the Board's oversight capacity by providing a revealing glimpse into the strategy execution efforts of the company, but today's directors, facing unprecedented pressure to adhere to leading-edge governance standards, require a tool to assess their own performance as well. Enter the Board Balanced Scorecard, an emerging tool in the arsenal of pioneering Boards wishing to maximize their contribution to corporate performance and sustain the ability to add value in the years to come through the identification and evaluation of key performance measures utilizing the proven Scorecard framework. As a first step in the Board Scorecard process, a strategy map of objectives, such as the generic example in Exhibit 7.4, should be constructed.[24] Let's work through the four perspectives of this map, outlining the considerations that must be made when selecting objectives.

Should the Board capably perform their required tasks, there is an assumption that those efforts will contribute to the corporation's ability to achieve financial success. Therefore, the *Financial* objectives comprising the Board strategy map should be drawn directly from the organization's corporate strategy map. As discussed in Chapter Four, this will normally include an overarching objective relating to shareholder value, as well as objectives that outline how the organization will achieve the dual objectives of increasing productivity (through cost reductions and improved asset utilization) and growing revenue (from selling new products or deepening relationships with existing customers).

The customer perspective for this map has been renamed to *Stakeholder*, in recognition of the many groups who have a stake in the Board's performance. Thus, the initial task in crafting objectives for this perspective is determining the stakeholder groups who must be satisfied as the Board works to fulfill its obligations. From the objectives appearing in Exhibit 7.4, we might infer that this Board has chosen shareholders and employees as the critical stakeholder groups. "Ensuring compliance and accountability" will allow stockholders to sleep a little easier, secure in the knowledge that the Board has their best interests at heart. While not explicitly stated, society at large will also benefit from this objective, avoiding the high costs of litigation, productivity declines, and unemployment that frequently result from corporate shenanigans. Shareholders will also be pleased to see the Board engaged in "Approving and monitoring corporate performance." Finally, all employees will benefit from the Board's "Counseling the CEO and monitoring executive performance."

The *Internal Processes* objectives articulate how the outcomes in the stakeholder perspective will be achieved through efficient and effective Board processes. In order to achieve compliance and accountability, as shown in the stakeholder perspective, this Board must ensure compliance with all laws and regulations, make certain the company has effective internal controls, and diligently work to improve disclosure practices, improving transparency and visibility into the firm's operations. Stakeholders also demand that the Board approve strategy and monitor corporate performance, thus internal processes must be developed to achieve this significant undertaking. In this example the Board will monitor performance using the company's corporate Balanced Scorecard, approve funding for, and monitor strategic initiatives to ensure that spending is aligned with

EXHIBIT 7.4   Board of Directors Strategy Map

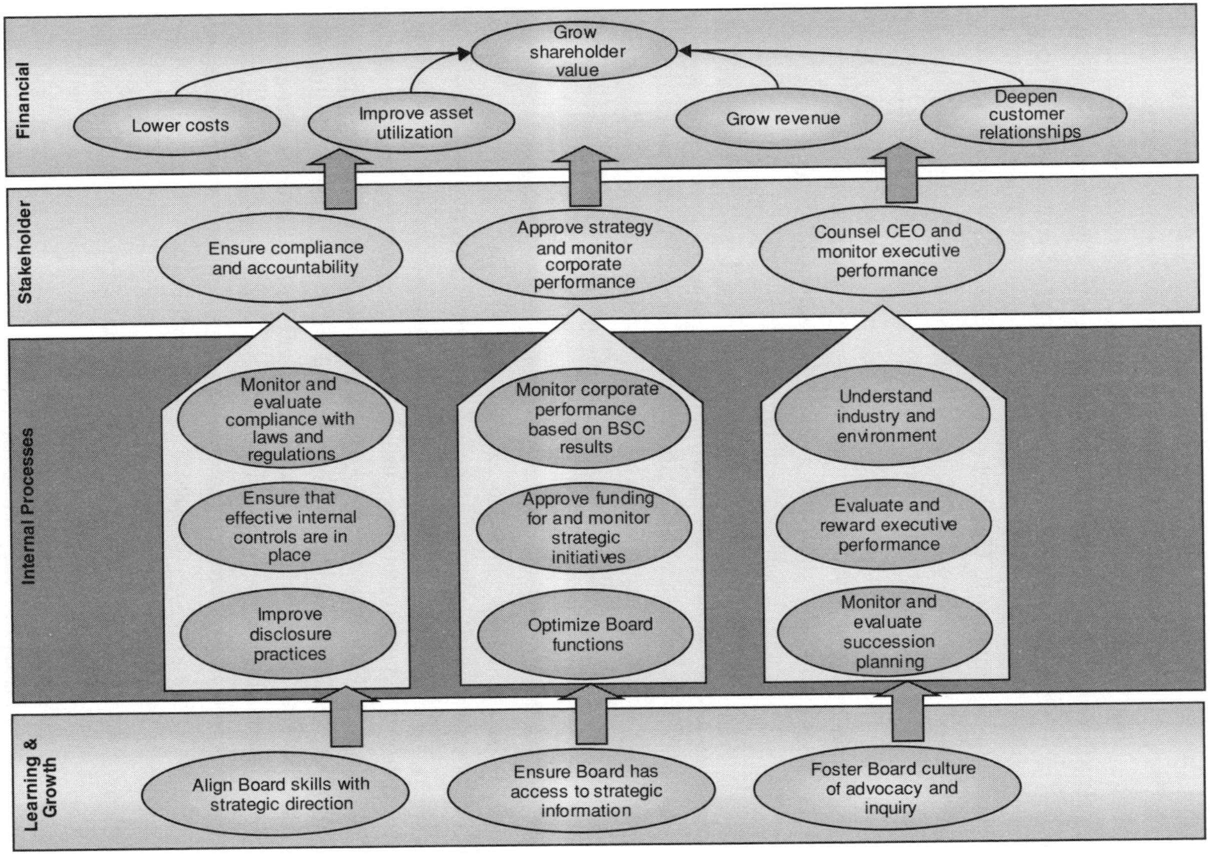

Financial

- Lower costs
- Improve asset utilization
- Grow shareholder value
- Grow revenue
- Deepen customer relationships

Stakeholder

- Ensure compliance and accountability
- Approve strategy and monitor corporate performance
- Counsel CEO and monitor executive performance

Internal Processes

- Monitor and evaluate compliance with laws and regulations
- Ensure that effective internal controls are in place
- Improve disclosure practices

- Monitor corporate performance based on BSC results
- Approve funding for and monitor strategic initiatives
- Optimize Board functions

- Understand industry and environment
- Evaluate and reward executive performance
- Monitor and evaluate succession planning

Learning & Growth

- Align Board skills with strategic direction
- Ensure Board has access to strategic information
- Foster Board culture of advocacy and inquiry

159

strategy, and finally, optimize their own functions such as Board structure and procedures in an effort to ensure that they function as efficiently as possible. A major endeavor of any Board is counseling the CEO and monitoring executive performance. This Board will attempt to achieve that objective by first ensuring that they have a firm grasp on the company's industry and underlying economic and political environment. Evaluating and rewarding executive performance and monitoring succession planning ensure that successful executives are rewarded for a job well done, and a pipeline of future leaders is waiting in the wings.

A well-constructed *Learning and Growth* perspective must contain objectives focused on three separate but integrated dimensions of capital: human, information, and organizational. Under the mantle of human capital, the Board represented in Exhibit 7.4 will work to ensure that its skills align with the firm's strategic direction. Board members must possess the requisite financial literacy and business acumen to contribute meaningfully in their capacity. Regarding information capital, the Board must press the company to provide access to strategic information if they wish to provide insight and effectively monitor corporate performance. Finally, it's vital for the Board to approach their work with a spirit of advocacy and inquiry. Some governance experts have suggested that Board members don't behave effectively in meetings, demonstrating an unwillingness to raise important issues and challenge the CEO on the firm's current performance and strategic direction. Boards must rise to this challenge by balancing the seemingly competing demands of advocating on behalf of the firm, acting as a tireless champion for it, while also serving the needs and preserving the trust and confidence of stakeholders by encouraging robust dialogue on challenging and potentially controversial issues.

The strategy map paints a compelling picture of the Board's endeavors, but for day-in and day-out tracking of performance, the Board must next translate the objectives into performance measures and targets. Strategic initiatives—the projects relied on to achieve targets—must also be brainstormed, funded, and monitored for effective performance. And what are the payoffs awaiting Boards that are proactive enough to make this leap of faith into the Balanced Scorecard world? For starters, effectiveness and efficiency of Board operations will benefit tremendously as Board members glean new insights into their core activities and are supplied with the ingredients they need to divert attention away from the perfunctory reviews of the past and squarely on the dialogue that will ignite the opportunities of the future. Stakeholders will undoubtedly applaud this intrepid move as well, because their interests are further highlighted with public commitments to safeguard their investments printed in black and white on the Board's Balanced Scorecard. This transparency and enhanced visibility not only ensures improved Board functioning but may also have positive financial ramifications for the company—one study recently suggested that more than 75% of institutional investors surveyed were prepared to pay a premium for well-governed companies.[25]

SELF-ASSESSMENT QUESTIONS

Strategic Resource Allocation:
The Balanced Scorecard and Budgeting

1. Before linking the budget process to the Balanced Scorecard, did we convene a planning council and communicate the new process to stakeholders throughout the organization?

2. Have we cascaded the Scorecard throughout the organization, ensuring the inclusion of objectives, measures, targets, and initiatives in all?

3. Have we created easy-to-understand and easy-to-complete budget submission forms for budget preparers?

4. Have we aggregated budget spending by strategy and objective?

5. Do we finalize our budget based on the strategic importance of initiatives appearing in Balanced Scorecards?

Linking Pay with Performance:
The Balanced Scorecard and Compensation

1. Before commencing our Balanced Scorecard and compensation linkage, did we communicate the purpose of the plan and clearly explain how rewards will be earned and distributed?

2. Do we have an accepted rationale for who could participate in the incentive compensation plan?

3. Do we base incentive awards on individual performance, group performance, or both?

4. Have we balanced incentive awards across the four perspectives of the Balanced Scorecard?

5. Does our incentive compensation plan contain the critical measures of our success?

6. Have we ensured that any leading indicators in the incentive compensation plan focus more on outcomes than activities?

7. Did we institute a financial threshold that must be met before any Scorecard-based incentives will be paid?

8. Have we supplemented financial awards in the incentive compensation pool with intangible rewards sought after by employees?

9. To ensure employee focus on Scorecard results, do we report results, and calculate payouts, frequently?

The Balanced Scorecard and Corporate Governance

1. Do we regularly share Balanced Scorecard results with our Board of Directors, ensuring that the Board agenda is shaped by the Balanced Scorecard?

2. Has our Board created a strategy map and Balanced Scorecard?

3. Do we regularly monitor Board performance using their Balanced Scorecard?

NOTES

1. Jeremy Hope and Robin Fraser, "Who Needs Budgets?" *Harvard Business Review*, February 2003, p. 111.

2. Ibid., p. 109.

3. Robert S. Kaplan and David P. Norton, *The Strategy Focused Organization* (Boston, MA: Harvard Business School Press, 2001).

4. Paul R. Niven, *Balanced Scorecard Step by Step for Government and Nonprofit Agencies* (New York: John Wiley & Sons, Inc., 2003).

5. Abigail J. Sellen and Richard H. R. Harper, *The Myth of the Paperless Office* (Cambridge, MA: MIT Press, 2001).

6. See note 4.

7. Nitin Nohria, William Joyce, and Bruce Robertson, "What Really Works," *Harvard Business Review*, July 2003, p. 46.

8. See for example: Elspeth J. Murray and Peter Richardson, *Fast Forward: Organizational Change in 100 Days* (New York: Oxford University Press, 2002), p. 112.

9. Tanya N. Ballard, "House Passes Pay for Performance Measure, *GovExec.com*, May 23, 2003.

10. Jack Welch with John A. Byrne, *Jack, Straight from the Gut* (New York: Warner Business Books, 2001).

11. Jonathan D. Day, Paul Y. Mang, Ansgar Richter, and John Roberts, "Has Pay for Performance Had Its Day?" *The McKinsey Quarterly*, Number 4, 2002.

12. Todd Manas, "Making the Balanced Scorecard Approach Pay Off," *ACA Journal*, Second Quarter, 1999.

13. Gary Loveman, "Diamonds in the Data Mine," *Harvard Business Review*, May 2003, p. 113.

14. Andrea Gabor, *The Capitalist Philosophers* (New York: Times Business, 2000), p. 319.

15. Fabio Sala, "Laughing All the Way to the Bank," *Harvard Business Review*, September 2003, p. 16.

16. Richard Alm, "America's Move to Mass-Customization," *Consumers' Research Magazine*, June 1, 1999.

17. Marc Knez and Duncan Simester, "Making Across-the-Board Incentives Work," *Harvard Business Review*, February 2002, p. 16.

18. Mercer Human Resources Consulting, *Study of Compensation Practices in 214 Companies*, 1999.

19. John M. Holcomb, "Corporate Governance: Sarbanes-Oxley Act, Related Legal Issues and Global Comparisons," *Denver Journal of International Law and Policy*, March 22, 2004.

20. Marc J. Epstein and Marie-Josee Roy, "Measuring and Improving Performance of Corporate Boards," *CMA Canada Strategic Management Accounting Practices*, 2002.

21. Robert F. Felton, "What Directors and Investors Want from Governance Reform," *McKinsey Quarterly*, Number 2, 2004.

22. R. Felton and M. Watson, "The need for informed change in the boardroom," *McKinsey Quarterly*, Number 4, 2002.

23. "Board Governance and Accountability," An Interview with Edward E. Lawler III, *Balanced Scorecard Report*, January-February 2003, p. 12.

24. In preparing this generic map, I have drawn on the work performed in this area by Michael Nagel of the Balanced Scorecard Collaborative, as presented in a Balanced Scorecard Collaborative NetConference on May 27, 2004.

25. McKinsey and Company, 2002 Global Investor Opinion Survey: Key Findings.

CHAPTER 8

Sharing Balanced Scorecard Results: Reporting and Strategy-Centered Management Meetings

O ne of my favorite old jokes is about a man who, in desperation, prays to the Almighty that he might win the lottery. In case you've never heard it, here goes: One Sunday, Gus walks into a church and kneels down at the altar and begins to pray to God, stating that he owes many people money, and asks to win the lottery. After he is done praying, he gets up and walks out. The next Sunday he goes to the same church and pleads with God through his prayers to let him win the lottery so that he can pay these people back. The next Sunday comes around and Gus enters the church very upset and close to tears. He kneels at the altar and asks why God is doing this to him and says that he has asked to win the lottery for three weeks now and nothing. Suddenly, there came a loud bang of thunder and God spoke, "Gus, meet me halfway: Buy a ticket!"[1]

Poor Gus could have spent an eternity praying for relief from his debts, but without a ticket, dashed hopes and sore knees are about all he could have expected. Building a Balanced Scorecard and not rapidly sharing results is similar to hoping to hit the jackpot on the lottery without troubling yourself to buy a ticket. When you develop a Scorecard system you have the highest of expectations: alignment from top to bottom throughout the company, a crystal clear focus on strategy, and better resource allocation decisions, to list a few. None of these admirable goals will be achieved if you don't widely communicate Scorecard results to employees and encourage the stimulating dialogue that results from an examination of your progress. I'm sure you found the challenge of developing the strategy map and performance measures comprising your Scorecard a thought-provoking and worthwhile endeavor, but until you take the steps of sharing results and discussing what those results tell you about your business, you're simply praying to win the strategy lottery, and your knowledge will be as bankrupt as our friend Gus waiting in vain to cash in.

In the first section of this chapter, we'll explore the mechanics of sharing Balanced Scorecard results, specifically examining the use of software designed for this capacity and other low-tech but no less creative methods in place at organizations today. But getting your results out is simply the bait you'll use to catch the big fish in this pond: strategic learning. For those of you who have yet to venture into the Scorecard software market, an appendix provides several elements to consider when making the purchase decision. The chapter also delves into the theory and practice of the new strategy-centered management meeting, one based on a discussion of the Balanced Scorecard, and designed to stimulate creativity and breakthrough thinking on the vital subject of executing your unique strategy.

REPORTING BALANCED SCORECARD RESULTS

Balanced Scorecard Software Systems

When discussing the topic of Balanced Scorecard software systems in my second book, *Balanced Scorecard Step by Step for Government and Nonprofit Agencies,* I noted that while writing I was curious about the number of hits I might find on the Web if I typed "Balanced Scorecard" and "software" into a search engine. My query returned 44,000 hits—an enormous number—but I predicted that by the time readers were turning the pages of the book the number would have mushroomed significantly. Interested in an update, I decided to run the test again as I write these words in late 2004, about two years after my last foray into this subject. The result: an astronomical 187,000 hits. Technology has become an integral part of virtually every facet of our professional and personal lives, and the Balanced Scorecard has not been spared in this tsunami of activity, with more than 100 vendors currently offering Scorecard solutions to the ever-expanding roster of organizations employing the tool. Software veterans are competing tenaciously alongside innovative niche players in an attempt to carve out a slice of this lucrative pie, but a question remains: Does the use of software significantly enhance the Balanced Scorecard experience?

Users and pundits unite in the rallying cry suggesting that Scorecard software is an essential ingredient to any successful implementation. Among the benefits they rightly trumpet are real-time information retrieval using Web interfaces, which have become increasingly popular in more recent offerings; the ability to drill down within the organization to acquire more detailed information on performance; enhanced data quality as a result of automatic interfaces; warning symbols to alert you when key metrics fall out of a desired range; and the ability to streamline cascading efforts, which can be accomplished much more swiftly thanks to technology. Today's leading software products also allow you to move beyond Balanced Scorecard reporting and draw in other critical aspects of the implementation, such as initiative tracking and human capital linkages to strategy. As the Scorecard continues to evolve, with practitioners and theoreticians pushing the envelope on creative applications for the tool, technology will continue to be a tremendous ally, enabling the important changes that allow organizations to learn about their strategy execution in real time. A screen shot from one of the many software vendors in this space is shown in Exhibit 8.1.

Technology isn't always a bed of roses brilliantly illuminated by the pretty colors coming from your monitor, however, and there are risks to be considered. One of the principal dangers of using Scorecard software is having the system "become" the Balanced Scorecard in the minds of users. Some organizations will launch Scorecard software tools in conjunction with the development of strategy maps and measures in an attempt to rev up support for the tool and enhance the Scorecard learning experience. Users, however, who are already inundated with change and its attendant technology offerings, often miss the finer points of the Balanced Scorecard, lost in a sea of dazzling graphics and sophisticated reports provided by the software system. I've seen this happen with damaging effects, as organizations fail to provide the requisite knowledge of the theoretical underpinnings of the Balanced Scorecard, electing instead to focus on the software, only to find themselves having to redouble their efforts later in the implementation as confused software users throw up their hands in despair, claiming, "I just don't get this Balanced Scorecard system." The key word to remember when investing in Scorecard software is *enabler*. The technology enables and enhances the Scorecard experience by providing many benefits not supplied by paper reports, but it is not the Scorecard and should not be billed that way.

One of the most seductive aspects of Balanced Scorecard software is its impressive array of functions, but it is also another potential trouble spot. Although we're living in the technology-crazed climate of the 21st century, many of the executives and senior-level managers at the helm of our organizations are computer neophytes, to say the least, and may even harbor a healthy dose of fear for what lurks beyond their computer screens in the land of bits and bytes. It's not uncommon for companies to spend vast sums of money for technology only to have executives—the very group that should benefit most from the tool— request all of their Scorecard reports on paper. Fortunately, a significant proportion of the risks associated with Scorecard software systems can be mitigated with thoughtful training, balancing the need to educate users on the theoretical con-

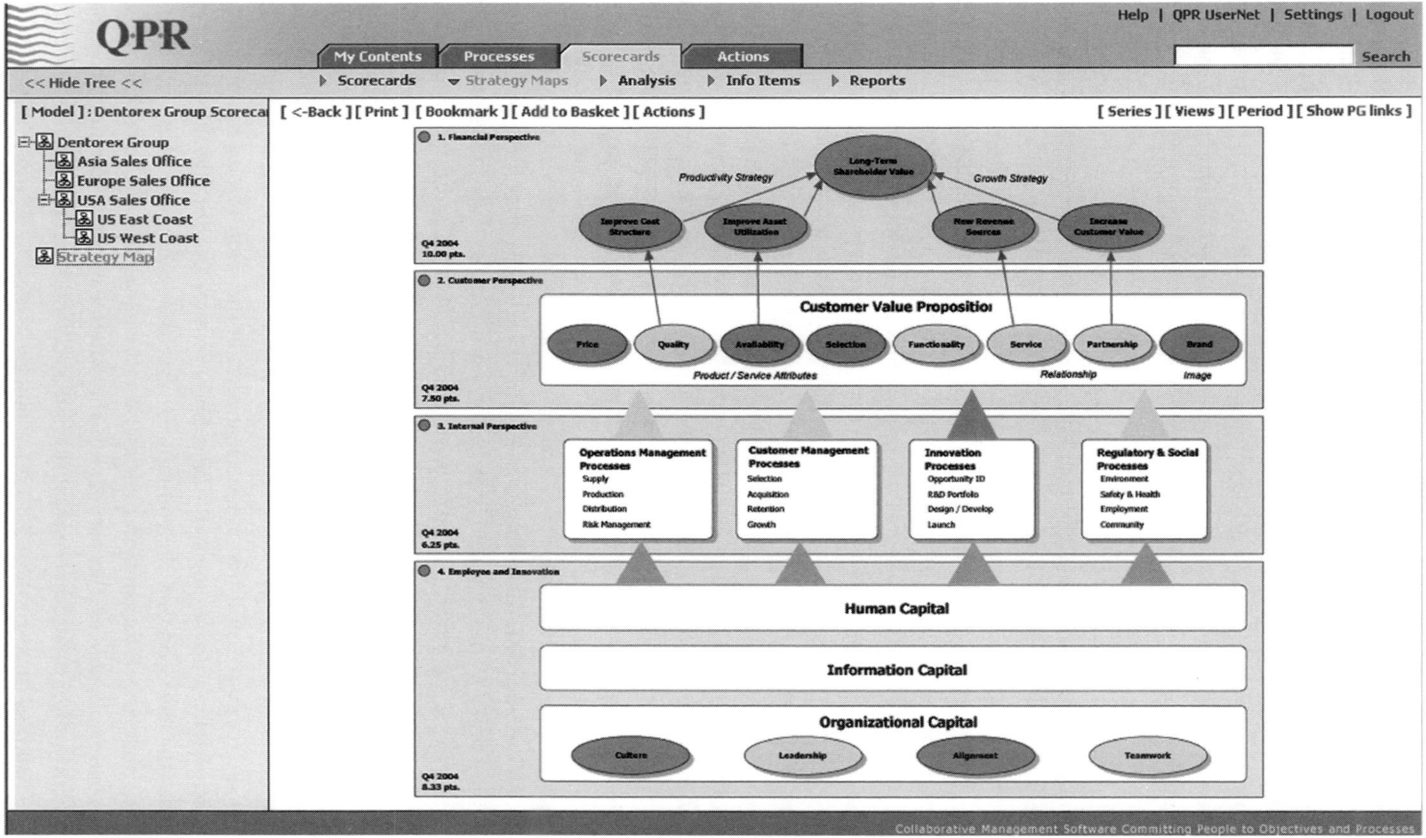

EXHIBIT 8.1 Screen Shot from a Balanced Scorecard Software System

structs of the Scorecard system along with the software, which will allow for maximum benefits to be derived from using the Scorecard framework.

Alternative Methods of Reporting Balanced Scorecard Results

Software isn't the only game in town when it comes to reporting Balanced Scorecard results. When you combine the potent forces of desktop publishing tools in place at most companies today with old-fashioned employee ingenuity, the possibilities for creatively sharing Scorecard results with your staff are virtually limitless. This low-tech option should not be viewed as software's poor cousin; in fact, many of the earliest Scorecard adopters, organizations pioneering the use of the system in the early 1990s, generated tremendous results for their firms in an age when Scorecard technology systems were still just a glint in the eyes of ambitious software programmers who were more familiar with baseball scorecards than Balanced Scorecards.

Homegrown Scorecard solutions come in a variety of shapes and sizes, but many will follow a familiar pattern: a cover page bearing a color-coded version of the organization's strategy map, followed by graph- and commentary-filled pages reporting results of each of the company's performance measures. These reports are relatively simple to complete, and they provide comfort to those of us preferring the tactile pleasures afforded by paper-based reports. Unfortunately, these reports also tend to suffer one of two equally ignominious fates at the hands of time-starved managers and employees: being sandwiched into a dust-collecting binder sitting on a cluttered shelf or, following a cursory glance complete with the requisite number of "umm hmmms" and head nods, being tossed into the nearest recycling bin.

Peter Murphy, CEO of EpicData, had another idea when it came to reporting Balanced Scorecard results at this information technology firm dedicated to the continuous advancement of integrated data capture, processing, and dissemination solutions. He understood the value of a piece of paper containing useful information, but he wanted to ensure that the Scorecard reports he issued had a shelf life longer than the duration of a typical coffee break. Working with a small team in the company, Peter developed one of the most innovative reporting vehicles—and vehicles is the operative word here—I've ever encountered: the Balanced Scorecard three-wheeled board. Mr. Murphy and EpicData Business Analyst Erin Dalzell are shown viewing recent results in Exhibit 8.2. Each month, Scorecard results are faithfully pasted to the roaming conversation piece, and it is sent on its way through the corridors of this dynamic technology enterprise. Managers have embraced the unusual reporting device and shuttle the board into all department meetings, referring to recent developments on the strategic indicators that grace its walls, and encouraging staff to engage in fresh thinking that will propel the company forward. When it is not serving as the tri-wheeled

EXHIBIT 8.2   Balanced Scorecard Results Board of EpicData

agenda for department meetings, employees will find the board gracing common areas of the company's offices, such as break and lunch rooms. Mr. Murphy has noticed employees congregating around the board, reflecting on results and engaging in informal conversations that frequently lead to questions being directed at him, which he welcomes as a signal that people are thinking about the company's strategy and customers—always a positive thing.

Realizing that information preferences vary widely within organizations, EpicData supplements the reporting board with intranet Scorecard reports and a monthly newsletter, "At Epic," which includes, among a host of topics, a schedule of the company's key initiatives. The latest progress, key milestones, and commentaries are posted to ensure that employees are fully informed of the company's efforts in creating a leadership position in their field. EpicData's reporting tools—the results board, intranet, and newsletter—work in concert to ensure that employees are fully informed of the latest results and have the data they need to facilitate strategic decision making.

The choice between investing in a Scorecard software solution and relying on paper-based reporting is predicated on several factors, including your sensitivity to the cost factor, comfort with manually loaded data, and the level of technical sophistication residing in your company, to name but a few. But regardless of how you report results, you must ensure that the reporting mechanism is being actively used by your employees. The most technologically slick package available today or the archetype of creative paper reports on their own will not help you execute your strategy—that desirable event occurs when people interact with the information contained in the system and take informed action as a result. Therefore, it is incumbent upon you to monitor the effectiveness of your reporting system through usage statistics. The ultimate lagging indicators are an increase in knowledge of vision and strategy and improved results on Scorecard measures. Leading indicators to track in the interim include the number of hits on your Scorecard intranet, number of questions posted to the site, downloads of Scorecard information, and number of presentations requested of your Balanced Scorecard team.

THE STRATEGY-CENTERED MANAGEMENT MEETING

At various points throughout this text, I've quoted from a book titled *Execution,* by former Honeywell International Chairman Larry Bossidy and consultant to the CEO stars, Ram Charan. The subtitle of the book is "The Discipline of Getting Things Done," which represents beautifully the essence of the new strategy-centered management meeting: sharing Balanced Scorecard results, discussing the implications, learning about the strategy, and taking action to execute it. Sadly, many organizations fall dreadfully short on this critical leg of the measurement journey. They go to the often significant effort of collecting data and dutifully producing the colorful charts, but rather than taking the next logical step of establishing a dialogue on what the results are telling them, the process comes to a screeching halt. As two researchers described it recently:

> The whole process of measuring performance is completely wasted unless action is taken on the performance data that are collected. Far too often, and in far too many organizations, management fails to do this. They produce the charts. They produce the reports, but then they fail to analyze the data and decide what they are going to do differently inside the organization to make sure that next month's figures are better than this month's figures. It is almost as if managers today have become so obsessed with measuring performance, that they no longer have time to act on the performance data once they have been gathered.[2]

Even those organizations that do carve out a sliver of time to discuss results frequently end up dwelling on operational details and budget line items, crowding out any room for the tough and honest questions that must be asked when assessing the business's progress and future prospects.[3] The real victim here is the company's strategy, laying to waste at the altar of operational effectiveness as executives endlessly debate the latest cost and budget figures rather than shining a light on the company's ability to differentiate itself and execute. Speaking more empirically, recent studies suggest that the top management of most companies spends a scant three hours per month discussing strategy, and as much as 80% of their time is devoted to issues that account for less than 20% of their long-term value. At one global financial services firm participating in the survey cited previously, a senior executive reported that top executives spent more time each year selecting the company's holiday greeting card than debating their strategy for the entire continent of Africa, where they had made significant capital investment.[4] Think of that the next time you open a card from your boss!

Even companies held in the highest regard of the business press and shareholders alike can suffer from the abject inability to effectively discuss performance results. Lou Gerstner discovered such a problem when he assumed the leadership of corporate icon IBM in 1993. He convened a strategy meeting—well attended by senior managers, each accompanied by legions of assistants—but was bitterly disappointed to see his team listening somberly to a PowerPoint presentation and engaging in virtually no discussion. Gerstner was so frustrated by the lack of dialogue that he turned off the overhead projector with what he called "the click heard around the world," and insisted on real conversation taking place.[5]

Success doesn't happen by accident. The companies that execute are those recognizing the vital role played by tenacious questioning of results in an atmosphere fused with both inquiry and accountability. Let's now turn our attention to how you can stage a strategy-centered meeting featuring the Balanced Scorecard, in the process taking your reporting to the next level of rigor and discipline. Those of you who are new to the concept of strategy-centered management meetings may have many questions; therefore, a question-and-answer format is used for the ensuing discussion.

How Often Should We Hold Meetings?

Hold your strategy-centered meetings at least quarterly, but even more frequently, monthly for example, if feasible. Are you rolling your eyes at that suggestion? It sounds aggressive, I know, but the fact of the matter is that you will find these meetings tend to be shorter than the marathon operation reviews you currently conduct. Such was the case with Brother Industries (USA), as Human

Resources director Stan Romanoff reported to me: *"Monthly meetings used to take hours because we reviewed very operational metrics. Now we use the Balanced Scorecard and simply go around the table discussing the metrics. The meetings are much simpler and more strategic."*[6]

Who Is Invited to Attend?

The strategy-centered Balanced Scorecard meeting signals a radical turn away from the antiquated command-and-control paradigm featuring meetings attended by only the most senior executives from your ranks. Strategy is the responsibility of everyone collecting a paycheck at your company, and therefore attendance should be a function of strategic contribution, not seniority or rank. Alongside your executive team, others filling the conference room for this exchange will be objective and measure owners (if other than executives) and employees possessing specific information that will shed light on performance measures or initiatives.

What Should We Do Before the Meeting?

Your primary responsibilities before the meeting consist of creating the agenda and distributing the materials that will be reviewed during the session. The Balanced Scorecard should not be *part* of the agenda, another item to be checked off in the endless list of to-do's stretching from here to eternity for most companies; it should be *the* agenda. Learning about strategy is the chief concern of this get-together, and because your Scorecard was derived directly from your strategy, what better tool to guide the discussion?

Materials for the session, in the form of Balanced Scorecard results, should be distributed to participants approximately one week in advance of the meeting. The package will normally include your strategy map, performance measure results, updates on initiatives, and any supporting material necessary to further illuminate what is contained in the Scorecard.

Who Facilitates the Meeting?

Your Balanced Scorecard champion or team leader should play the role of facilitator during the session. This individual is well-versed in the art and practice of the Scorecard, should be deeply involved in the preparation of results, and should possess an ability to liaise easily and comfortably with your executive team. Another compelling rationale for having your Scorecard champion lead the event is a lack of competing interests. While he or she hails from a specific department of the organization, first loyalty is to the Scorecard and its ability to execute strategy, not the esoteric concerns of a specific business unit.

How Do We Review Results?

You can follow several roads when determining specifically how results will be reviewed. If your strategy map relies heavily on strategic themes, knitting together objectives through all four perspectives, then you may wish to review results by those overarching vectors, focusing on the cause-and-effect linkages, and reviewing the hypothesis of your strategic story. Alternately, you could move sequentially through the map and measures, beginning with the Financial objectives and indicators and working progressively through the four perspectives. Finally, some organizations will conduct their reviews on an exception basis, choosing to focus first and foremost on those objectives and measures suffering from less than desirable performance. Of the three choices, the latter is the only one with which I have a problem. No one will argue the importance of learning from mistakes and gathering information when circumstances haven't turned out quite as you'd hoped; however, success can often be a wonderful teacher as well. The Scorecard relates to strategy, and if you discover strong performance on certain dimensions of your strategy, as indicated by breakthrough performance on your Scorecard, you can exploit that fortuitous turn of events by sharing best practices throughout your organization and ramping up efforts to sustain your success over the long haul.

Regardless of the choice you make, objective and measure owners should be prepared to present current results, outline the status of enabling initiatives, answer questions from the audience, and share their wisdom about how poor performance will be reversed or strong results sustained. The facilitator holds the responsibility for ensuring that the discussion remains at a strategic level and doesn't spiral into the quagmire of operational details. All objectives and measures should be reviewed during the session, not just those for which you currently have data. Any indicator that lacks data may have associated initiatives that can be examined, ensuring that once results can be tabulated they will reflect positive performance.

How Do We Establish the Right Tone for the Meeting?

The tone for any meeting is set primarily by the speech and body language of the most senior person present, and your strategy-centered Scorecard meeting is no different. In this setting, a spirit of discovery and learning from the past in order to execute effectively in the future is the most critical characteristic your leader can display. Participants must trust that bringing up bad news or challenging entrenched ideas will be accepted in an atmosphere of honest exchange and not supply them with a one-way ticket to the unemployment lines.

Civility is important, of course, but creative tension, and lots of it, is encouraged. Excellence should never be victimized by the unintended consequences of harmony, with a risk of hurt feelings given more weight than the potential benefits of putting a hard-hitting question to a colleague. In his study of companies that went from good to great, researcher Jim Collins found that those making the ascent shared the proclivity of passionate discussions: *"All the companies had a penchant for intense dialogue. Phrases like "loud debate," "heated discussions," and "healthy conflict" peppered the articles and interview transcripts from all of the companies."*[7] Your challenge is creating a haven of psychological safety in which attendees feel safe in voicing unpopular sentiments, while simultaneously fostering a culture that demands results and is willing to dig deep to get them. This may represent a cultural shift, perhaps of seismic proportions, for your company, so don't expect to hit a home run in your first meeting. With time and experience, and relying on both the facilitation skills of your champion and visionary leadership of your executives, you will find a tone that is right for you.

How Do We Ensure There Is Accountability?

This section began with a reference to the book *Execution*, so it's appropriate that we end with one as well. On the subject of accountability, and making the most of time spent in meetings, authors Bossidy and Charan are crystal clear: *"Never finish a meeting without clarifying what the follow-through will be, who will do it, when and how they will do it, what resources they will use, and how and when the next review will take place and with whom."*[8] Ideas are the currency of the knowledge economy, and during these sessions ideas will be flowing as freely as promises at a political convention. But as we all know, ideas are only as good as their execution, and they require directed action to reach fruition. Always compile a list of action items flagged during the meeting and ensure that updates are provided at the next gathering.

SELF-ASSESSMENT QUESTIONS

Reporting Balanced Scorecard Results

1. (For those using an automated reporting solution) Are we confident that our Balanced Scorecard software satisfies the criteria for design, reporting, technical, and maintenance considerations presented in the appendix of this chapter?

2. (For those using an automated reporting solution) Have we provided adequate training on both the Balanced Scorecard system and the software, allowing users to understand both, and do we recognize that the software tool is an enabler of the Balanced Scorecard?

3. (For those using either software or alternative reporting methods) Do we track statistics regarding our reporting tool, using both leading and lagging indicators?

The Strategy-Centered Management Meeting

1. Do we hold a strategy-centered meeting, using the Balanced Scorecard as an agenda, at least quarterly?

2. Do we open our strategy review meetings to anyone who is able to provide significant information on Scorecard results, or do we limit attendance to senior executives?

3. Are strategy-centered meetings strongly facilitated by our Balanced Scorecard champion?

4. Have we established a tone in our strategy review sessions that balances the psychological safety of participants with a desire to aggressively learn about our strategy?

5. Do we track action items raised during our meetings and ensure that they are reviewed at the subsequent session?

APPENDIX 8A: CHOOSING BALANCED SCORECARD SOFTWARE

The material appearing in this appendix is drawn from my two previous books *Balanced Scorecard Step by Step: Maximizing Performance and Maintaining Results* (Wiley, 2002) and *Balanced Scorecard Step by Step for Government and Nonprofit Agencies* (Wiley, 2003).

Selection of the right software for your organization is a crucial decision. Not only are you shopping for a system to report your Scorecard results and provide a platform for future evolution of the tool, but you must also ensure that whatever you buy will suit the needs of your workforce and be accepted as a useful tool. Software selection is typically done in five sequential steps:[9]

1. *Form a software team.* Just as we used a cross-functional team to develop your Scorecard, so too will we rely on several people to make the crucial software decision. Include your executive sponsor, Balanced Scorecard champion, a representative from your Information Technology (IT) group, and an individual representative of the typical Scorecard user. The team should begin its work by reviewing the current landscape of Scorecard software and speaking to end users regarding their requirements for this tool. Remember that different users will demand specific functionality. Execu-

tives may simply be interested in one-page summary reports, whereas analysts may focus on data input, retrieval, and complex reporting. The team should also develop a software project plan outlining key dates and milestones on the path to the software decision.

2. *Develop a short list of candidates.* You'll find dozens of potential vendors ready and willing to supply you with Scorecard software. Use the criteria presented in the following sections to help you determine three or four finalists.

3. *Submit a Request for Proposal (RFP).* Compile your needs and specifications into a document for distribution to your finalists. Each organization you contact should provide you with a written summary detailing how its product stacks up to your requirements.

4. *Arrange demonstrations.* Invite software candidates to conduct a demonstration of their product at your facility. To ensure that the demonstration is relevant to your needs, send a copy of your strategy map and measures to the vendor in advance, and have them base the demonstration on your data.

5. *Create a summary report and make your selection.* Determine which functionality and specifications are most vital to you, and rank each product against them. The software program that most closely matches your requirements should be selected.

Choosing the Software

Design Issues: Configuration of the Software

In this section we'll examine some Scorecard software setup and design elements:

- *Time to implement.* Software programs for the Balanced Scorecard can run the gamut from simple reporting tools to sophisticated enterprise-wide management solutions. Therefore, major differences exist in the time and resources necessary to implement the system. You must determine what your thresholds are in terms of timing and resource requirements necessary to have the system up and running.

- *Various Scorecard designs.* This book focuses exclusively on the methodology of the Balanced Scorecard; however, you may at some point wish to track other popular measurement alternatives such as the Baldrige criteria, total quality management (TQM) metrics, or any number of different methodologies. The software should be flexible enough to permit various performance management techniques.

- *User interface/display.* Most Balanced Scorecard software products will feature a predominant display metaphor. It may use gauges similar to those you'd see in the dashboard of a plane or automobile, boxes that are reminiscent of organizational charts, or color-coded dials. Some of these simply look better (i.e., more realistic and legitimate) than others. That may sound insignificant, but remember that you're counting on your workforce to use this software faithfully, and if they find the instrumentation unrealistic, or worse, unattractive, that could significantly impact their initial reaction and ongoing commitment.

- *Number of measures.* Some pundits suggest that the advent of sophisticated software tools has led to a proliferation in the number of measures appearing on the Balanced Scorecards of those employing such technology. I have mixed feelings on this criterion, because I believe too many measures can distort an organization's focus and blur what is truly important. However, your software must be equipped with the flexibility to handle a significant volume of measures to accommodate tracking results from across the organization.

- *Strategies, objectives, measures, targets, and initiatives.* As the backbone of the Scorecard system, you should be able to easily enter all of the above elements in the software. Additionally, the functionality of the tool should permit you to link objectives to perspectives, measures to objectives, targets to measures, and initiatives to targets.

- *Cause-and-effect relationships.* Your Scorecard software should provide a means of demonstrating the cause-and-effect linkages that describe your strategy. Capturing these strategy maps with compelling and easy-to-understand graphics is critical if you hope to benefit from the information sharing and collective learning to be derived from the Balanced Scorecard.

- *Multiple locations.* The software should accommodate the addition of performance measures from a variety of physical and nonphysical locations.

- *Descriptions and definitions.* Simply entering names and numbers into the software is not sufficient for communication and eventual analysis. Every field in which you enter information must be capable of accepting textual descriptions. Upon launching the software, the first thing most users will do when looking at a specific performance indicator is examine its description and definition.

- *Assignment of owners.* The Scorecard can only be used to enhance accountability if your software permits each performance indicator to be assigned to a specific owner. Because you may also have another individual acting as the owner's assistant and yet another as data enterer, it is beneficial if the software provides the ability to identify these functions as well.

- *Various unit types.* Your performance indicators are likely to come in all shapes, sizes, and descriptors, from raw numbers to dollars to percentages. The tool you choose must permit all measure types.

- *Appropriate timing.* Not all performance indicators will be tracked with the same degree of frequency. An item like sales could be tracked annually, quarterly, monthly, weekly, or even daily, while employee surveys are most likely conducted and reported only once or twice a year. However, you may wish to view past performance in different time increments than originally reported. For example, you may wish to view on-time delivery (reported monthly) annualized for the past two years. Your software should provide this flexibility.

- *Relative weights.* All measures on the Balanced Scorecard are important links in the description of your strategy. However, most organizations will place greater emphasis on certain indicators; perhaps financial measures are vital at the outset of your implementation. A good Scorecard tool should permit you to weight the measures according to their relative performance.

- *Aggregate disparate elements.* That description sounds a little complicated, but it simply means that your program should deliver the ability to combine performance measures with different unit types. This can best be accomplished with the use of weighting (see previous item). Measures are accorded a weight that drives the aggregation of results regardless of the specific unit type of each indicator.

- *Multiple comparatives.* Most organizations will track performance relative to a predefined target (e.g., the budget). However, it may be useful to examine performance in light of last year's performance, relative to your competition, or a best-in-class benchmarking number. Look for the software to allow several comparatives.

- *Graphic status indicators.* At a glance, users should be able to ascertain the performance of measures based on an easy-to-understand status indicator. Many programs will take advantage of our familiarity with red (stop), yellow (caution), and green (go) metaphors.

- *Dual polarity.* For the software to produce a color indicating measure performance, it must recognize whether high values for actual results represent good or bad performance. Up to a certain point, results might be considered good, but beyond a certain threshold they may be a cause for concern. For example, it may be perfectly appropriate for a call center representative to answer 15 calls per hour, but responding to 30 may indicate that the representative is rushing through the calls and sacrificing quality for the sake of expediency. The software solution should be able to flag such issues of "dual polarity."

- *Cascading Scorecards.* Users should be able to review Balanced Scorecards from across the company in one program. Ensure that your software allows you to display aligned Scorecards emanating from throughout the organization.

- *Personal preferences.* "My" has become a popular prefix in the Internet world, with My Yahoo, My Home Page, and so on. The information age has heralded a time of mass customization, and so it should be with your Balanced Scorecard software. If they so desire, users should be able to easily customize the system to open with a page displaying indicators of importance to them. Having relevant information immediately available will greatly facilitate the program's use.

- *Intuitive menus.* Menus should be logical, easy to understand, and relatively simple to navigate.

- *Helpful help screens.* Some help screens seem to hinder users' efforts as often as helping them. Check the help screens to ensure that they offer relevant, easy-to-follow information.

- *Levels of detail.* Your software should allow users to quickly and easily switch from a summary view of performance to a detailed view comprising a single indicator. Navigating from data tables to summary reports back to individual measures should all be easily accommodated. The user community will demand this functionality as they begin actively using the tool to analyze performance results.

Reporting and Analysis

Any software solution you consider must contain robust and flexible reporting and analysis tools. In this section we'll explore several reporting and analysis factors to be considered during your selection process:

- *Drill-down capabilities.* This crucial tool must allow users to drill down on measures to increasingly lower levels of detail. Drill-down ability might also be considered in the context of strategy maps, which should be easily navigable at the click of a mouse.

- *Statistical analysis.* Your software should include the facility of performing statistical analysis (e.g., trends) on the performance measures making up your Balanced Scorecard. Additionally, the statistics should be multidimensional in nature, combining disparate performance elements to display a total picture of actual results. Simply viewing bar charts is not analysis. Users require the ability to slice and dice the data to fit their analysis and decision-making needs.

- *Alerts.* You will want to be notified automatically when a critical measure is not performing within acceptable ranges. Alerts must be built into the system to provide this notification.

- *Commentaries.* Whether a measure is performing at, above, or below targeted expectations, users (especially management) need to quickly determine the root cause of the performance and be aware of the associated steps necessary for sustaining or improving results. Commentary fields are essential to any Scorecard software program, and most, if not all programs, will include them.

- *Flexible report options.* "What kind of reports does it have?" is invariably one of the first questions you'll hear when discussing Scorecard software with your user community. We're a report-based and dependent culture, so this shouldn't come as a surprise. What may in fact come as a surprise is the wide range of report capabilities featured in today's Scorecard software entries. Test this requirement closely, because some are much better than others. An especially important area to examine is print options. We purchase software to reduce our dependency on paper, but as we all know, it doesn't necessarily work that way. Ensure that the reports will print effectively, displaying the information clearly and concisely.

- *Automatic consolidation.* You may wish to see your data presented as a sum, average, or year-to-date amount. The system should possess the flexibility to provide this choice.

- *Flag missing data.* At the outset of their implementation, most organizations will be missing at least a portion of the data for Balanced Scorecard measures. This often results from the fact that the Scorecard has illuminated entirely new measures that were never before contemplated. The software program should alert users to those measures that are missing data, whether it is for a single period or the measure has never been populated.

- *Forecasting and what-if analysis.* Robust programs will possess the capability of using current results to forecast future performance. It's also useful to have the ability to plug in different values for various measures and examine the effect on related indicators. This what-if analysis provides another opportunity to critically examine the assumptions made when constructing the strategy map.

- *Linked documents.* At a mouse click, users should have the ability to put measure results into a larger context by accessing important documents and links. Annual reports, CEO videos, analyst reports, discussion forums, and a variety of other potential links can strengthen the bond between actual results and the larger context of organizational objectives.

- *Automatic e-mail.* To harness the power of the Balanced Scorecard as a communication tool, users must be able to launch an e-mail application and send messages regarding specific performance results. Discussion forums or threads may develop as interested users add their perspective on results and provide insights for improvements.

Technical Considerations

The following elements examine hardware and software technical dimensions:

- *Compatibility.* Any software you consider must be able to exist in your current technical environment. Most employ client/server technology and will run on Windows XP, 95, 98, 2000, and NT.

- *Integration with existing systems.* Data for your Balanced Scorecard will probably reside in several different places: financial data from your general ledger, customer information from your customer relationship management (CRM) system, and other measures from an enterprise resource planning (ERP) system. Your software should be able to extract data from these systems automatically, thereby eliminating any rekeying of data. Those users who appear reluctant to use the Scorecard software will often point to redundant data entry as a key detraction of the system. Therefore, a big win is delivered if you have the ability to automatically extricate information with no effort on the part of users.

- *Accept various data forms.* In addition to internal sources of data, you may collect performance information from third-party providers. The software should therefore contain the ability to accept data from spreadsheets and ASCII files.

- *Data export.* Sometimes getting information out is as important as getting it in. The data contained in the Balanced Scorecard may serve as the source for other management reports to Boards, regulators, or the general public. A robust data export tool is an important component of any Scorecard software.

- *Web publishing.* Users should have the option of accessing and saving Scorecard information using a standard browser. Publishing to both an internal intranet and the Internet is preferable.

- *Trigger external applications.* Users will require the capability of launching desktop programs from within the Balanced Scorecard software.

- *Cut and paste to applications.* Related to the previous item, users may wish to include a graph or chart in another application. Many programs will provide functionality enabling users to simply copy and paste with ease.

- *Application Service Provider (ASP) option.* An ASP is a company that offers organizations access to applications and related services over the Internet that would otherwise have to be located in their own computers. As information technology outsourcing grows in prominence, so does the role of ASPs. Several Scorecard software vendors now offer this service, which gives anyone direct access to the Balanced Scorecard for a monthly (normally) fee based on the number of users.

- *Scalability.* This term describes the ability of an application to function well and take advantage of changes in size or volume in order to meet a user's need. Rescaling can encompass a change in the product (e.g., storage,

RAM) or the movement to a new operating system. Your software should be scalable to meet the future demands you may place on it as your user community and sophistication grow.

Maintenance and Security

Ensuring appropriate access rights and ongoing maintenance are also important criteria in your software decision. Here are a few elements to consider:

- *System administrator access.* Your software should allow for individuals to be designated as system administrators. Depending on security (see later item), some of these users may have access to the entire system.

- *Ease of modification.* Altering your views of performance should be facilitated easily with little advanced technical knowledge required.

- *Control of access to the system.* My proclivities are toward open-book management with complete sharing of information across the enterprise. Organizations practicing this participative form of management give it glowing reviews for the innovation and creativity it sparks among employees. The Scorecard facilitates open sharing of information both through the development of a high-level organizational Scorecard and the series of cascading Scorecards that allow all employees to describe their contribution to overall results. However, not all companies share this view, and many will wish to limit access to the system. Therefore, a software program should allow you to limit access to measures by user and develop user groups to simplify the measure publishing process.

- *Control of changes, data, and commentary entry.* Related to the previous item, not all users will necessarily be required to make changes, enter data, or provide result commentaries. Only system administrators should have the power to change measures, and only assigned users will have access to entering data and commentaries.

Evaluating the Vendor

Chances are you'll be presented with a wide array of software choices from both industry veterans and unknown upstarts. Either way, performing a little due diligence on the vendor regarding the following points is always a good idea:

- *Pricing.* As with any investment of this magnitude, pricing is a critical component of the overall decision. To make an informed decision, remember to include all dimensions of the total cost to purchase and maintain the software. This includes the per-user license fees, any maintenance fees, costs related to new releases, training costs, as well as salaries and benefits of system administrators.

- *Viability of the vendor.* Is this provider in it for the long term, or will any vicissitudes of the economy spell their demise? Because they're in the business of providing Scorecard software, you would expect them to steer their own course using the Balanced Scorecard. Ask them to review Scorecard results with you. For reasons of confidentiality, they may have to disguise some of the actual numbers, but you should still glean lots of valuable information on the organization's future prospects.

- *References and experience.* By examining the profiles of past clients, you can determine the breadth and depth of experience the vendor has accumulated. Although no two implementations are identical, it will be reassuring to know the software company has completed an installation in an organization with some similarity to yours, whether it's the same industry or a comparably sized organization. References are especially important. When discussing the vendor with other organizations that have been through the process, quiz them on the vendor's technical skills, consulting and training competence, and ability to complete the work on time and on budget.

- *Post-sale service.* You will inevitably have many bumps in the road as you implement your new reporting software. Bugs hidden deep in the program will be detected, patches will be required, and thus a lifeline to the vendor is crucial. How much support are they willing to offer and at what cost? Do you have a dedicated representative for your organization or are you at the mercy of their call center? These are just a couple of questions to ask. And never forget that software companies owe a lot to us, the users. New functions and features are often the product of intense lobbying on behalf of function-starved users, who sometimes end up knowing more about the product than the vendor. So don't be shy with your requests!

NOTES

1. Adapted from material presented at www.jokes.com.
2. Andrew Neely and Mike Bourne, "Why Measurement Initiatives Fail," *Quality Focus,* Vol. 4., Issue 4, 2000, p. 3.
3. Michael Beer and Russell A. Eisenstat, "How to Have an Honest Conversation About Your Business Strategy," *Harvard Business Review,* February 2004, p. 84.
4. Michael C. Mankins, "Stop Wasting Valuable Time," *Harvard Business Review,* September 2004, p. 61.
5. See note 3.
6. From author interview with Stan Romanoff, July 26, 2004.
7. Jim Collins, *Good to Great* (New York: Harper Business, 2001).
8. Larry Bossidy and Ram Charan, *Execution* (New York: Crown Business, 2002), p. 128.
9. Christoper Palazzolo and Kent Smack, "The Four Steps to BSC Software Selection," *Balanced Scorecard Report,* November–December 2002, pp. 15–16.

CHAPTER 9

Building the Balanced Scorecard at Aliant, Inc.

Aliant is an information and communications technology company based in the Atlantic provinces (Nova Scotia, New Brunswick, Prince Edward Island, Newfoundland, and Labrador) of Canada. The company was formed in 1999 as the result of a merger of the four Atlantic telecommunications companies, each with more than 100 years of operating experience. The merged entity provides a wide range of voice and data communications services, including local, long distance, and cellular telephone, Internet, and wireless. Through its wholly owned subsidiary, x-wave, the company is active in the market of information technology services. Aliant employs more than 8,000 people and, with revenues exceeding $2 billion in 2003, is the third largest incumbent full-service telecommunications company in Canada.

Aliant pursues innovation to enhance and simplify the lives of Atlantic Canadians through world-leading telecommunications and technology solutions. Innovation doesn't stop with products and services, however.[1] The company believes strongly in applying proven management thinking and ideas in an effort to ensure that all employees benefit from established approaches to the business of business. Reflecting that spirit of inquiry was the decision by CEO Jay Forbes to introduce the Balanced Scorecard at Aliant in 2002. The organization had recently developed a new strategy, and Forbes was confident the Scorecard represented the right tool at the right time to align his entire workforce with the company's new direction. In the pages that follow, we'll examine the implementation of the Balanced Scorecard at this progressive enterprise.

I've chosen to highlight the Aliant experience for several reasons. Primarily, their work illuminates many of the principles I have put forth in this book, displaying clearly how an organization—even a large, multifaceted one—can, with discipline and focus, implement the Balanced Scorecard swiftly and effectively, generating rapid benefits. Additionally, through my ongoing consulting relationship with the firm, I have been provided the broad access necessary to critically examine the implementation, opening a window onto the many victories and vexing challenges that accompanied this significant change initiative.

POURING A FOUNDATION FOR BALANCED SCORECARD SUCCESS

Chapters Two and Three of this book were devoted to elements of the Balanced Scorecard that must be considered long before objectives are debated, measures created, or reports issued. To build a Balanced Scorecard that works, the rough terrain of your organization must be smoothly graded and prepared by examining the foundational elements of why you've decided to build a Scorecard, who will sponsor it, who will build it, and how you'll communicate this exciting, yet challenging, new change in performance management. In the sections ahead we'll learn how Aliant ensured that the critical pieces of this puzzle were in place before building its Corporate Balanced Scorecard.

Why the Balanced Scorecard, and Why Now?

Thanks to a highly successful implementation at an investor-owned electric utility, Aliant CEO Jay Forbes was well-acquainted with the concept of the Balanced Scorecard when he initially determined it would be the appropriate tool for the execution of Aliant's new strategy in 2002. Forbes realized, however, that his knowledge and confidence in the tool was not a guarantee of instant acceptance from 6,000 employees, many of whom had seen their share of change initiatives come and go at Aliant. From his cadre of senior leaders to linemen climbing poles, Forbes realized that everyone within the company had to be convinced the Scorecard was solving a legitimate business issue if they were going to accept and embrace the tool.

The business impetus appeared in the form of a new strategy developed by Aliant in recognition of the evolving dynamics of the telecommunications market in Canada and their unique place in that market. But employees had seen new strategies enthusiastically introduced in the past only to morph into a set of exclusively financial performance indicators shedding little light on how they could play a part in executing the strategy day in and day out. As one manager described previous strategy introductions: *"We'd have a huge slide deck and then just a couple of financial measures."*[2] Forbes and his executive team seized the opportunity to introduce the Balanced Scorecard as representing the dawn of a new day in the implementation of strategy at Aliant, explaining that the Scorecard would supplement traditional financial measures with the drivers of future success, and provide every employee from top to bottom with the opportunity of contributing to the company's triumphs.

The rationale was clear: an exciting new strategy was on the table, the effective implementation of which would be unlocked by a key in the form of the Balanced Scorecard. Aliant leadership quickly embraced the choice of the Scorecard, citing its ability to bring "strategic agility" to the organization, rally everyone around a core group of financial and *nonfinancial* measures that promised to spring the new plan to life, and provide them with an opportunity to actively participate in the execution of the strategy. They then set out to ensure the entire employee population understood the scorecard, linking it to all processes and workgroups, recognizing that it would take commitment and perseverance to fully integrate the scorecard and overcome suspicion and skepticism by some front line employees.

Executive Sponsorship

Quite simply, it all begins at the top. If senior executives do not understand the Balanced Scorecard, and more important, do not appreciate how it can be harnessed to solve real-world business problems, then it is doomed to mediocrity at best, failure at worst. At Aliant it begins with the CEO, who combines a deep understanding of the practicalities and nuances of the Scorecard method with a contagious passion for the tool. At the outset of the implementation, Mr. Forbes communicated this message to his employees: *"Given these uncertain times in our industry, Aliant needs greater alignment to focus on success. The Balanced Scorecard will help us successfully execute our new strategy by: establishing greater alignment of our strategic and operating objectives, fostering collaboration among lines of business, and engaging our people in its execution."*[3] Far from a sideline cheerleader, Forbes immersed himself in the Balanced Scorecard implementation from the outset, participating in strategy mapping workshops, offering guidance on the tool's evolutionary path at the company, and most important, ceaselessly promoting the Scorecard as a valuable tool in the execution of Aliant's new strategy. He took every available opportunity—town hall meetings, conference calls, and intranet messages, among them—to share his commitment and belief in the tool, encouraging employees, regardless of their position, to become actively involved in the implementation.

Forbes and his inner circle of executives also recognize, unlike many wide-eyed Scorecard adopters, that the framework is not a panacea for this or any organization. According to them, it's all about the execution of strategy, a mantra at Aliant that is echoed throughout the vast reaches of this innovative enterprise.

While the Scorecard may not cure every organizational ill, the executive team at Aliant is quick to underscore the crucial areas in which it does prove invaluable: shaping a culture of performance, facilitating open and active discussions of performance results, and creating an unrelenting focus on strategy.

The team at Aliant practices what it preaches, with every possible opportunity taken to use Scorecard results as a mechanism for learning about the company's strategy. Executive meetings, quarterly operational reviews, and Board of Directors meetings all feature agendas shaped significantly by the Balanced Scorecard. These interactive discussions provide a unique opportunity to gauge strategic progress and contemplate necessary course corrections along the way.

Aliant's Balanced Scorecard Team

Recognizing the importance of the Balanced Scorecard in the execution of their new strategy, the Aliant executive team, led by CEO Jay Forbes, quickly assembled a cross-functional team of high-potential individuals possessing the intellect, political acumen, and enthusiasm necessary to implement a change initiative of this magnitude. Resources, both human and financial, were not spared, and in fact the organization had the foresight to understand the necessity of a driving force behind the team, and thus hired a Balanced Scorecard champion to lead the implementation and the ongoing evolution of the Balanced Scorecard at Aliant.

The team worked closely together during the development of a corporate strategy map and measures, providing the voice of their respective business units while simultaneously ensuring that the product being created was greater than the sum of the individual parts represented. As the implementation moved to the stage of cascading and, later, linking the Scorecard to management processes, day-to-day responsibility for the Scorecard was ceded to Aliant's Corporate Development group, with the original team being convened at selected intervals to vet recent developments and provide updates from their home business units.

Getting the Word Out:
Balanced Scorecard Communication

Imagine you've got in excess of 6,000 employees spread over hundreds of miles, many of them, like their corporate brethren across the globe, "change weary" and viewing any corporate initiatives with a healthy dose of skepticism. Such was the challenge of communicating the Balanced Scorecard at Aliant. With typical enthusiasm and vigor, the Communications team at Aliant jumped head first into these chilly waters, unleashing a communications campaign aimed at informing, educating, and influencing every single Aliant employee.

As discussed in Chapter Three, Aliant began its communication efforts by determining the following goals and objectives:

Communications Goals

- Increase awareness of Aliant's strategic plan
- Increase awareness of Balanced Scorecard among Aliant employees
- Increase knowledge of the Balanced scorecard and how it will be used to manage Aliant's strategy
- Ensure consistent and persistent communication about the Balanced Scorecard, its role, and eventual results
- Encourage employees to ask questions about how the Balanced Scorecard relates to them—How does it affect me?

Communications Objectives

- Attain understanding among employee base of the Balanced Scorecard and how it affects them
- Have the Balanced Scorecard be used as a key strategic management, communications, and measurement tool
- Ensure that the Balanced Scorecard remains in place in Aliant as a key strategic and measurement tool

The team at Aliant worked diligently to ensure that communications were aimed equally at executives, managers, supervisors, and front-line employees alike, utilizing a multipronged approach to launch their Scorecard "brand." The centerpiece of their communication strategy is represented by the impressive Balanced Scorecard website. The site's home page is shown in Exhibit 9.1. As you can see, it hosts several pages, including an *overview* where employees can learn more about the implementation and how it affects them, copies of the company's strategy map and measures *(Aliant's BSC page)*, the latest Scorecard *news, resources* including many external websites of interest, *performance tracking*, a frequently viewed page where employees can find the latest Scorecard updates, and finally, the team encourages employees to *contact* them with any questions or comments, and thus an easy-to-complete contact form has been created.

The company's communication efforts aren't restricted to employees; all stakeholders are encouraged to learn about their Scorecard efforts. In that spirit, Aliant's 2003 annual report makes several references to its commitment to, and use of, the Balanced Scorecard, highlighted by a two-page section titled "Simple is Balance," reflecting on the importance of managing with balance in an effort to improve results for all stakeholders.[4]

Balanced Scorecard Training

Training at Aliant, as with communication planning, has been developed with care and the needs of the learner in mind. Rather than presenting a "push"

EXHIBIT 9.1   Aliant's Balanced Scorecard Home Page

| HOME | OVERVIEW | ALIANT'S BSC | NEWS | RESOURCES | PERFORMANCE TRACKING | CONTACT US |

Welcome

Welcome to Aliant's Balanced Scorecard Website.

There is no doubt about it, this website is your one-stop location to find out more about Aliant's Balanced Scorecard (BSC). The BSC site is filled with valuable information on the Balanced Scorecard model to help you better understand and contribute to Aliant's strategy.

I encourage you to visit each section - the **Overview** section highlights the Balanced Scorecard and how it will be applied. The **Resource** area contains **Q&A** and **Glossary** sections. And, **News** is where you'll find the latest updates from our Balanced Scorecard executive champion, David Rathbun. Finally, there's **Aliant's BSC**, where you can find the strategy maps and balanced scorecards for Aliant, Innovatia and xwave.

Jay Forbes
President and CEO, Aliant

You may be aware that last year Aliant outlined the 24 strategic initiatives that would be the focus for 2003 – now you have an opportunity to learn more about these initiatives.

I am pleased to introduce **Aliant's Strategic Initiative Profiles.** Published weekly, these profiles will help you understand the impact and contribution of each strategic initiative by providing the following details:

- the goal, benefits and rationale of the initiative;
- team members;
- current accomplishments; and
- future milestones.

Please read the eighth profile: **Create a safe and healthy work environment.**

If you have any feedback, please send your thoughts along to **balanced.scorecard@aliant.ca.**

Please join me in making these profiles, and this website, part of your weekly routine. The combined efforts of Aliant employees can make Aliant's BSC and the strategic initiatives successful!

Jay Forbes

method, the company has been responsive to the entire Aliant community. For example, it is recognized that front-line staff were more comfortable receiving their training from supervisors, rather than corporate staff. Acting on that knowledge, the Balanced Scorecard team developed a simple 12-slide presentation for supervisors to share with their staff, complete with slide notes and frequently asked questions. The objectives page of that education presentation is presented in Exhibit 9.2. As you can see, the focus is squarely on what the learner needs: *what the Balanced Scorecard is, why the company is using it, and how it directly affects them.* Aliant supplements its traditional learning channels with innovative e-learning opportunities, offering three Balanced Scorecard modules employees can access from their desktops at any time.

EXHIBIT 9.2   Objectives for an Employee Training Session

Objectives

Upon completion of this Education Session, you will have an appreciation of:

➢ <u>What</u> a Balanced Scorecard is, <u>why</u> are we using it, and <u>how</u> it is used to manage and improve Aliant's performance

➢ The components of a Balanced Scorecard

➢ The purpose of "Cascading" the Balanced Scorecard

➢ How your daily work activities are reflected in our BSC measures

➢ Your Team's Balanced Scorecard

ALIANT'S STRATEGY MAP, PERFORMANCE MEASURES, TARGETS, AND INITIATIVES

Aliant's Strategy Map: A Powerful Communication Tool

Aliant's corporate strategy map is shown in Exhibit 9.3. As you can see, the map is not overly complex, relying on the most vital of objectives to communicate the company's strategy to all 6,000 employees. Interestingly, that's not the way it began. When the Scorecard team completed the first draft of the strategy map, it contained several additional objectives in each of the perspectives. Upon reviewing the map, CEO Jay Forbes was impressed with the work of the team, citing the comprehensive nature of the objectives created and the robust cause-and-effect relationships evident throughout the map, but he challenged the team to revisit the map, simplify it, and transform it into a powerful communication tool easily grasped by linemen and executives alike. Mr. Forbes recognized that the map's inherent value is its ability to convincingly communicate strategy to a broad audience, while measures and initiatives handle the heavy lifting of performance monitoring and corporate resource allocation. The revised map shown in the exhibit resulted from several workshops featuring strenuous debate and discussion, but based on a foundation of commitment to creating a tool everyone in the organization could rally around as they worked to execute their strategy. Let's look briefly at each of the four perspectives of Aliant's strategy map:

EXHIBIT 9.3 Aliant Strategy Map

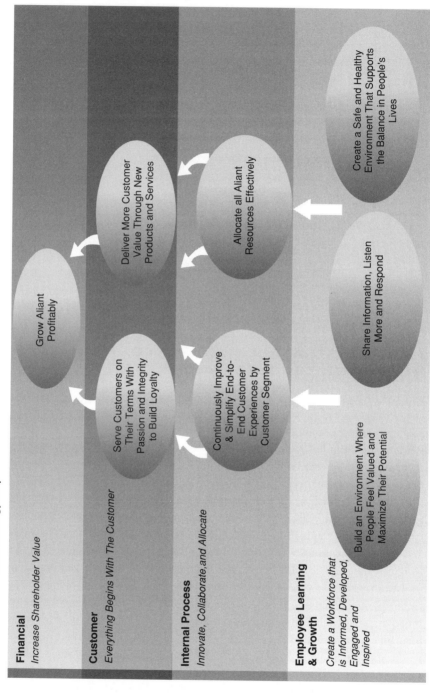

Financial
Increase Shareholder Value

Customer
Everything Begins With The Customer

Internal Process
Innovate, Collaborate, and Allocate

Employee Learning & Growth
Create a Workforce that is Informed, Developed, Engaged and Inspired

Grow Aliant Profitably

Deliver More Customer Value Through New Products and Services

Allocate all Aliant Resources Effectively

Create a Safe and Healthy Environment That Supports the Balance in People's Lives

Serve Customers on Their Terms With Passion and Integrity to Build Loyalty

Continuously Improve & Simplify End-to-End Customer Experiences by Customer Segment

Share Information, Listen More and Respond

Build an Environment Where People Feel Valued and Maximize Their Potential

- *Financial.* As discussed in Chapter Four, most organizations include financial objectives relating to both productivity and growth. Aliant has determined that it will manage that tension with a single objective, "Grow Aliant
profitably." As the title confers, the objective covers the growth dimension
through the inclusion of the word *grow*, while productivity is captured with
the reference to *profitably*, suggesting that not all growth will be pursued,
only that which will lead to greater profitability for the company.

- *Customer.* After casting a glance at Aliant's customer objectives, to which of
the three value propositions would you guess it is committed? If you said
customer intimacy, give yourself the rest of the day off. As one Aliant manager told me, *"Our choice of customer objectives reflects our history of being a full-
service provider to a core market. We're continuing a transition from a monopoly
provider to being more customer intimate. Customer intimacy is one of our major
strategic thrusts right now."*[5] Speaking of value propositions, operational excellence is not overlooked, as serving customers also relates to simplicity, as
we'll see in the Internal Processes perspective.

- *Internal Processes.* The objectives appearing in this perspective were chosen
as the representative processes that would ultimately drive the customer perspective and lead to the company's desired financial results. Narrowing the
broad universe of potential process objectives down to two is an aggressive
choice, but the company has benefited from its choice to err on the side of
simplicity, with each objective generating quick benefits. As an example, I was
told during my interviews with Aliant staff that,

  > Continuously improve and simplify end-to-end customer experiences
  > has had the greatest impact on our organization. For example, when a
  > customer service representative takes calls, they may have up to 42 dif-
  > ferent systems on their desktop. This information came to light because
  > of the Balanced Scorecard. As a result of committing to offering value
  > and "their terms" we've begun to look at our systems, and committed
  > $100 million dollars to fix system problems. That commitment resulted
  > from the Balanced Scorecard.[6]

- *Employee Learning and Growth.* At first blush, "Build an environment where
people feel valued and maximize their potential" may appear to be more of
an organizational capital objective, but Aliant considers it to represent their
dedication to human capital. The objective has resulted in a formal process
of measuring, monitoring, and evaluating the company's leadership, which
forms a foundation for succession planning. "Share information, listen more
and respond" is the company's information capital objective. What I like
most about this objective is the commitment of a response to employee
issues, a critical component of feedback that is often overlooked by companies zealously attempting to take the pulse of employee feelings with no

intention of acting on their findings. "Create a safe and healthy environment that supports the balance in people's lives" is an organizational capital objective focusing on health and safety, while also reflecting a desire to promote balance between work and family.

Measures, Targets, and Initiatives

For reasons of confidentiality, I cannot share Aliant's performance measures, targets, or initiatives with you. However, we can examine how they were developed. When choosing performance measures, the company adhered to several criteria, one of which was an insistence that most measures already exist within the business. Aliant's Director of Corporate Development explains the rationale for this and other measure factors:

> This approach ensured quality of information and established reliable cause and effect relationships based on historical data. It also resulted in the creation of only a small number of new measures and insured their lack of predictability did not add unnecessary risk to the implementation. Each measure also had to be quantifiable. There was no appetite for subjectivity. The executive team insisted measures be objective so they could be clearly defined and where appropriate, benchmarked against other companies. Lastly, the measures had to be few (i.e. less than twenty) and focused. In an effort to create clarity of focus, the executive team mandated that Aliant's Balanced Scorecard be based upon measuring the few things that are key to our long-term success.[7]

To ensure that the measures selected for inclusion in the Balanced Scorecard were in fact measurable, Aliant took the unorthodox step of creating a measure support team. The mandate of the group included formally documenting the measures (using a data dictionary similar to that in Chapter Five), testing their reliability, proposing processes for data collection, and suggesting targets. When creating targets, the team was supplied with guidelines from the executive team stipulating they should aim for best-in-class performance within three years and world-class within five. Best-in-class within this context was defined as being among the top 10% of the Canadian communications industry, while world-class translated to performance tantamount to that of the top 10% of all industries on that metric.[8]

Before implementing the Balanced Scorecard, Aliant's strategic initiatives were created from a bottom-up build, culminating in a broad list of initiatives spanning the company's units. The Scorecard ushered in a new day in the development and reporting of strategic initiatives, featuring the creation of a cross-functional planning council. During 2004 this cross-functional group facilitated a two-day session during which business unit Scorecards and accompanying initiatives were presented with the aim of determining strategic alignment, discovering organizational synergies, and calculating resource requirements. The council sessions proved to be a highly effective forum for discussing initiatives and have taken permanent root in the company in the form of monthly conference calls during which Aliant's critical initiatives are reviewed. A common template is used for each initiative, and during the call 10 minutes is allotted to each. During that time questions rain down upon the initiative's owner, milestones and budgets are reviewed, and risks are surfaced and mitigated.

CASCADING THE BALANCED SCORECARD TO BUILD ORGANIZATIONAL ALIGNMENT

Cascading the Balanced Scorecard brings the knowledge of strategy to life through the development of Scorecards at lower levels of the organization, which, while open to local opportunities and challenges, align with the overall strategy of the organization. For large organizations implementing the Balanced Scorecard, cascading represents more a necessity than a choice if they hope to drive alignment and focus from top to bottom. Aliant understood this distinction and chose an aggressive cascading path, developing a corporate Balanced Scorecard, line of business, business unit, and department-level Scorecards within the tool's first year of operation.

Those responsible for developing cascaded Balanced Scorecards were not left in the dark on this sometimes intimidating topic, but were provided both in-person facilitation assistance and an abundance of documentation to ease the process. Outlined as follows is an excerpt from one "cascading guide" issued to managers:

> The steps outlined below will help you develop cascaded Balanced Scorecards that drive action at your level while minimizing measures and ensuring understanding of corporate objectives.
>
> 1. Always begin cascading from the Scorecard "in front of yours." For Lines of Business (LOB) and Corporate Resource Groups (CRG) this would entail cascading from the Aliant Inc. Scorecard. For a business unit (BU) it would mean cascading from the LOB Scorecard.
>
> 2. Let's assume we're cascading from the Aliant Inc. Scorecard to a Line of Business. The LOB will begin by examining our financial objective of "Grow Aliant Profitably" and ask themselves, *"can we influence this objective in some way?"* If the answer is no, they will move on to the next objective. If, however, the answer is yes, the LOB must determine whether the current wording of the objective is appropriate for them. We encourage you to use the same (or very consistent) language whenever possible. Doing so will lead to greater transparency of objectives throughout the organization. And don't forget—even if you use the same wording for the objec-

tive, you can always use different and more specific language for the objective statement, the 2 or 3 sentence description of the objective. However, we do recognize that in some cases you may need to change the wording of the objective itself to capture your unique contribution and drive action locally. That's okay, but we ask that you carefully weigh the value derived from specificity against the loss of transparency across the organization.

3. With the objective determined you must next consider the appropriate measure or measures to track your progress. Again, we ask that whenever possible you use the measure appearing on the Aliant Inc. Scorecard. Doing so will limit the total number of measures tracked throughout the company and allow for more "linear" compilation of results. As with objectives, however, you may have to develop a substitute or "proxy" measure (or measures) that best describes how you can track the objective under question. For example, while Aliant Inc. will measure the objective of "Grow Aliant Profitably" using earnings per share (EPS), it would be impossible for a CRG to do the same since they have neither earnings nor shares. In this case they may use the proxy measure of "variance to budget." They would suggest that by controlling their costs they can help influence the total cost structure of Aliant, thereby contributing to the overall result of improved EPS.

4. With objectives and measures created you will turn to targets and initiatives. It is in these areas that we would anticipate very individual responses signaling your specific goals and plans. Your targets will reflect both past results and desired improvements, while your initiatives will determine the specific programs and plans you must put in place to drive success on achieving your target. As we evolve our BSC program at Aliant the initiatives we all develop will form a direct link to our budgeting process.

5. Work through all of the objectives on the Strategy Map from which you're cascading using the methods described in steps 2, 3, and 4.

6. Once you've worked through all of the objectives appearing on the map in front of yours you should have a strategy map of your own. It's very important at this point to perform a simple diagnostic ensuring the map you've created accurately reflects the value you bring to Aliant. There may be areas of significant contribution, or key operational processes that are critical to your success, which are not covered on your map. If that is the case, create any new objectives and measures necessary to ensure the map for your group clearly and convincingly portrays your contribution to Aliant's success. *As an interesting side note, it's important that we*

review all Scorecards to determine the number of new objectives appearing throughout the organization. If we see patterns forming among the newly created objectives we'll have to ask ourselves if they warrant inclusion on the Aliant Corporate Scorecard.

7. Review your Strategy Map and measures, ensuring they do in fact "tell the story" of your contribution to Aliant.

Ultimately, cascading is about alignment throughout the organization, and Aliant took great care to ensure that all Scorecards created within the company were in fact aligned with the overall strategy of the organization. During my work with the company, I had the opportunity to review documents that summarized the alignment of strategy maps, measures, and initiatives. One in particular made a strong impression on me: the strategy map for the department of the Chief Information Officer (CIO). Measuring information technology (IT) performance has become a hot trend in the business world, and many IT organizations are scrambling to become "world-class" service providers. At first glance this appears to be a noble goal, but on further reflection we must determine whether this pursuit of excellence furthers alignment within the organization. Some IT organizations have achieved world-class marks, but that is of little solace when the overall strategy of the organization fails—demonstrating there was never a link between IT and the overall strategy of the firm. With that in mind, it was encouraging to review the strategy map of Aliant's CIO, which included objectives such as "Enable Aliant to introduce new products, services & technology," "Create strong, effective partnerships," and "Maximize Aliant profitability by spending & investing IS/IT dollars wisely." These and other objectives on the map demonstrate a deep commitment to excellence, but excellence in the pursuit of overall strategy implementation.

Aliant's cascading experience was summed up best by a manager who, reflecting on past attempts to spread the strategic word, told me:

> Two years ago if you'd asked how my team is linked to the strategy I would have given a long answer, but not really known. But now my team has developed a Balanced Scorecard, and they can see how they link. They can now also look at other groups and see how they all link. There are greater connections with other functional areas because we all speak the same language.[9]

REPORTING BALANCED SCORECARD RESULTS

Aliant provides a great example of an organization that has derived tremendous benefits from the Balanced Scorecard without the aid of a sophisticated technology solution. They have chosen to drive reporting through existing processes (paper-based and intranet reporting) for two primary reasons. First, while they are open to the notion of using software, they have been unable, despite substantial investigation, to find a tool they feel has all of the functionality they require for an implementation of this scope. That is not to say such a tool is not available. I'm certain any of the Balanced Scorecard software vendors would beg to differ, but it simply reflects Aliant's desire to wait until they are 100% certain they've found the right technology product for them. Their decision also contains a timing element; they felt it was important to ensure that all employees understood the fundamentals of the Scorecard system and why it was being used at Aliant before introducing any enabling technology.

Balanced Scorecard results are reviewed and discussed frequently throughout the vast reaches of this geographically dispersed company. Every Monday morning, Aliant's executive team holds a virtual meeting, conducted by conference call, during which Scorecard results are reviewed informally. A more structured recap of results is held during the company's quarterly review process. In order to involve as many employees as possible in the ongoing strategy dialogue, this event is held at a different location each quarter and kicks off with a town hall session, during which the CEO uses the Balanced Scorecard to facilitate a discussion of performance for the preceding three months. The intensity is ratcheted up several notches over the next two or three days, during which executives and line-of-business management stage a deep dive into organizational results and gauge the progress of accompanying initiatives. Despite the heated discussions that occasionally flare up, the underlying spirit is one of learning from the results, not dispensing blame and punishment for "red lights." CEO Forbes uses lagging performance on measures to speak about what must be done to improve and to ensure that the company's strategy is executed. In addition to the corporate reviews outlined previously, all lines of business and business units review Scorecard results at least monthly. The Board of Directors is not neglected in this ongoing discussion, because Scorecard results are shared with them on a monthly basis as well.

EVERYBODY WINS: LINKING THE BALANCED SCORECARD TO INCENTIVE COMPENSATION

One word that cannot be used to describe the Aliant Scorecard experience is *conservative*. Within a year of introducing this dynamic management framework, the company had created more than 140 Scorecards organization-wide (with more on the way), reengineered the strategic initiatives process, and decided to link Scorecard results to their short-term incentive program. Many organizations struggle with the Scorecard and compensation link, suffering from inadequate measures or targets and complex payout formulas that lead to confusion and employee suspicion. Recognizing these potential deficiencies, Aliant created a simple-to-understand and relatively easy-to-administer program designed to make the Balanced Scorecard real in the eyes of employees and reward them for their contributions to corporate success.

Exhibit 9.4 provides a graphic representation of Aliant's linkage from the Balanced Scorecard to its short-term incentive program. Starting from the left-hand portion of the exhibit, we learn that an employee's award is based on several factors, beginning with the company's performance on a subset of Balanced Scorecard metrics. One indicator is chosen from each of the Scorecard's four perspectives and assigned an associated weight. Although four measures are included in the calculation, no payouts will be shared unless the minimum target for their financial metric is achieved. This widely adopted approach ensures that employees are cognizant of the importance of meeting financial commitments. Each of the metrics included in the compensation equation has three associated target levels: threshold, target, and stretch, each indicating increased levels of performance. Incentives at Aliant are also a function of the employee's performance appraisal, as indicated by the middle box of Exhibit 9.4. Finally, the employee's level—or "band" in Aliant parlance—is used to calculate the payout amount.

To illustrate the system, let's take the case of David, who is in band ten and earns $50,000 per year. This year David received an "achieves" rating on his performance appraisal, and the company has achieved all of its Balanced Scorecard targets. David's incentive compensation will be 100% (All Balanced Scorecard targets achieved) times 100% (David's performance multiplier) times 12% (the payout percentage for David's band) times $50,000 (David's salary) equals an incentive award of $6,000.

After breathing a collective sigh of relief, Aliant employees celebrated the achievement of their financial threshold and were the deserving recipients of a bonus payment in the first year of aligning the Scorecard with their incentive program. While everyone from Human Resources leaders to operations employees is pleased with the program, the company continues to tinker and benchmark best practices in the compensation field, ensuring a program that is linked to performance for all.

EXHIBIT 9.4   Calculating Incentives at Aliant

BSC Measure	Weighting		Individual Performance Modifier			Target			
Financial measure	%								
Customer measure	%		Exceeds	Up to 150%		Target			
		×	Achieves	100%	×	Band...	15%	× **Your earnings**	
Internal Process measure	%		Achieves most	50% to 75%		Band...	12%		
						Band...	10%		
Employee Learning & Growth measure	%		Does not achieve	0%					

Award =

ALIANT'S BALANCED SCORECARD RESULTS

Balanced Scorecard results have been both rapid and significant at Aliant, with indicators resident in all four perspectives demonstrating success. Financially, during 2003 the company's net income was up 28%, earnings per share increased 32%, and Aliant's share price rose 27%.[10] It would be unrealistic to attribute the entirety of these enviable occurrences to the company's foray into the Balanced Scorecard, but the positive ramifications of the investment are undeniable and are evident throughout the company's operations. Customer indicators such as reputation and perceived value both rose within percentage points of world-class performance, while internal metrics, including operational efficiency, did in fact meet world-class performance. Perhaps the strongest sign of the Scorecard's positive impact comes from an indicator within the Employee Learning and Growth perspective: employee knowledge of vision and strategy, a key leading indicator that rose about six percentage points in one year. A three-point increase would have been considered a significant improvement, thus the six-point climb provides strong evidence that the Balanced Scorecard message is being heard loud and clear through the many channels offered at Aliant.

Beyond the numbers, Aliant executives and managers point to a subtle yet unquestionable shift in the culture of the organization since the launch of the Scorecard. Many leaders have suggested that the company is transitioning to a culture of performance characterized by accountability, collaboration, information sharing, and a focus on strategy. Now, rather than approaching strategy and its execution from their individual and isolated cultural lenses, employees are provided with a wide-angle view of the company's operations, thanks to the objectives and measures of the Balanced Scorecard.

NOTES

1. From Aliant's 2003 Annual Report, p. 19.
2. From interview with Aliant employee focus group, March 24, 2004.
3. Allan A. MacDonald, "Implementing Balanced Scorecard to Create a Strategy Focused Organization," *Unpublished dissertation for Henley Management College,* 2004.
4. Aliant's Annual Report is available on their website at www.aliant.ca.
5. From interview with Aliant Balanced Scorecard team, March 22, 2004.
6. Ibid.
7. See note 3.
8. Ibid.
9. See note 2.
10. From Aliant's 2003 Annual Report.

Index